DATE DUE

NOV 30 '77			

How Far the Promised Land?

AMS PRESS
NEW YORK

Also by Walter White

How Far
the Promised Land?

by Walter White

New York · The Viking Press · 1955

Library of Congress Cataloging in Publication Data

White, Walter Francis, 1893-1955.
  How far the promised land?

    1. United States--Race question. 2. Negroes.
I. Title.
[E185.61.W6 1973]   301.45'1'042   73-153360
ISBN 0-404-06938-X

First AMS edition published in 1973
Manufactured in the United States of America

AMS PRESS INC.
NEW YORK, N.Y. 10003

BY WAY OF DEDICATION

The day before he died, Walter White said to his wife, "All afternoon I've been trying to think of some fitting way to dedicate this book to you, but all I can think of is,

'I love you,

I love you,

I love you, Poppy.' "

Contents

Foreword, by Ralph J. Bunche

This is the foreword to the last words of a great man and a stout-hearted leader of his people in the momentous cause to which his adult life was wholly dedicated. I was privileged over a long period to enjoy Walter White's friendship. I admired him highly and developed a deep affection for him. One so seldom meets a truly dedicated person, and when such a one is also keenly intelligent, vibrant, engaging, and warmly human—and this was Walter White—his going leaves a sorrowful void.

In this book are his last thoughts and written words on the progress of the Negro toward full equality in the American society. They are straightforward words which are vital and commanding for everyone who believes in democracy and freedom and the dignity of the individual man. They are the words of a man whose life, in fuller measure than that of any I have known, was devoted to making American democracy a complete and equal reality for the black as well as the white citizen. And, characteristically, they are words of utter frankness and full integrity, and also of hope.

He gave to this book a title in the form of a question: *How Far the Promised Land?*—how far off is the day when the American citizen of Negro descent will walk beside his white fellow citizen in full equality? Thanks to Walter White's vision, his leadership, and his unflinching devotion for more than three decades, the answer

today comes unmistakably clear: "It cannot be far." For he brought
the Negro close to the border of that land—perhaps even closer
than he himself realized. Moreover, the good fight led by him will
be carried on relentlessly by his surviving associates in the National
Association for the Advancement of Colored People, which continues to grow in strength and prestige throughout the country, due
to a steadily expanding body of sympathizers and supporters of all
races and creeds who realize that democracy to be true must be
color-blind. The basic element in Walter's faith in our country, in
the American way of life, and in the inevitable achievement of full
citizenship by the Negro was the conviction—and I believe it was
soundly based—that the vast majority of Americans really believe in
that democracy whose principles we profess and can therefore be
arrayed against practices of racial injustice. His task it was—and he
performed it well through the NAACP and the media of mass communication—to arouse the American conscience to the crude and
costly injustice in the treatment of its minority-group citizens, and
to mobilize sentiment behind the elimination of all undemocratic
practices and attitudes.

During the quarter-century of our friendship I had many and
long talks with Walter about all manner of things, but especially
race relations and democracy. Indeed, one could not talk with him
for very long at any time before he would embark with unique ani-
mation on the subject of race and democracy. His perspective on
such matters was world-wide. He was thoroughly conversant with
the problems of human rights and freedoms, racial and religious in-
tolerance, and colonialism all around the world. He was acutely
sensitive to reactions abroad to American racial injustices, and even
more so to American ineffectiveness in getting across to the world
the true story of American racial relations, the nature of the problem, and the sometimes striking progress made toward its solution.

I suspect that no man was ever more proud to be an American
than Walter White, nor have I ever known a more vigorous and
effective champion of American democracy. Despite the daily heart-

aches, setbacks, and frustrations in the Negro's historic forward march—each one of which during the past thirty years had been virtually a personal experience for him—he was ever insistent that the true story of the Negro's progress within the democratic framework of our society is the one convincing answer to the unceasing efforts of Communist propaganda to exploit the American racial situation. The answer to all such hostile propaganda, whatever its origin, he thought, could best be given by non-governmental sources. In fact, there are no better answers than Walter White's life itself—the saga of how, in a free society, a courageous and determined man, even though handicapped by identification with the race he chose to stand by, waged an effective fight for a people and a cause—and the record of the accelerated progress of that people in recent years as set forth clearly in this, his final book.

He was always "up front" and under fire in the cause of inter-racial democracy; he wrote from the trenches and the foxholes of the incessant struggle for equality for minority peoples. He lived that struggle for three decades. In a symbolic sense, he was that struggle in our times. Moreover, in his own never-failing confidence and belief he gave expression to the Negro's simple but unshakable faith in the American democratic process. Walter White, who has contributed so significantly to American social and political history of recent years, looked beyond the American scene and stated quite correctly that, "The Negro knows that the tide of world history is flowing in his direction." It is a rising tide.

This is dynamic history written by a man who was one of the most dynamic figures of our times. We do not go backward, we do not stand still, he said; American democracy moves forward. There is an ever-stronger current of democracy which eventually will carry *all* Americans into the "Promised Land." He left behind him the reasoned hope that Lincoln's work of emancipation, in its major aspects, can actually be completed by 1963—the centennial of Lincoln's signing of the Emancipation Proclamation.

A century, it would seem, is a long enough time indeed for a people to await fulfillment of the promise of the democracy which surrounds them. Walter White, I know, would agree that the emphasis today properly belongs on the urgency of fulfillment and not on the Negro's long-exercised and often abused quality of patience. As the "Promised Land" comes nearer, the pace of progress must be quickened.

How Far the Promised Land?

Why This Book?

Here is how and why this book came to be written.

It was a fiendishly humid day in New Delhi. The sun beat mercilessly down like a giant inverted copper hot-plate. It had been no less sticky and a little less hot when we of the "Town Meeting of the Air" arrived at midnight on the world tour that had already taken us through Europe, North Africa, the Middle East, and Asia. But our welcome had been as warm as the weather. Our hosts had given us cool drinks and whisked us through customs as they told us how pleased they were that we had come to India.

Freshened by sleep, we now were about to embark on our first official engagement—a mass press conference in the famous Constitution Club. As we entered, we were courteously handed copies of the morning newspapers. On each front page was a two-column feature story of our arrival—twenty-eight Americans representing as many national organizations who either at their own expense or that of the bodies they represented were traveling around the world. Our reasons for making the trip were explained in full detail: to learn through first-hand observation about the swift changes that two world wars had wrought, and to tell how democracy works in the United States.

But alongside the well-written and friendly story of our arrival was printed a Reuters dispatch about another group of Americans.

Its headline was printed in bold type, and read: HOMES OF EIGHT-
EEN NEGROES BOMBED BY KU KLUX KLAN IN BIRMINGHAM, ALA.,
U.S.A. A member of our party who represented influential business
interests looked at it, then turned to me in deep discouragement
and remarked, "We're wasting our time here. We might just as well
take the next plane out and turn Asia over to the Communists."

Later we talked about what would happen to the American industrial civilization should it become impossible for the Western
world to import from Asia those minerals and other materials so
essential to our own industrial and military production—tin, rubber, tungsten, cobalt, uranium, and so forth, to say nothing of the
moral as well as military catastrophe that would accompany loss of
the friendship and faith of more than a billion Asians. Someone
mentioned the grave danger that, if this happened, Africa would
swiftly follow Asia into the orbit of the Soviet Union. But at the
time we first saw the headlines we were not able fully to discuss
this situation, because we could hear the highly animated talk of
the journalists who awaited us inside the club. None of our party
needed to be told that the two front-page stories would be the tak-
ing-off-point for an interview in a continent where color consciousness runs high, particularly where the United States is concerned.
We had learned that a few days before in Pakistan, when lurid
stories had come over the cables about the rioting at Peekskill, New
York, involving Paul Robeson.

Our fears took no longer to materialize than the time it took for
the amenities of introductions. My wife and I remembered the
warning that Madame Vijayalakshmi Pandit, sister of the great Pandit Nehru and at that time Ambassador of India to the United States,
had voiced to us before we left New York. "You'll find India at its
hottest and worst in August, and you'll encounter some of the most
persistent and skeptical newspaper correspondents in the world."

We found her admonition an understatement. The questions
asked in crisp British accents softened somewhat by Urdu or Hin-
dustani tumbled over one another in a bombardment that neither
the heat nor the hum of ceiling fans nor the street noises lessened.

There were questions about Kashmir; about the American attitude toward Communist China; about Point Four aid and its motivation; whether the North Atlantic pact with Europe signified American backing of colonialism in Asian areas such as Indochina and Indonesia; whether the United States planned to use the atom bomb only against dark-skinned peoples. A few of the queries revealed obvious pro-Communist and anti-American convictions or sympathies; most of them, however, were clearly motivated by an honest desire to get at the facts. It was very clear that our questioners were implacable in their hostility to any and every form of condescension or exploitation of Asia by the white Western world and that they were passionately devoted to the social revolution that Gandhi had started and that their beloved Nehru was continuing.

The most persistent and difficult questions were those about the status of the Negro in the United States. These bowled over many in our party. The Indian newsmen appeared to possess encyclopedic knowledge of lynching, disfranchisement, segregation, Senate filibusters against such civil-rights legislation as Fair Employment Practices Committee bills, and the anti-Negro speeches of Americans such as Bilbo, Rankin, Talmadge, and Byrnes. Some of them appeared to be convinced that every one of the fifteen million Negroes in the United States had to get off the sidewalk when a white man came near, lived perpetually in terror of lynching, and generally occupied lower status than the Untouchables of their own country.

George Denny, the leader of the Round the World Town Meeting, turned over the questions regarding race to me as Secretary of the National Association for the Advancement of Colored People, about which, fortunately, some of the journalists had read. It was not an easy assignment. I remember particularly one tart-tongued man who apparently had memorized every detail of every race riot and lynching that had ever occurred in the United States, including some that I had personally investigated. I had to rack my memory to match his familiarity with the facts. There was little effort to

conceal his conviction—which some of the other reporters shared
—that America is barbarous in its treatment of all non-white human
beings.

All of us were handicapped and embarrassed because the facts
were indisputable. Some of our party were angered but tactfully
reserved their most vigorous comments until later, when we were
alone. One American was particularly bitter as he asked, "What
business have they attacking us for a few lynchings when they have
a caste system here which is worse than our racial discrimination
at home?" When I pointed out that the government of India had
outlawed discrimination based on caste or religion while our Senate
had successfully blocked anti-discrimination laws through filibusters, his anger against our Indian critics was such that he appeared
to see no relevance in the comparison.

What appalled us most was the almost total absence of information concerning the hard-won progress that had been made in the
fight for racial equality in the United States. All of the newsmen
had read of the notable work of Dr. Ralph J. Bunche as mediator
in Palestine. Joe Louis as world heavyweight champion was known,
though some were interested in him chiefly because the fact that
he was permitted to fight and beat white men puzzled them, being
a contradiction of what they believed the Negro's status to be. Mrs.
Eleanor Roosevelt's consistent, lifelong opposition to prejudices of
every sort was familiar to some of the journalists, but they made
it clear that they did not believe her to be typical.

Even the presence in the Town Meeting party of Mrs. Edith
Sampson, a successful Negro woman lawyer from Chicago, who
was to serve later as a member of the United States delegation to the
United Nations, and myself, as Secretary of the NAACP, seemed
to have little immediate effect in dispelling the journalists' concepts
of the inferior status of the Negro in America. We answered the
avalanche of questions as factually and as honestly as we could. It
would have been absurd to deny the truth. Bigots had built over the
years too damning a record, and that record was better known to
our inquisitors than it was to many in our own party. All of us were

decent Americans well informed on a variety of subjects, ranging from banking and agriculture through education and fraternal organizations to human rights. Most of the group had left the United States believing that the race problem, if not minor, was at least merely one of a number of questions facing the world. It had been a jolt of considerable proportions for the white members of the group to find themselves in a world where their faces were tiny pale specks among millions of dark faces.

We met the issue by saying something like this: No honest American denies the existence of racial and religious bigotry in the United States, any more than any honest citizen of the Commonwealth of India denies the fact that caste discrimination has not entirely been eliminated in India. Thoughtful Americans are not only heartily ashamed by the continuation of prejudice in their country, but many of them are effectively doing something about it. A few are doing much, more are doing a little, some are doing nothing or are actively working to perpetuate prejudice. In a democratic society where there is freedom of the right to protest against even the government itself, some progress toward abolition of the color line in jobs, voting, the armed services, and education is being made. Not enough of course. But with all its shortcomings a democracy does permit dissent, which is not possible in dictatorship of either left or right. Where all power is vested in a dictator or a small clique, however benevolent its announced objectives, protestants against government usually wind up, I reminded the newsmen, in prison or facing a firing squad.

Another episode that indicated the need to tell the true story of race occurred at a dinner party in Karachi given for us by the vivacious wife of a high government official. Both of them were widely traveled in Asia and Europe but at the time had not visited the United States. With tact and delicacy they and the other Pakistani guests approached questions about race they obviously were eager to ask. Their curiosity and perplexity were measurably heightened by stories in the Pakistan newspapers that my wife and I were an interracial couple, the possibility of such a marriage in the

United States being totally at odds with all they had heard. Confusion was compounded for them, apparently, by the fact that my wife is a brunette and I am blond. As we watched the eyes of the guests shift in increasing puzzlement from my wife to me and back again it was apparent that they were trying to figure out which of us was colored.

When finally our hostess accepted me as a Negro, she asked if I would be willing to answer some quite personal questions. I told her she could ask any question she wished.

"How did you obtain an education in the United States?" was her first query.

I told her how, with the aid of my parents and through working during summer vacations, I had paid for the modest formal training I possessed.

Impatiently she brushed aside my reply. "I know all about the Horatio Alger rags-to-riches tradition of you Americans," she told me. "That isn't what I meant at all. What I want to know is how you *as a Negro* got an education, since it is well known that Negroes in the United States are not permitted to go to institutions of higher education."

I told her about the establishment of Atlanta, Fisk, and Howard Universities after the Civil War, to give Negroes higher education.

She politely cut short my explanation. "Oh, what I meant was that you have laws and customs prohibiting Negroes from attending schools with whites."

Had our hostess been less well informed on a variety of subjects, her incomplete knowledge would have been understandable. But because she represented the best-informed opinion of Pakistan, her views were both disconcerting and startling in revealing American failure to tell the facts about the issue that creates more doubt than any other about America's sincerity among the two-thirds of the world's people who are non-white.

We told her and the other guests that Negroes were barred from tax-supported and private colleges and professional schools only in the South. One of the guests who had been in the United States asked somewhat acidly about the quota system affecting Negroes, Jews, and other minorities, and the domination of campus life by fraternities and conservative boards of trustees. We had to admit that such handicaps to democratic education exist.

But when we told them of the series of legal cases which were even then being carried to the United States Supreme Court—decisions which we were certain would lead to the admission of Negro students to state colleges in Southern States—there was incredulity on the faces of our audience. The following year we could have informed them that ten state universities in the South were open to students on a non-segregated basis, and that Negroes were faculty members of seventy-two non-segregated colleges and universities.

In India, Pakistan, Malaya, and the Philippines we found a willingness to listen to the facts. But when one encounters men and women from the Soviet Union or her satellites, there is usually found belligerent denial that treatment of Negroes in the United States is ever anything but foul. Here is the story of one such encounter.

In 1948 I attended in Paris the meetings of the General Assembly of the United Nations as one of the non-governmental-organization representatives. Of all the issues on the agenda, the most hotly debated were genocide and human rights. I was invited to do a world-wide broadcast over the UN radio on how the efforts for a human-rights covenant and a genocide convention appeared to an American Negro. I gladly accepted, and showed up at the agreed time at the broadcasting station in the labyrinthian bowels of the vast Palais de Chaillot. As I was about to begin, the argumentative chief of the Polish delegation, Juliusz Katz-Suchy, stormed into the studio to demand that he record a broadcast immediately. It seemed that he had been detained from keeping his appointment, which had been scheduled a half-hour ahead of mine. He was told politely that because he was tardy preparations had been made to permit me to do my chore.

His explosion at such an indignity would have done credit to the most temperamental actor. Seeing that the studio employees might get into difficulties with Katz-Suchy, I volunteered to step aside and do my broadcast after the Polish delegate had finished. Apparently such a concession from an American was more displeasing than being made to wait. Without thanking me, he glared silently at me as though I had insulted him and strode past me into the studio to deliver an impassioned diatribe against the war-mongering, capitalistic Americans who were attempting by force and bribes to dominate the United Nations and thwart the peaceful intentions of the Soviet Union and her allies.

When he was told that I would talk on human rights, curiosity to hear what would be said and the possibility of finding ammunition for future debates caused Katz-Suchy to go into the control room to listen. I found myself so fascinated by the changes of expression on his face that I had difficulty following the script. When I stated that as a Negro I would rather take my chances in a democracy, whatever its shortcomings, in preference to any dictatorship, the Polish delegate's mouth opened in astonishment.

As soon as I was finished, Katz-Suchy rushed from the control room to ask if he heard correctly when I stated that I was a Negro. When I assured him that his ears had not deceived him, he exclaimed, "You can't be—you have blue eyes, a skin whiter than mine, and none of the features of a Negro!"

Quite obviously convinced that I was an impostor, he poured out a torrent of statements—not questions—about the low and miserable status of the Negro in the United States. In all honesty, the basic facts of most of his charges were correct, despite the class-angling he gave to them. He concluded his indictment by demanding, half-pityingly and half-contemptuously, how I as a Negro could possibly hold on to faith in a capitalistic, prejudice-ridden nation like the United States.

I knew the futility of denial of the accuracy of the gloom-filled picture he had painted. Another approach was obviously necessary. "Monsieur Katz-Suchy, what would happen to you," I asked him quietly, "if in your native Poland you criticized or attacked the Russians? How long would you remain in power if you appealed to the courts in opposition to policies set by the Soviet Union?"

His face reddened. Without another word, he left the studio. I was not particularly happy over matching the relative shortcomings of our governments. But I had learned from the encounter how universal and effective a weapon against the United States and democracy everywhere had been forged by the Communists out of the material that America herself had furnished by two and a half centuries of human slavery and three-quarters of a century of second-class citizenship for its Negro citizens.

Nor are questions of our treatment of Negroes confined to Asia and Africa and to the far side of the Iron Curtain. There is, for example, a friend of ours in Italy. He is a man of substance, and a member of an old and distinguished family. Because one of his ancestors fell in love with and married a beautiful woman who was part Jewish, retribution descended upon him generations later when Hitler took over Italy and Benito Mussolini. He refused to follow the example of many of his class who bowed to the new regime to save their properties, so he slept in a different place every night for six months to escape certain imprisonment and possible death as he rallied resistance to fascism and nazism. Always he had kept American democracy as an ideal. But one night as we sat after dinner in the restaurant that had been the villa of Apuleius, near Rome, he asked us if we could answer a question that had been bothering him.

"You in America are the greatest technicians the world has ever known," he told us. "You are superb businessmen. When disasters occur anywhere in the world you give aid generously and immediately. You have youth and vigor and buoyance, which we no longer possess. We want to believe in you and follow your example. But how can we, when you mistreat and abuse your own people when they have a different color of skin? What's wrong is that we just can't believe you when you talk about democracy and don't practice it."

One more incident from Asia. As we left Pandit Nehru's home in New Delhi we asked him if there was anything we could do to repay his hospitality when he came to America. We were delighted when, instead of the customary declination, he told us there *was* something we could do.

"I want to meet with some Negro leaders to ask them the answers to the questions which puzzle us in Asia," he told us. "I discussed this last year in Paris with Ralph Bunche. Will you and he arrange such a meeting?"

We told him we would not arrange a Jim Crow conference because we believed that he and other visitors to the United States interested in the race question should have an opportunity to learn that both white and Negro Americans are concerned with doing something about it.

Pandit Nehru agreed but insisted that the conference be held away from crowds and newspapermen, so that, "I can ask the questions—not answer them." He added another proviso—that no more than sixteen persons be invited, "because when there are more, everybody, including myself, will make speeches, and I won't get the information I need to answer the questions they're asking all over Asia about the color question in the United States."

We did manage to keep the number down to twenty. Ralph Bunche skillfully managed to keep those of us who were inclined to talk too long or too often in line. Mary McLeod Bethune, the foremost woman Negro of America, answered movingly Pandit Nehru's informed questions on the status of colored women in American life. Judge William H. Hastie, and Arthur B. Spingarn, President of the NAACP, tersely told of the fight through the courts that so materially was changing the pattern of American life; Robert C. Weaver described housing and the acute problems in that field which Negroes face, in which discussion he was joined by Albert M. Greenfield of Philadelphia. Lester Granger of the National Urban League talked about employment, while others of us answered Mr. Nehru's and Madame Pandit's searching inquiries about the Negro's growing political independence and power.

The Prime Minister repeated what he had told my wife and me in New Delhi about the frequency with which he encountered in Asia great skepticism about the United States because of reports of mistreatment based on skin color. "Whenever I warn against acceptance of Soviet promises of equality because they are so frequently broken, I am answered quite often by questions about America's attitude toward dark-skinned people. The people of Asia don't like colonialism or race prejudices. They resent condescension. When Americans talk to them about equality and freedom, they remember stories about lynchings. They are becoming increasingly aware that colonialism is largely based on color—and, for the first time in the lives of many of them, they realize that they are colored. With what is happening to the dark-skinned native population of South Africa at the hands of Malan and what the French are doing in Indochina our people are developing a sense of sympathy and unity with dark-skinned victims of exploitation all over the world."

It was a somber warning to all of us gathered there in the deepening dusk at Kitty Lehman's spacious apartment, which she had generously offered for the meeting. The traffic of New York, many stories below, suddenly took on the ominous sound of tumbrils, symbols of a civilization that had fancied itself unaffected by the demands of hundreds of millions of brown people in Asia and black people in Africa. The words of the gentle brown man were quiet ones, but behind them were the marching steps of millions tramping out of the bogs of bondage.

Yet none of us felt the terror that one instinctively feels when the way of life to which he has become accustomed is threatened. On the contrary, the vast wisdom and courage that flowed out of the great spiritual leader of nearly three times as many people as live in the United States was reassuring. We knew that hundreds of millions of non-Indian Asians and Africans were influenced in some fashion by his words and acts. We felt that the correction of imbalances between peoples based on economic circumstances, geography, language, tradition, race, and religion, which Nehru espoused and fought for, was assuredly part of the answer to the world's grave illness.

The talk continued long past the time limit that the Prime Minister's schedule permitted. But he insisted on our taking him on a tour of Harlem. We went first to Harlem Hospital, where the late Dr. Louis T. Wright, famed surgical director and world authority on brain injuries, antibiotics, cancer, and lymphogranuloma, conducted the Prime Minister's party through the huge institution. As Pandit Nehru animatedly asked innumerable questions about the hospital's methods of operations and especially about the relations between the white and Negro members of the staff, I became aware as never before how measurable was Dr. Wright's contribution to America in his thirty-year fight against racial segregation in New York hospitals. What he saw with his own eyes at Harlem Hospital, the Prime Minister told us afterward, did more than anything else to convince him that the picture of the Negro's status which he had previously held had not been entirely accurate.

Unfortunately the elaborate security regulations that had been arranged by the Secret Service and the New York police, in addition to the shortage of time, permitted only a swift automobile tour of upper Manhattan. We were eager to show Mr. Nehru some of the churches and social-welfare agencies, as well as some of the better housing and some of the worst. We could not show him the latter because we were not allowed to drive on Lenox Avenue, as Benjamin J. Davis, Jr., a Communist candidate for the New York City Council, was addressing a street-corner meeting there.

I had to leave New York early the next morning for a speaking engagement in Arizona, but Mr. Nehru told my wife at a dinner party before he left that the brief glimpses we and Ralph Bunche had given him of the Negro's position in American life in relation to white America constituted the most significant and valuable experience of his trip to the West.

Many other factors have made me want to write this book, to tell as simply as I can the true story, which I hope will counteract at least some of the half-truths, misconceptions, and outright falsehoods about the Negro's place in American life that are current all over the world.

Unfortunately far too many misleading and often quite untrue general statements that are based on the race question made in anti-American propaganda are accompanied by specific documentation of the all too horrible facts. For example, I remember well a leaflet dropped from German planes in North Africa during World War II which I picked up in Algiers. On the front of it was a photograph made in Detroit during the bloody race riot of 1943. The central figure was an elderly, slender, sad-eyed Negro whose arms were pinioned by two husky policemen. Behind them were two mounted officers, one of whom held an upraised club aimed, not at the frenzied mob of whites, but toward the skull of the helpless Negro. As the four officers made sure no member of the mob was hurt, a brutish, shirt-sleeved, muscular white man smashed his fist full in the face of the Negro.

The photograph, I am sorry to say, was an accurate picture of a horrible event. The use to which it was put was typical of the techniques of Nazi propaganda. With incredible arrogance, in view of Hitler's racist doctrines, which then dominated German thinking, the obverse side of the leaflet carried an inflammatory message asserting that if the Allies won the war, the dark-skinned inhabitants of Africa would all be subjected to treatment identical with that given to the Negro in Detroit, but that if Germany won, all men of every race and color would be given justice and freedom.

I asked the Algerian who translated the leaflet from Arabic if such patently insincere propaganda was influencing any North Africans.

"We don't trust the Germans, and we take whatever they say with a grain of salt," he told me thoughtfully. "But this picture of the way Negroes are persecuted in the United States isn't the first one we've seen. We've read for years about your lynchings. We've seen how some of your white GIs act toward your Negro troops. Some of our people have been to your country and have come back with stories about being turned away from restaurants and hotels. Naturally we are puzzled, and we wonder what kind of treatment you'll give us because we aren't white."

Like an evil malady, the same kind of questioning is found all over the world. During World War II, I found it in Japanese anti-American propaganda in Guam, the Philippines, Okinawa, the Marianas, and other areas in the Pacific. I remember well a beautifully printed poster in Guam that had been displayed all over that unfortunate island during the Japanese occupation. It called on Guamanians in impassioned verbiage to join in driving out the "bigoted, imperialistic American white man," whose sole purpose was subjugation of colored peoples. It urged Guamanians to join Japan, "the champion and defender of the colored peoples of the world." Had not the Japanese been as cruel in their treatment of the people of Guam, the appeal might have had a serious effect on the war efforts.

Americans know that it is not the purpose of the United States to subjugate the colored peoples of the world, yet it is difficult to say this convincingly to a member of one of the dark-skinned races of the East, when at the same time one must answer yes to such questions as: "Is it not true that Negroes have the worst housing in America; that they almost invariably are forced to live in segregated areas; that they are excluded from many restaurants and schools; that it is almost impossible for them to make any significant headway in some occupations; that there is still violence against them?"

Anti-American propagandists see to it that information about the sordid facts of widespread racism in the United States and the dramatic horror of some of its worst expressions spreads far more rapidly and widely than the equally dramatic, and equally true, story of advances in the fight against the evils of discrimination, or the fact that a large body of intelligent white Americans are fighting side by side with the Negroes.

It is the purpose of such propagandists to make American discriminatory practices seem a unique phenomenon in human relations and universal in all aspects of our national life. In many instances they have been widely successful. Actually while the situation has been improving in the United States, it has worsened in some other parts of the world—even among some highly enlightened social groups. Ever since World War II there has been a rising tide of antagonism in England, not only against Negroes, but actually against all foreigners. Dr. Malan's *apartheid* policy in South Africa is an example of the depths of cruelty to which racism can descend, and is, to the world's eternal shame, an official policy of the government. Other examples could be cited.

Ever since peoples of different skin pigmentations, different religious beliefs, and different hereditary cultures have mingled, the evils of concepts of superiority and inferiority, of exploitation and subjugation, of discrimination and segregation, have been serious stumbling blocks in the path of humanity's progress toward social maturity. And though it is tragically true that the race situation in the United States of America still furnishes the world with some of its most horrible examples of ignorance and savage inhumanity, it is equally true that much that has been accomplished in the last fifteen years in the struggle to eliminate these evils has set a salutary example for other social groups throughout the world. The heads of intelligent Americans have long been bowed in shame over the situation of the American Negro, but they are now being raised a little—at least in hope.

We returned to the United States from the Round the World Town Meeting tour deeply concerned by the fact that outside of the United States the world is studiously being kept unaware of the not inconsiderable progress which has been made since the Civil War, and particularly since the outbreak of the Second

World War, while the stories of violence and denial of justice to the American Negro are being well publicized.

It is important for us to let the world know that there have been gains. Many of them have come about, not through, but in some cases even in spite of, official government action. They have been won by persistent, heartbreaking, organized, and frequently expensive action by citizens' organizations and individuals. Much has been achieved by Negroes themselves, often in the face of odds that have seemed insuperable.

We came home convinced that it was imperative that the story of America's success as well as that of its failures needed to be told. We had learned from scores of incidents that it should be told by non-governmental agencies and individuals, because the modern world since the days of Hitler's "big lie" technique has grown increasingly suspicious of all governmental statements and counter-statements on controversial issues. This did not mean that we advocated abolition of official agencies such as the United States Information Service or the Voice of America, for undoubtedly the efforts of these agencies bring about some favorable results. But we found that the materials on the race question in United States libraries, embassies, consulates, and USIS offices in various parts of the world were fragmentary and apologetic.

Inquiry on our return about the poor selection of such literature on a question that is increasingly emphasized by those in whom distrust of the United States is growing disclosed a fundamental weakness of the American information service. Edward W. Barrett, at the time Assistant Secretary of State in charge of public information, described the conditions under which that agency was forced to operate.

Continuous attacks by certain members of the Congress against all governmental programs instituted to tell the facts to a doubting world had created an atmosphere of fear in the department. At frequent intervals, Mr. Barrett related, demands would be made on him to deliver the texts of VOA broadcasts and other literature published by the department to Congressional critics and enemies of the program. All the material would be closely and critically examined. Whenever any material that was not innocuous in its discussion of race relations was found, it would promptly be passed on to a senator or congressman from the South addicted to race-baiting. Almost immediately Mr. Barrett would begin to receive abusive telephone calls and letters threatening drastic cuts of appropriations or abolition of the public information program altogether.

"The result is that I have a gun-shy staff," Mr. Barrett concluded, "which writes about the race question with an eye on how its words will read to a bigoted Southern opponent of civil rights and not how they will answer the honest questions of people in Asia or Africa."

The same pressures were later enormously expanded when Senator Joseph McCarthy of Wisconsin used them against all those who did not conform to his views. It was apparent that effective presentation of the facts—even favorable ones—by the United States would be impossible until the Congress and the executive agencies of government found an acceptable and workable formula for cooperation.

Meanwhile the field was being left clear for anti-American critics and propagandists. For generations the attitude of smug and unrealistic Americans—that the United States could exist regardless of what happened to the rest of the world—had bred an indifference which at times bordered on contempt for what other peoples might think of Americans. This dead weight of apathy had similarly afflicted many of the philanthropic foundations and other agencies that possessed funds to do something tangible about the problem. The majority of American business concerns operated on the assumption that when they had paid the lowest price obtainable for raw materials and other goods and had sold their own products at the best price obtainable their responsibility was ended.

At a dinner in New York honoring Dr. Ralph Bunche after he had received the Nobel Peace Prize, I sought to point out that the relations between highly industrialized America and the so-called "underdeveloped" areas such as Asia, Africa, and Latin America must not be considered a one-way street. Only at its own peril could the Western world with its machine civilization continue to regard itself as a generous benefactor that dispensed crumbs from its well-laden table to less fortunate peoples as mendicants or inferiors. Technological aid through programs such as Point Four and the Ford Foundation's aid to India were essential, I pointed out; much more important was abolition of dangerous concepts too frequently held by the white Western world of its own moral and mental superiority. The consequences of continuation of such ideas, I warned, could result in the loss by the colored peoples of the world of what remained of their faith in democracy, causing them to turn in despair toward whatever system of society appeared to offer more hope. That action could mean the loss of man power, raw materials, and markets, without which the industrial West could not survive.

This simple and obvious statement of fact so shocked one industrialist that he left the dinner. Another and more important manufacturer, who ranks among the top ten businessmen in the United States, made the astonishing statement after the dinner that he had not thought of any connection between America's racial practices and the sources of her raw materials until I pointed it out that evening.

Unawareness such as this of the seriousness of the problem is more baffling and more difficult to combat than acts of violence and discrimination perpetrated by those who do not care what their actions do to the reputation of their country. Mobbists who murdered Mr. and Mrs. Harry T. Moore at Mims, Florida, on Christmas night in 1951, or those who staged a reign of terror in Cicero, Illinois, in the same year are more easily understood in their panic at having their racial "superiority" challenged. Less easy to understand and to awaken are those presumably more intelligent people who fail or refuse to understand that their own security is threatened.

Far beyond the interests of the American Negro himself, it became increasingly evident that whatever could be done—however little—by private organizations and individuals to portray America, pockmarks included, in a truer light must be done.

The first need, of course, was to step up in every possible way the process of elimination of prejudice and barriers based on race, color, religion, or national origin in the United States. Without such action it would be utterly impossible to convince the rest of the world that American democracy could be trusted and emulated.

The second step seemed to be to tell the United States about the decline in prestige that is affecting the United States all over the world because of the one-sidedness of the story as it is known, and to let the rest of the world know, through all possible media of communication, the facts as they really are, rather than as our enemies would have others believe that they are.

I was asked by the editor of one of America's most successful magazines, which has a very large circulation all over the world, to write the story as I had seen it. I accepted with eagerness, and devoted much time to research and to the depiction of the progress that had been made in various areas. Because the picture would have been neither convincing nor honest without mention of the vast job yet to be done, that part of the story was naturally included.

The editor, however, wanted all mention of the fact that Utopia had not been attained eliminated on the ground that, "Our enemies have seen to it that our faults have been well publicized; I want this to be exclusively a story of our accomplishments in combating race prejudice." Naturally I could not with integrity permit that to be done. I would have been charged quite properly with writing a whitewash of the truth and with giving a picture as unbalanced on one side as critics of the United States, wittingly or otherwise, had portrayed on the other. Quite practically, I knew from experience that such an article would have been brushed aside or ridiculed and could have done more harm than good.

Fortunately Norman Cousins, editor of the highly regarded though less widely circulated *Saturday Review*, published the article under the title, "Time for a Progress Report," and it has had considerable circulation in various parts of the world.

My wife and I also arranged a conference at our Connecticut home, Breakneck Hill, in September 1950 to discuss what effective action could be taken on the problem. Among those who joined in the all-day discussion were Mrs. Franklin D. Roosevelt; Ralph J. Bunche; Dr. Louis T. Wright, Chairman of the Board of Directors of the NAACP; Admiral Chester Nimitz, who as commander of the fleet in the Pacific during World War II had had considerable contact with the peoples there; Victor Reuther, the erudite CIO leader; Judge J. Waties Waring, who in South Carolina had recently handed down two courageous decisions, which had applied the *coup de grace* to disfranchisement of Negro voters through the "white, Democratic primaries" system; Elmo Roper, economic analyst; Norman Cousins, who had traveled widely and who knew from experience of the deterioration of respect for the United States because of its racial practices; Dowdal Davis of the Kansas City *Call,* who was also President of the Negro Newspaper Publishers' Association; Dr. Robert C. Weaver, former War Manpower Commission official and authority on housing for minorities; Sig Mickelson of the Columbia Broadcasting System; Judge William H. Hastie of the Federal Circuit Court of Appeals; Senator William Benton of Connecticut; and Henry Lee Moon, director of public relations of the NAACP. Messrs. Waring, Nimitz, Wright, Benton, and Reuther were accompanied by their wives, who also participated in the lively discussions.

We had emphasized in the invitations that those who attended were to participate as individuals rather than as representatives of any organizations with which they might be connected, in order to insure as free comment as possible. President Truman on this basis asked the late David K. Niles to attend the conference, while Secretary of State Dean Acheson asked Mrs. Margaret Carter to represent him and Assistant Secretary Barrett, since both of them were detained by the prolongation of the Council of Atlantic Ministers, which was then in session. Francis Russell of the State

Department's Office of Public Affairs attended, to contribute his intimate knowledge of the problem. Nelson Rockefeller, Henry Ford, Jr., David Sarnoff of the Radio Corporation of America, Clarence Pickett of the American Friends Service Committee, and several others expressed interest in the meeting but were unable to be present.

It was good talk, honest and frank. For example, Norman Cousins focused the discussion of anti-American Communist propaganda by remarking that, "The heart of the propaganda against America is in America itself," and Judge Waring by his observation, "When it comes to propaganda we are not as good as the Russians. We have sold automobiles throughout the world, and we have to sell democracy. The reason we sell automobiles is because we make and sell *good* automobiles. We can tell the truth when we say we make the best. Are we making the best democracy? Are we making it good enough to advertise? If automobiles are defective, you'd better not advertise them too much. The same goes for our democracy. We have been free since 1776. We have made progress, true —but so slow it is nothing to boast about."

Ralph Bunche emphasized that the United States and its people are inextricably involved for all time in the struggle for the free association of free people and that this means not only mobilization of government and industry, but preparation of the people for the new role of world responsibility that has been thrust upon them.

"The stakes in this struggle are people—hundreds of millions of people all over the world, and particularly in Asia, Africa, and the Caribbean, who throughout human history have been deprived and whose lives have been lives of misery. We come to them and say we have a concept of freedom and democracy which we believe is the only way of life. But we have to keep in mind that most of these people know nothing about it. They can't eat it. It is just a propaganda battle. Unless we live our principles of democracy and freedom, we can't possibly win."

With reference to an observation that the United States could not justifiably criticize India for not having wholly eliminated caste discrimination until there were Negroes in the President's cabinet, as there were two Untouchables in Pandit Nehru's official family, Mrs. Roosevelt pointed out that during the formative years in the life of a young nation it is often possible for the head of the state to bring about important changes through his own authority or influence, whereas in governmental structures that have existed for some time, and have achieved a fuller measure of suffrage, the head of the government cannot act independently.

All were fully agreed, however, that there was a job to be done to accelerate the pace of reform at home and thereby to turn out a brand of democracy that could be honestly publicized abroad as worthy of respect and emulation. A committee was appointed, as is customary when Americans meet to consider problems of any nature. My wife and I believed, possibly overoptimistically, that the conference had not been in vain, because all of us appeared to exhibit more willingness to urge upon others the need of doing something. But tangibly and measurably the meeting appeared to be one that could be written off as a "nice try."

Almost three years later, as this book was being written, however, solemn evidence arrived from Freedom Village in Korea— where Operation Big Switch, the exchange of war prisoners, was going forward—indicating that we should not have been deterred from doing the job. A news dispatch reported that the Chinese Communists in the North Korean prisoner-of-war camps had made particular efforts to win United States Negro troops to communism by installation of a new type of segregation through separation of Negroes from their white fellow Americans. Intensive indoctrination was directed at the Negro captives, with detailed reminders of such tragedies as the bomb murder of the Harry Moores. They were told: "There is no reason for you to like America, as you are black men and you are treated badly there. You should come over to our side, where you will be treated fairly."

In spite of the second-class citizenship that had been forced upon most of the Negro veterans prior to service in Korea, very few of them succumbed to the Communist lure of existence free of racial discrimination. None of them harbored any illusions that on returning to the United States there would be full and unrestricted opportunity to live without handicaps because of race. Why did men offered a new life after fighting for a democracy many of whose benefits they have seldom enjoyed refuse?

Home, parents, wives, sweethearts, a language and a way of life with which they were familiar—all the understandable reasons were present. But for Negroes there was something more—a loyalty and a patriotism of a somewhat special quality beyond that of their white fellow Americans, who had never experienced the humiliation of being set apart solely because of skin color. Many of the white Korean veterans had known discrimination because of religion or place of birth or poverty. But none of it had had the quality that crushes the spirit and robs the individual of ambition and hope. None of them had heard from home of new humiliations that had sprung up since their departure, such as a soft-drink vending machine with separate coin slots marked "White" and "Colored." None had received, as had the Negro troops, news of the murder by a nitroglycerine bomb of a man and his wife of their race for the "crime" of working for the fair treatment of Negroes. All of them had at least some reason for hope that their status would be improved on returning home because of the heavy sacrifices they had made.

Why did so few Negroes respond to the Communist overtures? Why did so many pay the penalty of death from starvation or lack of medical care when by even pretending to be receptive to the stories of race discrimination back home that they knew to be true they could have obtained food, tobacco, and treatment of their wounds? What gave them the faith and strength to return to struggle again for opportunity that had been grudgingly and only partially given them and their ancestors for more than three centuries?

The answer to these questions is what this book hopes to give. The complete story cannot, of course, be told in one book. An entire volume, for example, could be devoted to a single phase of one of the factors that caused Negro soldiers in Korea to spurn the blandishments of the Chinese Communists—abolition of the color line in the American armed forces and recognition on a basis of equality of opportunity as well as of danger and privation. It has been my intent to tell the story in terms of human beings and to avoid as far as possible dreary recitals of court decisions and the texts of laws.

It is also my hope that the picture of the continuing struggle will be one that will give an over-all view instead of the segmented account that scholars have written. Too often students of the question have concentrated on the short view or on one aspect, so that even they could not see the woods for the trees. As a result, much of what has been written has been slanted toward the gloomily pessimistic or the unjustifiably optimistic. As in military campaigns, the lines of battle have moved forward, then backward. But the net movement has been steadily forward and has demonstrated—even to the American Negro, who has had far less than his share of the benefits of democracy—that any form of totalitarianism with all its blandishments and promises is destructive not only to the oppressed but also to the oppressor, and that, with all its imperfections and infringements of freedom, a free society is the best hope of all mankind.

I have written this book in the hope that it will add substance to this faith. It is addressed to two audiences.

One is composed of peoples outside the United States who have had little or no contact with America's race problem and whose information on the subject is either fragmentary or made up largely of news of conflict.

The other audience is in the United States. It is my conviction that many more Americans oppose prejudice than favor and practice it. As Gunnar Myrdal points out, the basic principle of human equality, which is written into every important document of state, from the Declaration of Independence through the Emancipation Proclamation to the Charter of the United Nations, acts as a force of compulsion on the American conscience. Even when the average American neglects or fails to live up to these pronouncements, he suffers from a sense of guilt that harasses him to such an extent that even lynchers construct elaborate rationalizations to explain and justify their crimes. This pressure on Americans, collectively and individually, to deal justly with their fellow citizens is markedly different from that on citizens of countries like the Union of South Africa, where inequality is written into law and precept.

Progress against racial injustice, unfortunately, has been slowed more by inertia than by calculated determination to keep the Negro on a lower level of society. One of the chief causes of that inertia is the belief that the problem is so complex, difficult, and long-lived that it is useless to attempt to do anything toward its solution. It is hoped that the gains which are recorded here may disabuse the minds of the fainthearted, even though we have a long way to go before we reach the goals of equality set for us by the founders of the nation. At least we are nearer to them. As for those impervious to idealism or so engrossed in advancing their own fortunes without regard to the well-being of others, it is hoped that what is reported here may cause them to realize that they may lose all they have gained if the majority of the world's people who are colored turn against the democracies because we in the United States continue to give them reason to distrust and hate us.

Modern science has virtually eliminated national and racial protective barriers based upon time and space. This fact makes peculiarly applicable to our times a statement made by a Negro speaker in the pre-A-bomb days of less than ten years ago. He concluded a speech to a select audience in the exclusive Back Bay section of Boston with the quiet remark, "Your ancestors came to the United States on the *Mayflower*. Mine came on a slave ship. But we're all in the same boat now."

Since that day the atom has been split, to release more physical power than mankind ever dared dream was possible. Pilotless guided missiles of constantly increasing range and accuracy are being devised that in time may be able to wipe out any city anywhere on the globe. Hydrogen bombs have been manufactured capable of annihilation of every object, animate or inanimate, within a twenty-mile radius. On the other hand, nuclear fission, which has made humanity's most horribly destructive weapons possible, is capable of providing abundant energy for a world in which no man need be ill fed, ill housed, or ill clad. All these things expand the figure of speech used by the speaker in Boston. All the peoples of the world are in the same boat now. Today that vessel is unseaworthy because we have not yet mastered the science of living together. Through a major leak caused by color prejudice the waters of hate are rushing in. Our survival may depend on how swiftly and expertly that leak is caulked.

I. Decision Monday

Precisely at noon the ceiling-high red velvet curtains opened silently behind the tall bench and the nine chairs of the justices of the United States Supreme Court. The justices filed in to their seats. It was May 17, 1954. The austere but beautiful room was filled to the decorous capacity permitted by the court. The spectators seemed to be permeated with an electric sense of anticipation that the day might bring one of the most important decisions in the court's one-hundred-sixty-four-year career—possibly the most decisive ruling on human equality since the first Negroes arrived in North America in 1619.

On the faces of the justices there was, as usual, no indication that history was about to be made by a decision capable of altering the course of American race relations more profoundly than any event since the American Civil War. The customary routine of announcement by the clerk of procedural rulings and of admission of lawyers to practice before the high tribunal were given perfunctory attention. Attorneys-general from several Southern states sat in apprehensive silence, while lawyers for the Negro plaintiffs in the five public-school-segregation cases were equally grave as they awaited the ruling that would announce either victory in the long legal battle to abolish the color bar in tax-supported schools, or another postponement of the clear-cut decision that had so long been sought. Outside the courtroom stood long lines of would-be spectators who, by some strange intuition, had sensed that May 17 might be Decision Monday.

Chief Justice Earl Warren leaned forward and began to read. Four of the five cases, he announced—those originating in South Carolina, Kansas, Virginia, and Delaware—had been consolidated in a single opinion, because a common legal question underlay all four cases, although they were based on different facts and different local conditions. In admirably terse and clear fashion, as free of legalistic phraseology as possible, the decision summarized the history of racial segregation in American public education.

Particular stress was laid on the course of such education during the fifty-eight-year period since 1896, when the Supreme Court had ruled in the case of *Plessy* vs. *Ferguson* (163 U.S. 537) that, "Equality of treatment is accorded when the races are provided substantially equal facilities, even though those facilities be separate."

Noting that not only had there been no equality but that separation of students solely on the basis of race and color in and of itself constituted a denial of rights and opportunities guaranteed by the federal Constitution, Chief Justice Warren read:

"We cannot turn the clock back to 1868, when the [Fourteenth] Amendment was adopted, or even to 1896, when *Plessy* versus *Ferguson* was written. We must consider public education in the light of its full development and its present place in American life throughout the nation. Only in this way can it be determined if segregation in public schools deprives these plaintiffs of the equal protection of the laws. . . .

"We come then to the question presented: Does segregation of children in public schools solely on the basis of race, even though the physical facilities and other 'tangible' factors may be equal, deprive the children of the minority group of equal educational opportunities?"

The Chief Justice paused to lend emphasis to the momentous opinion that followed. Quietly, but with deep conviction, he pronounced in five crisp words the court's epochal decision: "We believe that it does."

Two paragraphs later Mr. Warren spelled out on behalf of the court the doctrine which thereupon became the law of the land.

"Whatever may have been the extent of psychological knowledge at the time of *Plessy* versus *Ferguson*, this finding [that segregation has a detrimental effect upon children and particularly upon Negro children as a badge of inferiority] is amply supported by modern authority. Any language in *Plessy* versus *Ferguson* contrary to this finding is rejected. We conclude that in the field of public education the doctrine of 'separate but equal' has no place. Separate educational facilities are inherently unequal. Therefore, we hold that the plaintiffs and others similarly situated for whom the actions have been brought are, by reason of the segregation complained of, deprived of the equal protection of the laws guaranteed by the Fourteenth Amendment. This disposition makes unnecessary any discussion whether such segregation also violates the Due Process Clause of the Fourteenth Amendment."

The rules of the Supreme Court forbid demonstrations of approval or disapproval. There were none on May 17. But no one in the court that day was unaware that both approval and revolt were of such intensity that, though silent, they surpassed in muted volume the wildest demonstration of a political convention. There were anger and bewilderment on the faces of the Southern legal officials, although most of them had anticipated that the court would rule against segregation. There was quiet jubilation on the faces of those, both Negro and white, who had fought for many decades against overwhelming odds for the victory this day won.

Chief Justice Warren began to read again, giving the court's decision in the case involving segregation in the schools of Washington, D.C. Although this case was of equal importance with those from the four states, now that the latter had been decided against segregation, it was a foregone conclusion that schools located on federal property would not be allowed to discriminate either. The District of Columbia case decision seemed, therefore, anticlimactic, despite its importance.

"In view of our decision that the Constitution prohibits the states from maintaining racially segregated public schools, it would be unthinkable that the same Constitution would impose a lesser duty on the federal government. We hold that racial segregation in the public schools of the District of Columbia is a denial of the due process of law guaranteed by the Fifth Amendment to the Constitution."

Thus was legal victory finally won for the Negro American in his long fight for educational opportunities equal to those enjoyed by whites. There remained the question of how promptly and wholeheartedly the decision would be implemented by action, especially in the South (which is discussed later in this chapter), but now it was an undisputed fact, on the authority of the nation's highest court, that any community that provided segregated educational facilities did so in violation of the Constitution of the United States of America. Northerners who live in localities where it is a commonplace for Negro and white children to attend school together may not realize how many Americans were affected by the decision. At that time in seventeen states[1] and the District of Columbia segregation in public schools was required by law. In four others[2] it was permitted by law. By one device or another it had been practiced elsewhere.

From the beginning the fight against educational segregation has been interwoven with that against segregation in other fields.

A decade after the Civil War (1873) the Supreme Court ruled (*Railroad Company* vs. *Brown*) that separate but identical railroad coaches for Negroes constituted a denial of equality. But, beginning in 1881 and continuing for a quarter of a century thereafter, Southern states passed laws compelling racial segregation on railroad trains, streetcars and in schools, and disfranchising Negroes. Bit by bit oppressive laws such as these, bitterness over the Confederate "Lost Cause," the Ku Klux Klan, fear of the emerging educated Negro's power, and Northern indifference to the plight of the Negro had changed the attitude of the entire nation.

Thus when Homer Plessy, a Negro, refused to ride in a Jim

[1] Alabama, Arkansas, Delaware, Florida, Georgia, Kentucky, Louisiana, Maryland, Mississippi, Missouri, North Carolina, Oklahoma, South Carolina, Tennessee, Texas, Virginia, and West Virginia.
[2] Arizona, Kansas, New Mexico, and Wyoming.

Crow coach in Louisiana, and carried his appeal to the United States Supreme Court, the stage was set for expression through the court that the majority of Americans were no longer enough interested in real equality to protest against its denial. In 1896 the Supreme Court reflected the moral decline of the nation in ruling that as long as the segregated railroad car in which Plessy was ordered to ride was reasonably equal to those assigned to white people, there had been no denial of his constitutional rights in forcing him to ride in a separate coach solely because of race.

One courageous member of the court, Justice Harlan of Kentucky, dissented vigorously and enunciated the doctrine to which the court was destined to return more than half a century later. He declared:

> Our Constitution is color-blind, and neither knows nor tolerates classes among citizens. . . . We boast of the freedom enjoyed by our people above all other peoples. But it is difficult to reconcile that boast with a state of law which practically puts the brand of servitude and degradation upon a large class of our fellow citizens, our equals before the law. The thin disguise of "equal" accommodations . . . will not mislead anyone, or atone for the wrong this day done.

The anti-Negro South gleefully seized upon the decision in *Plessy* vs. *Ferguson* to fasten racial segregation upon Negroes not only in railroad trains, streetcars, and schools but in every other phase of human existence—public halls, employment, hospitals, clinics, railroad waiting rooms, restaurants, hotels, drinking fountains, even cemeteries. Such was the climate of moral apathy and lack of organized and intelligent opposition that more than three decades passed before this doctrine and practice were challenged.

Twenty years after the *Plessy* vs. *Ferguson* decision had been rendered the separate-but-equal theory had resulted in such inequality that seventeen Southern states were spending $10.30 for the education of each white child and $2.89 for each Negro pupil annually. For the higher education of whites $6,429,991 was appropriated in 1916; $350,000 for Negroes. School terms for most Negroes had shrunk to no more than three to four months a year, against six to nine months for whites. Many of the Negro schools were housed not in school buildings with appropriate equipment but were held in churches, lodge halls, and vacant stores or houses. To obtain a mite more of education for their children, it was common practice for Negro parents to raise money by giving suppers, charades, concerts, and shows to pay for one or two additional months of schooling and to supplement teachers' salaries, which frequently ran as low as twenty-five dollars to thirty dollars per month for a four- or five-month school "year."

Four years later, almost a quarter of a century after the separate-but-equal doctrine had been legalized, a study by the National Education Association revealed that application of the doctrine of inequality was becoming constantly more effective. South Carolina, for example, was spending annually to educate each white child $45.45; for each Negro child, $4.48, or less than one-tenth; Alabama, $37.63 and $5.45; Georgia, $35.34 and $7.44; Louisiana, $46.67 and $8.02; Mississippi, $42.17 and $9.34; North Carolina, $36.70 and $11.06; Florida, $75.07 and $11.41; Arkansas, $21.15 and $11.60; Virginia, $54.21 and $14.86; Tennessee, $33.47 and $20.15; Texas, $40.04 and $28.34; and Maryland, $59.70 and $29.58.

These were the figures at the elementary-school level. Above that the discrepancy was even worse. Even large Southern cities such as Atlanta provided no high-school education or higher education for Negroes until 1917, when colored voters defeated two school-bond issues and forced the concession of a high school for Negro youth. Some states had created state colleges for Negroes, stressing agriculture and mechanical trades. But there were few of these schools, and the curricula and amount of funds available to them were greatly inferior to those allotted to schools for whites. At the graduate- and professional-school level there was not even a pretense of supplying any training whatever for colored citizens. What was worse, the gap at all levels was swiftly widening as the South built more and better grammar schools and high schools, colleges, graduate schools and professional schools, constantly increasing the per capita expenditure for whites, while that for

Negroes remained virtually stationary. Both quantitatively and qualitatively the discrepancy progressively proved the evil of the Supreme Court's blessing and legalization of separate but never equal schools.

These and other important facts were revealed by a study made for the NAACP in 1930 by Judge Nathan Margold, financed by a grant from the Garland Fund. A more disheartening task than that posed by the Margold study would be hard to imagine. The same pattern of inequality and injustice in education was revealed to be present in every other phase of life. The study covered all court decisions rendered up to that time dealing with apportionment of school funds, denial of justice in courts of law, property holders' covenants, discrimination in employment, segregated public carriers, disfranchisement, and mob violence. Its analysis of trends —most of them downward during the preceding thirty-five years —was the basis of the shift by the NAACP from the defensive to the offensive in its attack on educational and other injustices. Its board of directors decided to attack the evils at their sources, which meant a planned and continued attack upon segregation itself in its every manifestation.

Fortunately the grant that financed the Margold study was sufficient also to enable the NAACP to employ, for the first time in its history, a full-time lawyer, Charles Hamilton Houston, Harvard Law School graduate, Phi Beta Kappa, and the first Negro editor of the *Harvard Law Review*. He immediately started planning an uncompromising, sustained campaign of utilization of every legal procedure possible to reverse the anti-Negro course of history and to win complete equality. Along with the legal battle, the board voted to conduct an intensive campaign of education of public opinion on the extent and nature of the inequalities the Negro suffered.

The first gun was fired in 1933 in behalf of a young Negro, Thomas Hocutt, who wanted to study dentistry at the University of North Carolina. In a highly dramatic trial, in which five of the leading lawyers of North Carolina headed by the attorney general were assigned to defend the university, the basic facts of undeniable inequality were placed unanswerably on the record.

But officials of the state school for Negroes from which Hocutt had graduated, perhaps fearing that the legislature might cut appropriations for the school, refused to give Hocutt a copy of the transcript of his scholastic record to be attached to his application for admission to the University of North Carolina School of Dentistry. Because of the absence of this transcript, the court held that Hocutt had not met the dental school's requirements in filing his application for admission, and ruled against him.

The second case was that of Donald G. Murray of Baltimore, who sought to enter the University of Maryland Law School. Again the case was lost in the court of first instance, but the Maryland Court of Appeals ruled that the state must either establish a law school for Negroes equal to that for whites or admit Murray to the existing school. Because the cost of another law school was prohibitive, Murray was admitted in 1935 to the university, where he received a warm welcome from his fellow students, made an excellent record, was graduated, and, following his graduation, practiced his profession successfully in Baltimore.

Next in the series was a suit in Missouri in 1938 in behalf of Lloyd Gaines, who had been refused admittance to the law school of the University of Missouri. The Missouri Supreme Court affirmed the lower court's denial of mandamus asked by Gaines to compel the law school to admit him. The United States Supreme Court, however, reversed that decision and ordered Missouri to supply Gaines and other qualified Negro Missourians with a law school or admit Gaines to the university. Missouri hastily set up a makeshift school of law, which was picketed and boycotted. White students from the University of Missouri and other institutions participated in the picketing in protest against the inequity the makeshift school demonstrated. While action was being instituted to require Missouri to prove to the Supreme Court that the facilities set up for Gaines were equal to those at the university, Gaines mysteriously disappeared. His whereabouts fifteen years later is still unknown. The disappearance stopped further action in this case.

Another Missouri case, in behalf of Lucille Bluford of Kansas City, who wished to study for a Master's degree in journalism, forced that state to establish at considerable cost a school of journalism at the Negro college at Jefferson City. The effect of focusing public attention on the difficulties faced by Negroes in obtaining education was interestingly exhibited in Miss Bluford's case. When she arrived on the campus of the university to register she was welcomed by a large crowd of students, who gave a luncheon in her honor after she had been turned down.

The next suit, against the University of Kentucky, brought about the creation of a makeshift engineering course at the state Negro college.

An action against the University of Tennessee was lost on the technicality that the six applicants for admission to graduate schools "had not exhausted their administrative remedies."

The cases brought up to this time were predicated upon the theory that the most effective way to abolish segregation was through demonstration that establishment of completely or even approximately equal physical facilities, faculty, and curricula, in accordance with the *Plessy* vs. *Ferguson* edict, would cost so fantastic a sum that segregation would be proved too expensive to maintain. This was especially true of the seventeen Southern states, because they were the poorest states in the Union. When it became clear that states such as Missouri, Kentucky, and probably all the others would refuse to follow Maryland's example in the Murray case and would attempt the financially impossible job of supplying separate-but-equal facilities the strategy of those opposing discrimination and segregation was revised. It was decided by the board of directors of the NAACP and by vote of its annual convention that henceforth no further actions would be brought to attain equal facilities but that instead segregation itself would be attacked.

Another consideration was taken into account at this stage—that even if the economically impossible equal facilities were furnished, there would still be inequality, since one of the chief benefits of an education is the interchange of ideas and competition with other students. A new ingredient was added—the expert testimony of social scientists to prove the harm done by segregation to the segregator as well as to the segregated.

Ada Lois Sipuel, an honor graduate of Langston University, the Oklahoma state college for Negroes, sought admission to the law school of the University of Oklahoma in 1944. As was the experience of Lucille Bluford in Missouri, Miss Sipuel was greeted cordially by many white students when she appeared on the campus to register. The Oklahoma courts denied her petition on the grounds, first, that the Gaines decision did not require a state with segregation laws to admit a Negro to its white schools, and, second, that the state was not obligated to set up a separate-but-equal school unless the Negro seeking a legal or other education specifically requested the state to do so. The United States Supreme Court bluntly reversed the Oklahoma courts, especially with respect to their edict that Negroes be required to ask for segregation, and ordered Oklahoma forthwith to admit Miss Sipuel to the university's law school. The anger of the Supreme Court at the Oklahoma evasions was evident in its handing down its decision in an unprecedented hurry—five days.

But Oklahoma's bag of tricks was not exhausted. Although the Board of Regents voted 7 to 1 to admit Miss Sipuel forthwith, the attorney general of the state held that the Oklahoma laws forbidding whites and Negroes to attend the same school took precedence over the United States Supreme Court's ruling. White students numbering over a thousand staged a huge demonstration in protest of the delay, solemnly burned the Fourteenth Amendment, and mailed the ashes to the President of the United States to show their indignation against the exclusion of Negroes from the university. Miss Sipuel's attorneys were forced to take her case again to the Supreme Court, before she was eventually admitted to the law school. But admitted she was—to be graduated in 1952.

Much of the cost of fighting the Sipuel case was contributed by Miss Sipuel's fellow Oklahomans, some of them white.

Up to this time approximately eighty per cent of the costs of these and other legal and legislative struggles had been borne by Negroes. But during this period other Americans became aware of the importance of the fight to themselves as well as to Negroes. The Committee of 100 was organized under the leadership of the late Dr. William Allan Neilson, President of Smith College at Northampton, Massachusetts. Its purpose was to accelerate public concern with the problem and to raise the necessary funds for the costly court battles. Such was the nationwide respect for Dr. Neilson that distinguished men and women of both races eagerly joined with him in the work of the committee, which has raised during the past decade much of the money to finance the cases the NAACP has fought.

In 1950 the seventeen-year struggle against segregation, which began with the Hocutt case in North Carolina, achieved its most significant victory up to that time, when the United States Supreme Court in two unanimous and sweeping decisions ordered the University of Texas School of Law to admit Heman Sweatt, a Negro, to the existing institution, and the University of Oklahoma to admit G. W. McLaurin to the Graduate School of Education. The decisions said nothing about creation of schools of law and education substantially equal but separate—the court had passed beyond that. Today more than two hundred fifty Negroes attend the University of Oklahoma.

During the early 1950s, under the skilled leadership of Thurgood Marshall, who had been a student at the Howard University Law School in Washington when Charles Houston was dean, the technique of using the social sciences to demonstrate the harm of enforced segregation on the basis of race was strikingly demonstrated. Let Thurgood Marshall tell the story.

"It was necessary to demonstrate that segregation on the basis of race was an unreasonable classification within the accepted rules for measuring classification statutes by the states," Marshall told a

three-day seminar on "The Courts and Racial Integration in Education" at Howard University in 1952. "Experts in anthropology
were produced and testified that given a similar learning situation
a Negro student tended to react the same as any other student, and
that there were no racial characteristics which had any bearing
whatsoever on the subject of public education. Experts in the field
of legal education testified that it was impossible for a Negro student
to get an equal education in a Jim Crow law school because of the
lack of opportunity to meet with and discuss problems with other
students of varying strata of society. These witnesses also testified
that even if two law schools could be made absolutely equal inso-
far as physical facilities, equipment, curricula, and faculties, the
Jim Crow law school would nevertheless not offer an education
equal to that offered at the other school."

When the Hocutt case was first contemplated there were dark
prophecies of violence if Negroes were ever enrolled in Southern
white schools. Even as late as 1950, when the Sweatt and McLaurin
cases were pending in the Supreme Court, the attorneys general of
the Southern states with somewhat dubious morality and taste filed
a joint brief on the two cases in which they declared: "The Southern states trust that this court will not strike down their power to
keep peace, order, and support of their public schools by maintaining equal-but-separate facilities. If the states are shorn of this
police power and physical conflict takes place . . . the states are
left with no alternative but to close their schools to prevent violence."

By mid-1953 more than fifteen hundred Negroes were attending
Southern graduate and professional schools. There had been no
untoward incidents. At about this time a national picture magazine
decided that an interesting story could be photographed and written
on how well Negro and white students got along together, so the
editor dispatched a photographer and a writer to the schools in ten
Southern states where the color bar had been abolished. Almost
everywhere they went they encountered astonishment that anyone

would think there was any news whatever in American students of different races studying, eating, playing games, and otherwise associating.

Nevertheless the story is not by any means all one of harmony. During these critical years of heartening advance in some quarters there were Southern governors, such as Byrnes of South Carolina and Talmadge of Georgia, who still shouted fiery predictions of the violence that would rage if Southern Negroes and whites attended common schools together below the graduate and professional level. And the states of Alabama, Georgia, South Carolina, Mississippi, and Florida continued to refuse to follow the examples of their sister states in admitting Negroes to their graduate and professional schools, even though it would have meant saving vast sums of money. They refused to abandon the specious notion that they could afford separate-but-equal schools for their Negro citizens.

Victories at the highest levels of education caused jubilation, of course, but all who were engaged in the fight knew that these victories would be of little value to Negroes generally or to democracy itself unless the cleansing process was extended downward to the lowest elementary schools. The gross disparities in both quantity and quality of training afforded Negroes in grammar schools and high schools as well as at the college level fitted only a small percentage of Negroes to qualify for more advanced courses.

There were other very material factors. If, for example, Negroes in the South or the North are confined to ghettos by "gentlemen's agreements" or other extra-legal devices, the pattern of school segregation at lower levels is not materially altered, even though that pattern does not apply in colleges and universities because its students come from all over the state. If inferior training is given down below, the handicaps thereby inflicted will hobble the Negro when he seeks to qualify for highly technical education.

For such reasons, the Sweatt and McLaurin decisions were promptly followed by an attack on racial segregation at the elementary-school level. I will not bore you with details of the tortuous path that was trod over the years since Justice Harlan warned in 1896 that, "The thin disguise of 'equal' accommodations . . . will not mislead anyone, or atone for the wrong this day done."

President Mordecai W. Johnson of Howard University stated the problem more succinctly than anyone else. The greatest difficulty which college presidents face with respect to Negro students from the South, he declared in 1952, is "the fact that our students come to us from such a wretched system of high schools and primary schools." He spelled out the problem in this fashion.

"An examination of the whole structure of American education a few years ago showed that in New York State the average primary and secondary schools had a support of four thousand dollars a year for a classroom of twenty-three, while the average Negro school all over the former slave states received four hundred dollars for the same classroom of twenty-three students. . . . If a Negro with one son started walking from Mississippi and just walked moderately [northward], at about every state line he crossed he would improve the educational advantages of his child by one-tenth; and by the time he got to New York he would have multiplied his child's educational advantages by ten."

Beginning in the 1930s legislative and legal attacks were made on such inequalities as teachers' salaries, school facilities, bus transportation, length of school term, and per capita expenditure. Considerable success was achieved in the matter of salaries in some states. Between 1936 and 1951 suits challenging the differential in salaries paid white and Negro teachers doing the same type of teaching and meeting the same professional qualifications were filed and argued in Maryland, Virginia, Florida, Alabama, Kentucky, Arkansas, Missouri, Texas, South Carolina, Illinois, Tennessee, Louisiana, and Mississippi.

The extent of discrimination is illustrated by the amounts added to the salaries of Negro teachers through winning the legal suits. In nine out of twenty-three counties in Maryland the added pay won in 1938 was in excess of $100,000. In 1940 the city of Norfolk, Virginia, was ordered by the court to pay Negro teachers in the public schools an additional $129,000 a year. In 1942 Chattanooga, Tennessee, was required to pay $80,140.25 more to Negro teachers per year than it had been paying. In Louisville, Kentucky, the gain by Negro teachers of additional pay in excess of $100,000 annually led to abolition also of differentials of pay to white women teachers. This was an action for which white women teachers had fought unsuccessfully for many years.

Some fifty such cases in the fifteen-year period between 1936 and 1951 won for Negro teachers more than $3,000,000 of additional salary that had been denied them solely because of race and color.

But these were merely ameliorative measures. The real fight was against the basic principle of segregation itself.

The legal cases naturally formed the most publicized part of this campaign. There were other and equally vital concurrent activities toward the same goal at the national, state, and local levels. A continuing campaign was conducted in Congress by the NAACP and other organizations to include in appropriations bills effective provisions against discrimination. Even though Congress continued to refuse to vote for so simple a method of abolishing inequities, testimony before Senate and House committees and debate on the floor of Congress with all the attendant publicity shamed some states and forced others to lessen differentials.

Constant watch was maintained on the operations of administrative agencies, both federal and state. Many if not most of the officials charged with the administration of educational funds were personally opposed to discriminatory practices but were often powerless under the political pressures imposed upon them. Numerous conferences were held with public officials, from the President down. Thousands of mass meetings and other conferences were held to acquaint the public with the facts. Ministers, rabbis, and priests were supplied with materials and urged to use them in sermons and other communications to their congregations. Speakers were supplied for various organizations, to enlist their interest and support. Authors of newspaper, magazine, and professional-journal articles and those of books and radio and television scripts were given the facts, often at their own solicitation, as public interest in the struggle grew.

Possibly most important of all was the fact that the fight for educational equality was not isolated from other phases of the over-all struggle. The continuing drive to increase registration of Negroes and other voters concerned with human equality was a most important factor. The increasing power of the Negro vote, which is discussed at length in Chapter II of this book, played a major role in achieving results.

Among the changes in the field of education which the Negro vote helped materially to bring about were these:

1. An increased awareness on the part of school officials, even in the Deep South, of the Negro's demands for better school facilities.
2. The inclusion of Negroes on local boards of education in a number of cities, both in the North and in the South, and on state boards in North Carolina, Maryland, and other states.
3. President Truman's appointment of a Committee on Higher Education, whose report, in 1948, condemned segregation in higher education.
4. Abandonment of segregation in the public schools of East St. Louis, Cairo, and Edwardsville, Illinois; Alamogordo and Hobbs, New Mexico; Harrisburg, Pennsylvania; Tucson and other cities of Arizona; and in certain types of schools in Baltimore, Maryland, and Glendale, Ohio.
5. Repeal of laws making segregation compulsory, or passage of laws forbidding it, in several states, including New Jersey, Illinois, Wisconsin, Indiana, Oregon, Kentucky, Arizona, and New York.
6. The passage of Fair Educational Practices Acts in New Jersey, New York, and Massachusetts.
7. President Truman's veto (November 2, 1951) of a federal-aid-to-education act that required racial segregation on federal property in seventeen states and the District of Columbia.
8. The 1953 action of the American Federation of Teachers, which

voted 219 to 80 to expel any local union that barred any qualified teacher from membership because of race or color.

The Negro vote contributed greatly to the considerable change in public opinion on the subject of segregation, which was measured and reported by Elmo Roper in 1950. He found that outside the South averages ranging from 43.5 per cent in the Far West, to 57 per cent in the Northeast, favored total integration. It is doubtful that half that number would have so expressed themselves in 1940. Even in the South itself 17.1 per cent favored immediate integration. This conceivably may be even more revealing of change than the national average of 41.3 per cent.

Thus by 1951 it was evident that material progress had been made. Yet a survey of the seventeen states requiring segregation by law made by Benjamin Fine for the *New York Times* revealed that teachers' salaries had been equalized only in Louisiana, North Carolina, and West Virginia, though the differential between white and Negro teachers' salaries in Alabama, Florida, Georgia, and Virginia had been reduced. The gap had also been lessened in Mississippi, but white teachers' salaries were still twice those of Negro teachers.

Fine reported some efforts to reduce the gross inequality of physical facilities through belated construction of schools for Negroes in an attempt to forestall integration. A few of the new buildings were of superior quality. But he and others disclosed that in these states needed additions to funds spent for white education, which was far below the national average, were maintaining the differential in some states and even widening it in others, because of increasing building costs and rising populations. North Carolina, for example, could have equalized schools in 1900 at a cost of $265,-000. To do so in 1925 it would have cost $21,000,000. In 1951 it would have cost $50,000,000.

The President's Committee on Civil Rights had gone straight to the heart of the matter when in its 1947 report it declared that, "The cost of maintaining separate, but truly equal, school systems

would seem to be utterly prohibitive in many of the Southern
states." Since the South could not afford the expensive luxury of
segregation unless it received federal aid, which the opponents of
segregation were determined it should not have, and since Negroes
would receive real equality of education as far as physical facilities
were concerned only in the very distant future, if ever, several legal
suits were filed to challenge segregation itself during 1951. An incredible amount of drama and physical courage was involved in
some of them, particularly the one that originated in the remote,
rural area of Clarendon County in South Carolina.

John C. Calhoun, the "great nullifier," and most famous of South
Carolinians, must have had counties like Clarendon in mind when
he uttered the last words he spoke: "The South, the poor South!"
It is the sort of region of racial taboos and prejudices that the young
colored girl was thinking of when, having been asked during World
War II how Hitler could be most adequately punished for his sins,
she answered, "Paint him black and send him over here!"

Located in the most ill-favored section of the state, Clarendon
County is a region chiefly distinguished by eroded farms, unpainted
ramshackle farm buildings, and poor whites weakened by pellagra
and the more malignant malady of race hatred. It is not surprising
that the Ku Klux Klan rode higher and longer in Clarendon County
than in most other parts of the state and the South, or that politicians like James Byrnes, "Cotton Ed" Smith, Strom Thurmond,
and Cole Blease, who built their careers on abuse of the Negro,
received their biggest majorities in counties like Clarendon.

One would think that such a region, where mobbism had always
been a weapon close at hand for use against any Negro who
"stepped out of line," would be the last place where Negroes would
institute the legal action that many Southerners consider to be the
most revolutionary ever to come before the courts. But it was in
Clarendon County that the first of the school-segregation suits,
acted upon by the Supreme Court in 1954, originated, having been
instituted by a group of parents of Negro schoolchildren.

Reprisals were not long in coming. The banks called mortgages on the farms and homes of Negro participants in the suit. Fires of unknown origin mysteriously broke out in the dead of night. Shotgun blasts from swiftly passing automobiles ripped into Negro homes. A courageous young Negro minister was driven out of the county because it was suspected, quite accurately, that he favored the legal action.

Despite long nights of silent vigil and days of undisguised hostility not one of the Negro parents weakened. That they were not isolated in their determination to do away with segregation is illustrated by the story told by Spottswood W. Robinson, III, of Richmond, Virginia, NAACP attorney in the Prince Edward County, Virginia, anti-segregation case, which paralleled the Clarendon County one.

Robinson went with some trepidation to a meeting of Prince Edward County Negro parents to tell them, as he put it, that the NAACP had decided to "hit segregation head on and no longer fool around with the separate-but-equal business. . . . I took great pains, and I will readily confess that perhaps I belabored the question in pointing out why we felt this necessary. I told them that if they were not ready to make the decision immediately, they could go home to think it over and then come to another meeting to decide."

A father in the rear of the little country church rose to ask, "I have one question. As I understand the position of the NAACP, it is impossible for our children to get equality so long as we have segregation. Is that correct?"

"Yes, sir," answered Robinson.

The parent looked quietly at Robinson and told him, "Well, we have known that in this county for a long time and we have simply been waiting for you and the NAACP to find out the same thing."

Thurgood Marshall and his associates introduced in the trial of the Clarendon County case the most impressive array of authorities ever assembled to testify as experts on the unreasonableness of segregation and the impossibility of attainment of equality in segregated education at lower as well as at higher levels. Irrefutable testimony was presented in proving that segregation means ine-quality at the elementary and secondary levels just as it does at the graduate- and professional-school levels when measured and judged by the same standards that the United States Supreme Court had used in the Heman Sweatt and G. W. McLaurin decisions.

Two of the three judges, however, closed their minds to the evidence, to follow the precedent of the 1896 *Plessy* vs. *Ferguson* decision, and ruled that the facilities for Negro pupils were not equal to those of the white, that they were entitled to equal-but-separate facilities, and that South Carolina should give them equal-but-separate facilities. They ordered the school board to provide equal facilities within six months and to report back to the court at the end of that period on what had been done.

One judge did not concur. He was J. Waties Waring, Charleston-born descendant of a Confederate Army general. He wrote a most vigorous dissenting opinion in which he declared that the place to stop segregation "is in the first grade and not in graduate colleges." He proceeded to assert: "If the courts of this land are to render justice under the law without fear or favor, justice for all men and all kinds of men, the time to do it is now and the place is in the elementary schools, where our future citizens learn their first lesson to respect the dignity of the individual in a democracy."

Such heresy to Southern tradition brought ostracism and abuse to Judge Waring and his wife, even to the point of stoning by hood-lums of their home on sacrosanct Meeting Street in Charleston. But far more important was the jolting of many Americans into realiza-tion that Judge Waring had sharply brought them back to the morality and justice of the 1873 decision of the Supreme Court and the era that that decision reflected, instead of the 1896 separate-but-equal doctrine. For Negro Americans, Judge Waring was living proof of their faith, often badly shaken, that they had some depend-able friends among white Southerners.

A direct appeal from the majority opinion was made to the United States Supreme Court, which on January 26, 1952, sent the case back to the federal court in South Carolina to determine whether South Carolina had equalized school facilities and to "take whatever action it may deem appropriate." Meanwhile Judge Waring had been replaced by Judge Dobie of Virginia, who joined the other two judges in refusing to rule the segregation statutes of South Carolina unconstitutional. The court again ordered that state to equalize facilities.

Back went an appeal to the Supreme Court, where argument was postponed to December, 1952—after the presidential election. Meanwhile four other cases had reached the court and were joined with the South Carolina case for simultaneous argument, and still another was waiting to be handled separately.

One was from Prince Edward County, Virginia, where for the first time the defenders of segregation produced and presented expert witnesses to oppose immediate abolition of segregation but who admitted, under cross-examination, that inequality is inherent in segregation regardless of facilities, and admitted also the inequality of physical facilities. The federal district court in Virginia had refused, however, to rule out the segregation statutes and, as had been the case in South Carolina, contented itself with ordering equalization of facilities.

Another case had come from Topeka, Kansas, home state of John Brown, the unappeasable abolitionist. There the lower court had reached unanimous agreement among the three judges that segregation "has a detrimental effect upon the colored children"; that its hurtful effect is increased by legal sanction of the practice; that its practice deprives Negro children "of some of the benefits they would receive in a racially integrated school system." Nevertheless, the court followed the precedent of the separate-but-equal doctrine handed down by the Supreme Court in 1896.

Kansas's attorney general freely admitted to the Supreme Court during argument that no harmful consequences would follow integration. The Topeka Board of Education did attempt to intimidate Negroes by terminating the contracts of six of its Negro teachers, but swiftly withdrew when punitive action appeared imminent from NAACP attorneys.

A fourth case reached the court from Wilmington, Delaware, where Chancellor Collins J. Seitz in a historic twenty-six-page decision brushed aside legal hairsplitting to order immediate admission of Negroes to previously all-white schools. Although the order had been complied with without difficulty, purists afflicted with *status quo ante* concepts had insisted on appeal of Chancellor Seitz's ruling.

The fifth case was in its fashion as unique and significant as the one from Clarendon County. What made it so was the fact that it arose in Washington, D.C., capital of "the world's greatest democracy," where segregation provided an ironic twist to that appellation. It had been initiated by Charles Houston and, upon his untimely death, had been taken over by two able Negro attorneys of Washington—George E. C. Hayes and James N. Nabrit, Jr., of Howard University. Messrs. Houston, Hayes, and Nabrit had been retained by the Consolidated Parents Group of Washington to challenge, on Mr. Houston's recommendation, the legality of segregation on federal territory, on the ground that Congress did not have the right to require or enforce segregation through appropriation bills.

Six months of anxious waiting for decision followed the arguments. In June of 1953 the Supreme Court announced that the five cases must be re-argued on October 12. Later it announced that the date had been postponed to December 7, to permit the Attorney General of the United States to prepare more thoroughly. In its order the court requested attorneys on both sides and the Attorney General to discuss the intent of members of the Congress who voted for the Fourteenth Amendment, and that of the members of the thirty-seven state legislatures who had voted ratification of the amendment, as to whether they had meant the amendment to forbid racial segregation. If so, the court asked the lawyers to debate whether Congress intended that body or the courts to have power to abolish racial separation in schools, public conveyances, and other facilities. The court further asked discussion as to when and how segregation could be wiped out.

Public reaction to the court's postponement of decision and the questions it wished answered was immediate and varied and in a few instances violent. The Governor of South Carolina, James F. Byrnes, angrily announced that the public schools of his state would either be turned over to private agents or abolished altogether before white and colored children would be permitted to attend the same schools. The Governor of Georgia, Herman Talmadge, was even more explosive. He declared that blood would "flow in rivers" should Georgia be forced to abandon segregation, and stated that he did not have enough state troopers or the United States government sufficient soldiers to prevent this.

Possibly the most significant reaction was the fact that so few bombastic threats such as those of Byrnes and Talmadge were made, and that so many of opposite tenor came forth. Georgia's senior senator and former chief justice of the state supreme court, Walter F. George, voiced the opinion that at least two of the court's questions indicated that it had decided to end segregation over a period of time. Others pointed to the ease with which Negro students had been integrated in graduate and professional schools in the South, and in elementary and high schools in southern Illinois and Missouri, where race relations were identical with those in the South.

Although most white Southerners didn't like the prospect of seeing segregation go, many of them resigned themselves to the inevitable. This was notably true, according to a survey made by *Newsweek*, in cities where the growth of Southern industrialization had habituated white Southerners to mingling with Negroes at work and in union meetings. In such places, the survey reported, "they don't feel nearly so intensely about segregation as white Southerners in the back country." *Newsweek* attributed the resigned acceptance of the unavoidable by white Southerners to the impossible cost of equalization and the growing political power of the Negro.

The latter ingredient, coupled with the new Republican strength in the South, posed one of the most important problems of the entire issue. By asking—which means requiring—the United States Attorney General to join in the re-argument, the Supreme Court placed the Eisenhower administration in a difficult position. It had sought immediately upon entering into office to convince the pivotal Negro vote that it would be advantageous to return to the Republican party. Should the Attorney General fail to take an unequivocal stand against segregation, *Newsweek* asserted, the Republican party's chances of recapturing the Negro vote would be materially decreased. If he did make a strong plea to abolish segregation, his party's progress toward building a two-party South would be impeded.

As for the threats of Byrnes and Talmadge to turn public schools over to private groups, few took them for more than a tactic to postpone the inevitable. One reason for such belief was the certainty that the Supreme Court would swiftly repudiate so patent an evasion as soon as a test case reached the court. One basic principle of law is that a person cannot deputize another to do that which he himself is prohibited from doing.

The second reason, to quote Thurgood Marshall, was that, "The white citizens in those states are not insane enough on the segregation issue to be willing to turn over millions of dollars of their tax money invested in schools to private institutions, where they will have little, if any, control over the education of their children."

Even before the cases were re-argued, two of the cities—Topeka, Kansas, and Washington, D.C.—prepared to eliminate segregation. The schools of Delaware had already done so. Others prepared to follow suit. As Allen Rankin observed in the Montgomery, Alabama, *Journal*, "Personally, we think mountains are being made out of molehills on the segregation issue. We have long since lost this fight, if we consider it a fight. While some diehards bawl about the 'impossibility' of anti-segregation laws, the South is quietly becoming unsegregated."

If Allen Rankin was right, the 1940–1954 campaign of the American Negro and an increasing number of American whites, to achieve what seemed preposterously impossible at the beginning of the struggle, seemed close to success. None believed the task finished.

The far-reaching decision of the United States Supreme Court on May 17, 1954, promptly produced reactions that outlined the unfinished task. Within a few weeks this reaction became manifest in three quite clearly delineated patterns.

The first of these was the anticipated defiance by diehard politicians. They had elevated themselves in most cases to political prominence and maintained their control of state and local political machines by appeals to race prejudice and the maintenance of white supremacy. None of them was unaware of the importance of the increasing Negro vote and the enlightened white Southern vote or of the fast-changing economic pattern of the South, beginning with Roosevelt's New Deal and accentuated by World War II, which transformed materially the economy of the South from an agricultural to an industrial one. But faced by the unanimous and unequivocal decisions of the Supreme Court on racial segregation in education, public housing, and recreation, some of the politicians took refuge in silence. A few, however, screamed defiance at the Supreme Court as they searched for legal or other methods to circumvent or negate the court's rulings.

In a small Texas city fiery crosses were burned, but investigation proved that the perpetrators were in the main a group of thrill-seeking teen-agers. There were dark mutterings in a few other rural communities, notably in South Carolina, Georgia, and Mississippi, whose governors had been most vocal in asserting that the court's decrees could not be enforced and would be defied.

In most of the Northern states the Supreme Court decision merely gave federal legal recognition to a situation that was already established by law or custom. But even in the South, where opposition was fully expected, it was far from absolute.

As is unfortunately universally true in such situations, the reactionaries were most voluble. Here is a sample of the kind of thinking that pervaded their ranks, in excerpts from one of six articles in a symposium on the subject in the *Antioch Review*, Winter, 1954–55.

As far as the Deep South is concerned, the court's decision has not settled anything. . . . It seems to me that amalgamation is feasible now in Alabama only at the highest level, in the graduate school. . . . Would white parents allow their children to be taught by Negro teachers? . . . The Negro long ago lost his African culture, but he never replaced it effectively with the Western culture that comes from Greek, Roman, and Judeo-Christian roots. . . . Can we white people of Alabama trust our cultural heritage to Alabama Negro teachers?

The writer then pointed out, as an evidence of the Negro's unfitness to teach and mingle with white children in schools, statistics that proved only the very need for desegregation and the lifting of the degraded status forced upon the Negro by white supremacists.

Census figures of 1950 reveal very clearly, for example, the Alabama Negro's status. Thirty-two percent of the population of Alabama is Negro, but in 1950, whereas 3094 white people were accountants and auditors, only 21 Negroes held such positions. . . . Chemists, 662 to 16; dentists, 560 to 42; designers and draftsmen, 979 to 7; engineers, 4981 to 38; pharmacists, 1077 to 21; physicians, 2004 to 126. White members of the professions in Alabama totaled 53,517, Negro members, 11,321. . . . Thus it is evident that the Negro, especially in the Deep South, has not developed a middle class.

Then follows this fine collection of clichés:

Most Alabama Negroes live in crowded huts and shanties, they are ignorant, they are dirty, they are frequently drunk and immoral, their reading matter is trashy or non-existent, their speech is an ungrammatical patois. We may instantly acknowledge that they are often kind and lovable, that many of them work hard, and that they deserve respect. But such acknowledgment is beside the point. . . . The Negro woman walking by the courthouse jets a great splash of tobacco juice on the sidewalk . . . girls who are sexually experienced at the age of twelve create a school problem uncommon in most white schools. . . . Most Negro families are started casually with no father in evidence. . . . The Alabama Negro is not civilized in the sense that the whites are

. . . the Negro homicide rate runs to five times that of whites in the South. . . . Alabama Negroes are still primitives . . . who have taken over the vices of civilization but not its virtues.

Such is the usual character of the emotional opposition to desegregation in the South. But it is somewhat startling to learn that these words were written by Norman A. Brittin, a member of the faculty of Alabama Polytechnic Institute, who was born in New York and had spent only six years in the South.

Mr. Brittin is an advocate of "gradualism" in desegregation. "We might," he suggests, "in the first year increase the enrollment by five per cent who are Negro, and then gradually allow more Negroes to enter the mixed schools, say two per cent of the Negro school population each year. At this rate the amalgamation . . . would take place . . . over a period of about fifty years."

Actually it does not need more than elementary mathematics to see that even his gloomy prediction of full integration in fifty years is extravagantly optimistic if his suggestion were to be followed. By that method it is obvious that complete abolishment of segregation would never be accomplished.

Admission of Negroes to integrated schools, according to Mr. Brittin's plan, would depend "upon their having qualified, or their families' having qualified, for admission by reaching a satisfactory cultural level. The qualifications should include home conditions, education of parents, economic position, performance on standard achievement tests, good record of law observance, church membership, and high standing in the Negro community, possibly in terms of holding office in church or lodge."

One wonders how many white children, in Alabama and elsewhere, would be barred from decent elementary education if their admission to tax-supported schools were determined by the same qualifications.

The five other articles in the symposium, however, while recognizing difficulties involved in full educational integration in the South, pointed out that these were results of the great complex of evils that arose from a way of interracial life based upon Jim Crow

principles, and drew rather different conclusions from those voiced
by Mr. Brittin. Peter A. Carmichael, for instance, professor of
philosophy at Louisiana State University, wrote:

Enlightened citizens whose minds are not subverted by inscrutable
passion will hardly feel any qualms about the new freedom. The decision
makes no imposition on them, but lifts a dark burden from their conscience. . . . For the conscientious, reflective Southerner, this is a new
day.

Though no one expected desegregation to be accomplished
overnight, some Southern and border states—New Mexico, West
Virginia, Delaware, Arkansas, Missouri, and Oklahoma—immediately set to work to implement the decision.

At a meeting in Atlanta, on June 24, 1954, representative church
women from fifteen Southern states adopted a resolution: ". . . to
promote a Christian society in which segregation is no longer a
burden upon the human spirit . . . we accept with humility the
outlawing of separate schools and feel that such should work toward
a Christian society."

The Georgia Conference of the Methodist Church and other
groups have publicly gone on record in support of the decision.

But this is unfortunately only part of the story.

Three days after the Supreme Court decision was announced,
flaming crosses, symbol of the Ku Klux Klan, appeared in several
Florida towns. In Mississippi a Citizens' Council was formed, with
chapters in many of the state's eighty-two counties, to prevent desegregation by means of "economic pressures." Other similar groups
have emerged, with such names as The National Association for the
Advancement of White People; The National Association for
the Preservation of the White Race, Inc., of Augusta, Georgia; The
National Association for the Advancement and Protection of the
Majority of White People, Inc., of Griffin, Georgia; The Southerners, of Mobile, Alabama; Florida States Rights, Inc., of Miami,
Florida; and so forth.

Old habits of physical force to maintain unfair status for the
Negro are not easily obliterated. But a number of factors give basis

for belief that whatever outbreaks occur will be relatively short-lived and few in number. Where local peace officers fail, refuse, or neglect to take action, the Federal Department of Justice and the Federal Bureau of Investigation have been alerted to take whatever steps are possible under existing federal law.

It soon became clear that various legislative and legal devices will be adopted over a period of years in attempts to offset the court's decision. At the urging of Governor James F. Byrnes of South Carolina, the South Carolina state legislature voted in 1952 for a constitutional amendment to nullify sections of the state constitution that obligated the state to provide education, thus paving the way for abolition of all public schools should the Supreme Court rule against segregation. This was approved by the voters in 1952.

The Louisiana state legislature in June 1954 voted to invoke the police-power reserve of the state under the federal Constitution on the tenuous assumption that any effort to integrate a public school would result in disorder, which the legislature claimed to believe they were authorized to prevent by invocation of the police powers.

A Mississippi congressman and a senator from the same state, angered by the Supreme Court decisions, introduced a constitutional amendment into Congress to abolish the United States Supreme Court. This gesture of angry defiance evoked only laughter, in view of the fact that a constitutional amendment must be approved by two-thirds of the members of both houses of Congress and ratified by thirty-six of the forty-eight states.

Another proposed device was to turn over the schools to private organizations or individuals. This proposal to date has, for quite practical considerations, met with little enthusiasm. Although the schools of the South are below the standards of those in other sections of the United States, many hundreds of millions of dollars have been invested in them. Taxpayers are therefore unwilling, whatever their racial views may be, to transfer ownership and management of the South's educational system, ranging from small rural schools to huge universities, to private individuals or organizations. Obviously, such a transfer would attract educational racketeers with debased standards who would exploit the situation for their own financial benefit. Should any state intervene to protect students or property, it would immediately make itself subject to federal action.

Still another device that has been discussed is the subsidization of individual students, leaving to each the choice of the school he attends.

A detailed report of reactions to the new situation in the Southern and border states would require a book in itself. But a brief state-by-state survey of conditions as they existed at the opening of the 1954–55 school year, as reported by the *Southern School News*, is interesting.

Alabama. Segregation continued. A special commission appointed by Governor Gordon Persons recommended that sections of the state constitution be revised to permit the abolishment of public education.

Arkansas. Charleston and Fayetteville admitted a few Negroes to schools that had formerly been all white. Otherwise the old pattern of segregation was continued.

Arizona. Entered the final phase of an integration program that had been begun in 1953.

Delaware. Within a week of the Supreme Court's decision Governor Boggs sent a letter to the state Board of Education asking that it "proceed toward the objective" of implementing the decision. At about the same time the Republican party of Delaware issued a statement promising "orderly transition to integrated schools." As schools opened in the fall, integration proceeded without incident in Wilmington. In Milford, however, strong protests and threats of violence brought about temporary closing of the schools.

District of Columbia. Before the end of 1953 plans had been made for complete integration by the end of 1955, and a parent-teachers group had removed all racial bars. As school opened in the

fall of 1954, 111 of 161 schools were integrated without incident.
Florida. Schools opened according to the old pattern of segregation, but it was announced that they would be integrated gradually.

Georgia. Immediately following the court decision, Georgia's state legislature created a Commission on Education to make plans "to provide education consistent with both state and federal constitutions." An amendment to the state constitution was proposed that would provide funds for education to individuals, thus making it possible to abolish public schools.

Georgia had been improving its separate facilities for Negroes, but was dedicated to the separate-but-equal doctrine. In 1940 the state spent $46.70 a year for the education of each white child, and $14.60 for each Negro pupil. By 1952 the expense of educating each white child was $163.76, a little less than four times as much as in 1940, while that of educating the Negro had risen to $110.59, or about eight and a half times that of 1940. Thus it had been making efforts, in its own way, to better educational opportunities for Negroes. But desegregation, according to Governor Herman Talmadge, was something the state would never accept.

The matter became a primary issue of the gubernatorial campaign. Each candidate had a plan: to enforce segregation at the local level; to amend the federal Constitution to strengthen state control of schools; to give students the right to decide whether to attend all-white, all-Negro, or mixed schools, and to subject those who chose the latter to psychiatric tests; to move all Negroes out of Georgia; to abolish the Supreme Court; and so forth. Only one candidate, a woman lawyer of Atlanta, advocated compliance with the Supreme Court decision.

As school opened in the fall, the old pattern of segregation remained in effect.

Kansas. Ten cities in the state had maintained segregated schools before the Supreme Court decision. As school opened, most of these were integrating their students without incident.

Kentucky. In the fall of 1953 School Superintendent Omer Carmichael opened exploratory discussions of integration, in anticipation of the court decision. As school opened in the fall of 1954, segregation was continued, but Governor Taunton announced that the state was awaiting a further ruling by the Supreme Court, and that it would do what was necessary.

Louisiana. The 1954–55 school year began with segregation as formerly. A constitutional amendment was proposed that would declare segregation a matter of "health and morals" and thus properly under the "police power" of the state.

Maryland. In Baltimore, where Negroes and whites had long worked together in the Public School Teachers Association, the Teachers' Union, and the Principals' Association, and white and colored pupils from different schools had joined in various projects, the city segregation ordinance was declared void immediately after the court decision. A "voluntary" system of integration was adopted. After the opening of school, officials announced that about 2.5 per cent of Negro students chose to go to formerly all-white schools. There was some rioting, but only a very small percentage of the city's public-school students were involved.

Mississippi. Following the court decision, state officials announced that the state would not accept the order, and would abolish the public schools rather than integrate them. School opened in the fall with complete segregation as formerly.

Missouri. Following the court order, St. Louis and Kansas City, which have two-thirds of the state's Negro school population, announced plans for gradual integration, to be completed in 1955. Other smaller cities announced similar plans. Some began the school year with integrated school attendance.

New Mexico. Completion of integration. The last three communities in the state that had practiced segregation discontinued it. There were no incidents.

North Carolina. Here, as in Georgia, the separate educational facilities for Negroes has been noticeably improved since 1940.

In that year $41.09 was spent for the education of each white child, and $24.05 for that of each Negro. In 1952 the expenditure per capita for whites had risen to $158.73, and that of Negroes to $135.38, a lessening of the differential.

When the Supreme Court decision was announced, Governor William B. Umstead said he was "terribly disappointed," and the Board of Education voted to make no immediate attempt to desegregate the schools. Several religious groups urged compliance with the decision. In Rocky Mount, Raleigh, and Greensboro interracial citizens' committees formed to plan ways to implement the decision. As schools opened in the fall of 1954, segregation was continued.

Oklahoma. At the time of the decision school leaders announced, "We'll follow the law, but it would be disastrous to do it right now." In the fall of 1954 public schools opened on a segregated basis, but state colleges and parochial schools were integrated.

South Carolina. In Rock Hill, a small community, there was integration for the first time in the fall of 1954 in a parochial school. In public schools throughout the state segregation was continued.

Tennessee. In Nashville parochial schools, formerly all white, were opened to Negroes. In the public-school system throughout the state segregation was continued. The petition of the parents of three white children in Nashville to allow their children to attend a Negro school was denied.

Texas. Segregation continued. Negro students in Dallas, Fort Worth, and a few other communities attempted unsuccessfully to enroll in white schools.

Virginia. Segregation continued.

West Virginia. Twelve counties completely integrated; thirteen partially so; eighteen waiting for further court action; eleven have no Negro students.

It is obvious that the Supreme Court decision wrought no miracle, but rather that it speeded up a process already under way in some areas and made the eventual inevitability of it in others apparent. For it is clear that among the reactions to the decision in the South and the nation as a whole is one of profound relief, even among many of those who did not favor the abolition of segregation. One reason for this is, as I have pointed out, the economic impracticability of segregation. Southern newspapers, educators, and other molders of public opinion have come to realize that the states that either required or permitted educational segregation could no longer provide grossly unequal Negro and white schools. An unbroken series of court decisions over a period of nearly two decades held that there must be substantial equality of all educational facilities for the two races even though there were separate facilities. The cost of physical plants alone was estimated as close to the staggering total of two billion dollars, with an additional cost of one-quarter of a billion dollars to maintain the dual system.

The impossibility of maintaining such expensive duplication forever was best expressed by the president of one of the South's leading universities when he stated in the late forties, "We can't afford to build a cyclotron for a single student." This very practical reasoning was one of the major factors behind the peaceful admittance of more than two thousand Negro students to graduate and professional schools of twelve Southern states, and more than four times that number to summer schools, during the period beginning in 1950 when the United States Supreme Court ordered admission of qualified Negroes to the Universities of Texas and Oklahoma.

In 1954 a power revealed itself in the South that has not been hitherto sufficiently recognized. That force is the moral conscience of the predominantly evangelical Protestant South. The students of the social sciences, and particularly psychologists, have long recognized that the extreme sadism of lynching mobs and other perpetrators of violence against the Negro in the South revealed the subconscious torture of men and women who believed themselves to be devout Christians and whose consciences were troubled by what they were doing to their Negro neighbors.

It was this moral discomfort that caused a distinguished Southern newspaper correspondent to state recently that Southern whites instead of Negroes should celebrate on January 1 the signing of the Emancipation Proclamation, because Abraham Lincoln's act had emancipated the South from the sin of slavery. In similar fashion, the Supreme Court's decision of 1954 measurably advanced the freedom of the white South from the corrosive effect of segregation and the fallacy of racial superiority.

High Catholic prelates in New Orleans and in Missouri and Texas had anticipated the decision by orderly abolition of segregation in schools, hospitals, and other church institutions. Soon after the decision Southern Presbyterians, Baptists, Methodists, and Congregationalists voted overwhelming approval of the court's ruling and pledged their support to its enforcement.

Because Baptists are numerically in the majority in the South, the action of the Southern Baptist Convention at St. Louis in June 1954 is significant. The principal speech advocating compliance with the anti-segregation decision was made by a profoundly respected leader of Southern Baptists, Dr. J. H. Weatherspoon of the Southern Baptist Seminary at Louisville, Kentucky. He climaxed an eloquent appeal for compliance by declaring, "We will not move backward, but"—at this point he turned dramatically and pointed to a huge banner above the platform of the Kiel Auditorium—"FORWARD WITH CHRIST." Only thirty of the delegates voted against the resolution of compliance. Nine thousand voted for it.

Of increasing importance on the issues of compliance and fuller acceptance of the Negro on a basis of full equality in the South is the steadily growing Negro vote. There were fewer than 200,000 registered Negro voters in all the South when the United States Supreme Court in 1944 ruled that no qualified voter could be barred on the basis of race or color from participation in the so-called "white, Democratic primary" of Southern states. By 1948 Negro voters had increased in the South to 1,300,000 and had set for 1956 a goal of 3,000,000 voters.

Even the most intransigent Southern politicians had become

aware by 1954 that the Negro vote was becoming a factor that could not be ignored any longer. Accompanying this increase in Negro registration was the increase in younger, better educated, and less biased white voters. Some of these had served with Negroes in non-segregated branches of the armed services and had thereby learned a new pattern of racial thinking. Others had attended the recently opened graduate and professional schools in the South or non-segregated schools in other parts of the country. Some were becoming aware of the fact that the Negro buying market in the United States had reached the staggering total of fifteen billion dollars annually, and, as ambitious and enlightened businessmen, were increasingly interested in exploiting, rather than antagonizing, a purchasing power greater than that represented by United States trade with Canada or Latin America. Others among this new electorate were increasingly sensitive to the ridicule to which the South was being subjected because of its attitude toward Negroes. And, like the rest of the country, the South was becoming increasingly concerned with anti-American sentiment, which was growing throughout the world—and particularly in Asia, Africa, and Latin America—because of the race problem in the United States.

All these forces—economic, religious, moral, political, and international—were creating in 1954 a new climate of opinion that no one would have dared to predict even ten years before. No national teachers' organization had voted for segregation; on the contrary, the powerful National Education Association and the American Federation of Teachers, among others, had voted almost unanimously against segregation.

It is doubtful whether so basic and so bloodless a revolution of public thinking has ever previously occurred in human history.

II. The Negro Votes

Those who have been determined to maintain a degraded status for the Negro have shrewdly concentrated on taking from him his most potent weapon and defense—the right to vote. With comparable determination, and with a heartening measure of success, the Negro has striven to regain the ballot, his right to which was confirmed with the ratification of the Fifteenth Amendment at the close of the Civil War. Later, reactionary elements in the South conspired to deprive him of this right. In his efforts to defeat that conspiracy the Negro has been forced to combat federal and state legislation, legal chicanery, administrative trickery, biased decisions by the courts, discriminatory regulations unashamedly designed to disfranchise him, and mob violence. But he has met them all in open combat, and, though he has still not reached the goal of full suffrage, he has advanced so far along the road toward it that it may be said to be in sight.

The going has been rough, even as advances have been made. Harry T. Moore was assassinated as recently as 1951 because he had labored for years to increase the Negro vote, and otherwise to better the status of the Negro. Many lynchings and race riots as well as mobbings by such organizations as the Ku Klux Klan have been perpetrated to frighten the Negro from the polls. An estimated five hundred thousand dollars has been spent by Negro citizens on legal cases challenging disfranchisement, many of them ending in defeat. Other sums have been raised and expended over the years in efforts in Congress and in state legislatures to obtain passage of laws against practices and devices such as the poll tax. Political campaigns have been waged, at a great cost of time and money, to elect candidates pledged to enfranchisement and against those hostile to it. Unknown amounts have gone into meetings, literature, citizenship schools, travel, postage, telephone calls and telegrams, radio programs, research, and other methods of public education.

One of the earliest objectives of the NAACP after its organization in 1909 was to outlawing the iniquitous "grandfather clauses," enacted into law by Louisiana and Mississippi and later by Oklahoma and other states. These laws disfranchised any "illiterate" person, unless he, or an ancestor, had had the right to vote prior to the adoption of the Fifteenth Amendment, which forbids the abridgment by any state of the right to vote "on account of race, color, or previous condition of servitude." Since, as chattel slaves, Negroes in the South did not have the right to vote before emancipation, none of their descendants could ever be voters unless they were able to pass stiff and capricious "literacy" tests not required of whites with the correct ancestors. Under the brilliant leadership of its first president, Moorfield Storey, an able constitutional lawyer of Boston, the young association, small in numbers and limited in resources, won a historic victory in a Supreme Court decision which ruled in 1915 that the Oklahoma grandfather clause was unconstitutional.

But a new challenge faced the NAACP in 1923 when the all-white legislature of Texas enacted a law forbidding Negroes to vote in primary elections. Since in that day of the "solid South" selection of a candidate by a Democratic primary was tantamount to election, the new device was quite patently a method of disfranchisement adopted as a substitute for the outlawed grandfather clauses.

In order to test the constitutionality of the new law it was necessary to find a Negro who was willing to try to vote in a Texas primary. This was more difficult than it may seem at first glance. Racial tension had been mounting frighteningly during the six years since the United States had entered World War I. Southerners terrified by the possibility that Negroes who had fought for democracy in France should return to demand for themselves a larger share of its benefits had revived the Ku Klux Klan, which was waging throughout the South a campaign of violence and bloodshed not only against Negroes, but also against Jews, Catholics, Northerners, Negro-sympathizers, and anyone else who incurred the Klan's displeasure. John R. Shillady, white-haired Irish-American Executive Secretary of the NAACP, had been beaten almost to death on the main street of Austin, the state capital, in daylight. There was very grave danger that extreme, possibly fatal, violence would be visited on any Negro who, in defiance of the new law, attempted to vote in a Texas primary.

There was the additional problem of finding lawyers of requisite experience and reputation to handle a test case effectively. They also had to be men of such integrity that we could be sure they would not sell out.

The combination of obstacles was enough to dishearten almost anyone. But they were not too great for the courage and initiative of Dr. L. A. Nixon of El Paso. A thoughtful, well-educated, quiet man, he, like most Negroes of his generation, had spent his early life in incessant struggle against poverty and hardship. But, having done well in business, he had by 1923 achieved a measure of economic prosperity. For many years his drugstore was the only place in El Paso where Negroes could receive courteous treatment, and it became a gathering place where increasing racial tensions and opposition to the enfranchisement of Negroes were often discussed.

It was in such gatherings that Dr. Nixon rekindled hope and stimulated courage after the passage in 1923 of the law barring Negroes from primaries. And in the face of dire prophecies from his friends, threats from a few whites in El Paso, and the concern of his family, he volunteered to provide the NAACP with a test case by attempting to vote in a primary election. He was of course prevented from voting, but fortunately the dire prophecies of physical violence were not fulfilled.

His suit for redress of denial of the right to vote went through the seemingly interminable and costly journey of four years to the United States Supreme Court, which on March 7, 1927, decided in his favor. Justice Oliver Wendell Holmes in writing the decision declared: "It is too clear for extended argument that color cannot be made the basis of statutory classification affecting the right set up in this case."

The publicity attendant upon the long-drawn-out case had focused public attention on the fact that to deprive any American of the right to vote on the basis of race or color was a violation of the Constitution. But now advocates of disfranchisement, proceeding as though the illegality lay in the method, rather than with objective, sought other means of keeping colored voters from the polls. The Texas legislature was promptly called into special session to enact a law giving the executive committees of political parties the power to establish qualifications for participation in party primaries. Almost simultaneously—such was the patent collusion between the legislature and the Democratic party—the executive committee was summoned to meet and pass a resolution that, "All white Democrats who are qualified under the Constitution and laws of Texas . . . and none others be allowed to participate in the primary elections."

Dr. Nixon again attempted to vote, was again summarily denied that right; and another legal action in his behalf was instituted by the NAACP. Five years later, on May 2, 1932, after another tortuous and expensive journey through lower and intermediate courts, the United States Supreme Court ruled that no state could delegate to others power that it did not itself possess.

Again the disfranchisers sought a legal method of evading the law. What the state executive committee could not do, the party itself in convention assembled reasoned beyond reason that it had the right and authority to do. Seven Southern states besides Texas believed confidently that they had found the solution. Their state conventions voted unanimously that only whites would be allowed to participate in party primaries and Democratic party formulation of policy and selection of candidates.

Unfortunately for Negroes, a case (*Grovey* vs. *Townsend*) carried to the Supreme Court in 1935 by interested citizens in Texas was lost. But six years later, in a case originating in Louisiana, where election officials refused to count the ballots of a group of white dissident voters, the Supreme Court held that the primary is an integral part of the election process and that, where a primary is decisive in determining the general election, such a primary comes within the prohibitions of the federal Constitution. This was known as the Classic case.

Again the NAACP came to the aid of a Texas citizen, Dr. Lonnie E. Smith, a dentist of Houston, by filing suit in his behalf when he was not permitted to vote in a primary. The association did this on the basis of the Classic decision. Three years of litigation were necessary for the journey from the court of first instance through the Supreme Court of the United States. Much of the expense was paid through contributions by Texas Negroes ranging from a few cents to a few dollars. The legal work was done by NAACP attorneys.

On April 3, 1944, the Supreme Court reversed its own position in the Grovey case (*Smith* vs. *Allwright*), to rule that Dr. Smith and all other qualified Negroes must be allowed to vote in primary as well as general elections. Justice Stanley F. Reed in a sweeping majority opinion bluntly told the disfranchisers: "The United States is a constitutional democracy. Its organic law grants to all citizens a right to participate in the choice of elected officials without restriction by the state because of race. This grant to the people of the opportunity for choice is not to be nullified by a state through casting its electoral process in a form which permits a private organization to practice racial discrimination in the election."

Despite this unequivocal edict by the Kentucky-born justice,

and a steadily changing climate of opinion in the South and the
nation, certain Southern states were doggedly determined to con-
coct some formula that the courts could not overturn and so perpetuate an all-white electorate. South Carolina was the first to act.
Its legislature in an emergency session voted repeal of all statutes
referring to primary elections, hoping thereby to make the Democratic party a voluntary private club.

Success of such a stratagem would have disfranchised not only
Negroes but many whites as well, concentrating power dictato-
rially in the hands of a very small clique. So brazen a challenge to
the orderly processes of constitutional government had not been
attempted since the firing on Fort Sumter, in the same state, which
provided the spark that developed into the conflagration of civil
war. It was a stunning setback to those who for generations had
fought for Negro enfranchisement. Every court victory and the
many thousands of dollars so sacrificially contributed to the long,
heartbreaking struggle would have been forfeited had the device
proved successful.

Other Southern states studied the South Carolina action and put
their best legal brains to work in a desperate effort to find a formula that would work. The mildly liberal Governor M. E. Thompson of Georgia mustered courage enough to veto a bill backed by
the Herman Talmadge forces that was identical with the law enacted in South Carolina. Arkansas voted to set up two primaries,
one for federal offices and another for state ones, but prohibitive
costs forced the abandonment of the plan within a year. Mississippi
enacted a law requiring a loyalty pledge by primary voters to support opposition to federal civil-rights laws and to meet whatever
tests of literacy and understanding were required by registrars.
White applicants for registration who were approved by the local
political machines were passed immediately. Negroes were ordered
to answer such questions as, "How many bubbles in a bar of
soap?" and, "What is due process of law?"

Texas and Florida accepted the inevitable and abandoned further efforts to disfranchise the Negro. But Alabama came up with

the Boswell Amendment, which required that voters be able not only to read and write but also to "understand and explain any article of the Constitution of the United States to the satisfaction of the registrar." Prospective voters were also required to prove themselves to be persons of "good character . . . who understand the duties and obligations of citizenship." Some registrars demanded that Negro registrants be accompanied physically by two white voters to vouch for their moral character and reputation in the community.

To the dismay of politicians 'who expected enthusiastic approval of their attempts to evade the clear mandate against disfranchisement that the Supreme Court had rendered in the *Smith* vs. *Allwright* case, public opinion in the South and elsewhere in the nation was sharply divided, with a surprisingly large volume of vigorous disapproval. The climate of anti-Negro and pro-disfranchisement opinion that had dominated the South since the Civil War had changed, the politicians discovered, far more than they had realized—a warning that the old order was no longer sacrosanct.

The following are factors that the diehards had neglected to note or understand. The continuous campaign of public education accompanying the legal battles had materially altered the views of many white Southerners, even as it had deepened the determination of Negroes to vote. The South had become the butt of ridicule, which was causing sensitive Southerners to become increasingly aware that their section of the nation was being branded as backward and bigoted. This sensitiveness to criticism was increasingly reflected in the Southern press, although many of its editors continued to cry out against "Northern interference" and to claim that the South itself could and would correct its faults. But more and more of them were saying that the South might just as well recognize that it could not fly in the face of the Supreme Court and national opinion much longer by attempting to perpetuate disfranchisement.

Particularly effective in shaping opinion was the utter refutation of dire prophecies by Southern politicians that enfranchising the Negro would inaugurate an era of political corruption. They said this in spite of the fact that it would have required rare genius to improve on the techniques that had been developed over the years under the all-white "rotten-borough" political system of the South. Ralph Bunche wrote in 1940: "In many of the Southern communities today, the small Negro vote is the most independent and free from purchase in the electorate." Seven years later Ralph McGill confirmed Mr. Bunche's opinion when he wrote in the Atlanta *Constitution*: "It is interesting to observe the comments over the state [Georgia] with regard to the Negro vote in those sections where they have participated. In not a single instance have they voted in any number on the side of bad government or in behalf of racketeers. They have voted each time with the reform, or so-called better elements."

The Columbia, South Carolina, *Record* declared in 1950 that, "The Negroes of South Carolina came out of the contest [the senatorial elections] with flying colors. Under great provocation they have conducted themselves with proper restraint."

To jump ahead of our story, the white voters of Atlanta in 1953 joined with colored voters in a city-wide election to place a Negro college president, Dr. Rufus E. Clement, on the Board of Education by a 2-to-1 vote over his white opponent. The extraordinary adherence of the new Negro voters to high principle had taken away from the politicians a weapon on which they had counted to rabble-rouse public opinion against Negro voting.

World War II had also played a major role in influencing public opinion. Just as Asia and Africa had been stirred by noble phrases and high principles, so had the South. No one could see or read of men dying in Europe to stop Nazi racism without being somewhat uncomfortable about the domestic brand. Stories from the Pacific of Japan's self-election as the leader of the colored peoples of the world and her use of instances of American bigotry against the Negro added to the discomfort. The enlightened South became increasingly aware that Southern behavior toward Negroes was not helping America win the war. Even when Southerners, and Americans generally, said or did little to correct evil practices, their sense of guilt deepened.

More immediately, the Roosevelt administration accelerated the slow demise of disfranchisement. New Deal members of Congress stepped up their efforts to obtain laws against the poll tax, lynching, and discrimination in employment.

Four times, beginning in 1942, the House of Representatives passed anti-poll tax laws by better than 2-to-1 votes. Each time the Senate permitted the bills to be killed by filibusters, led by Southern senators but made successful by surreptitious aid from conservative Republicans. But although the measures had never become federal law, the agonized cries of Southern senators that the South should be left alone and not forced by federal action to clean up its discriminatory practices became less convincing. The steady pressure of the possibility of federal action has forced all but five of the Southern states to abolish the tax.

New Deal agencies such as the Agricultural Adjustment Administration included special grants in federal aid to enable sharecroppers to pay poll taxes (actually little or none of the money found its way to Negroes). This helped to enlarge and liberalize voting. Negro and white workers participated in National Labor Relations Board elections; familiarity with the process thereby increased, and interest in such participation in government widened. A new surge of liberalism permeated the South along with the rest of the country as a result of the economic and social philosophy of the Roosevelt administration.

Especially stirring was the moral leadership of Mrs. Eleanor Roosevelt on human rights. Her enemies and critics used every device of criticism and slander to stop her, but, undaunted, she continued to speak and act as her conscience dictated. She gave to many Americans, particularly Negroes, hope and faith which enabled them to continue the struggle for full citizenship.

Other circumstances were contributing to the slow change of attitude on disfranchisement in the South. New industries, especially textiles, were moving there. Some of them were lured from the North by inexpensive or free land and water power, by tax holidays, and especially by quantities of cheap and unorganized labor. Union organizers followed the industries, of course, and made some progress, although impeded by hostile legislatures, unfriendly local officials, and even mob violence.

But the considerable industrialization of the South, added to the many huge Army, Navy, Air Force, and Marine Corps installations, as well as other federal plants, such as atom- and hydrogenbomb plants—which for reasons of climate have been located in the South—changed the economic pattern of the region. The shift from a one-crop agricultural economy to one dominated by industry and commerce had wrought more change than politicians were wise enough to comprehend. The new masters of the region began to think that they might need a somewhat higher type of politician. The old ones found themselves on the way out.

Their fears that their day was passing were enormously increased when the Missourian President, Harry S. Truman, moved far beyond Franklin Roosevelt on the civil-rights issue. In 1946 he placed his political fortunes on the line when he named a fifteen-man Committee on Civil Rights, instructing it to conduct a thorough and honest examination of the status of those rights and to recommend action to make them secure. The anticipated protests from the conservative South materialized immediately. Vehement charges were made that the President was infringing sacred states' rights. Almost without exception, Mr. Truman's political advisers from both South and North were certain that his authorization of inquiry into the explosive issue of civil rights was nothing short of political suicide.

Mr. Truman stood firm. He wisely chose an eminent and unassailable committee of men and women representatives of business, labor, church, educational, political, and minority interests to make the inquiry. Charles E. Wilson, President of General Electric Company, served as chairman. The other fourteen members were Mrs. Sadie T. M. Alexander, an able Negro lawyer of Philadelphia;

James B. Carey, Secretary-Treasurer of the CIO; President John S. Dickey of Dartmouth College; Morris L. Ernst, lawyer and authority on civil liberties; Rabbi B. Gittelsohn; President Frank P. Graham of the University of North Carolina and later United States Senator, who was defeated for re-election partly because of having served on the committee; the Most Reverend Francis J. Haas of the Roman Catholic Church and former Chairman of the Fair Employment Practices Committee established by President Roosevelt; Charles Luckman, then the president of Lever Brothers; Francis P. Matthews, Omaha attorney and later Secretary of the Navy and Ambassador to Ireland; Franklin D. Roosevelt, Jr., who later was elected to Congress from New York; the Right Reverend Henry Knox Sherrill, Presiding Bishop of the Protestant Episcopal Church; Boris Shishkin, economist of the AFL; Mrs. M. E. Tilly of Atlanta, Georgia, active in church, women's, and racial movements in the South; and Dr. Channing H. Tobias, then executive director of the Phelps-Stokes Fund.

A particularly able staff headed by Robert K. Carr of Dartmouth College was engaged by the committee, and its published report, "To Secure These Rights," is one of the most frank and hard-hitting official documents that has ever been published by the United States government. While it must be admitted that at the time this book was written, Congress had not enacted into law even one of the several recommendations for corrective legislation urged by the committee, in numerous other areas, which are discussed in other chapters, action has been considerable.

On the issue of voting, the committee noted such progress toward a free ballot as had been made but commented acidly: "In fact there are many backwaters in our political life where the right to vote is not assured to every qualified citizen. The franchise is barred to some citizens because of race; to others by institutions or procedures which impede free access to the polls. Still other Americans are in substance disfranchised whenever electoral irregularities or corrupt practices dissipate their votes or distort their intended purpose. . . . The denial of the suffrage on account of

race is the most serious present interference with the right to vote."
Such refreshing bluntness and integrity has had a profound effect
on many Americans who hitherto paid scant attention to the infringements of civil rights. It has also become clear to some politicians that their political fortunes may be gravely affected by the
power that disfranchisement gives to bigots. Three Southern states
—Tennessee, South Carolina, and Georgia—have abolished the
poll tax as a prerequisite to voting since 1947, leaving five states—
Alabama, Arkansas, Virginia, Mississippi, and Texas—still requiring
such payment. Although this tax is only one of the methods used
to deny qualified citizens the right to vote, the existence of sufficient pressures from within and without the states that have abolished it is significant. In time the five states that retain it will either
yield of their own volition or Congress will be forced by public
opinion to act.

"To Secure These Rights" has been made the basis of intensive
study of the problem of civil rights by churches, labor unions, colleges, universities, high schools, civic organizations, and minority-
group associations. It has been widely discussed in newspaper
editorials and columns and from pulpits. It has clarified and guided
the thinking of many writers of articles and books. It has helped
create sentiment in support of court decisions dealing with the
franchise. Virtually every aspect of American life except the Congress has responded to its call for a more democratic America.

It is no derogation of any of the forces, organizations, or individuals in high places or less exalted ones, however, to say that the
greatest influence working on behalf of full enfranchisement for
the Negro in the South has been the rising power of the Negro
vote itself in the Southern and border states. It would not be an
overstatement to say that almost a revolution has occurred during
the past two decades, both in the political outlook of the Negro
himself and in the recognition by political parties of the value of
the Negro vote.

A second Emancipation Proclamation for the Negro, this one
written largely by himself, came into being as a direct result of the

use of the Negro issue in the presidential campaign of 1928. It is generally believed that Herbert Hoover won over Governor Alfred E. Smith the electoral votes of seven traditionally Democratic border and Southern states—Florida, Texas, Virginia, North Carolina, Tennessee, Kentucky, and West Virginia—on the issue of Catholicism. But Governor Smith's religion played a lesser role than did the use of incredibly vicious anti-Negro propaganda.

At that time Harvard-educated Ferdinand Q. Morton, a Negro, was Civil Service Commissioner of New York City. Hundreds of thousands of copies of a photograph of Mr. Morton dictating to a white secretary were circulated throughout the South with predictions that, should Northern Democrats gain control of the party, social equality and intermarriage between the races would become a firmly fixed policy of government.

This was only one of the appeals to racial and religious bigotry that were spewed throughout the South. The flood of race prejudice mounted as the campaign neared Election Day. "Incidents" were deliberately created to form the basis of newspaper and radio stories of rising tension between the two races. Minor disputes between whites and Negroes that would have passed unnoticed in normal times were exaggerated into "race riots" or "threatened race riots." Seemingly unlimited funds were expended on legitimate and illegitimate campaign expenses in the bitter contest between the Hoovercrats—as Democrats favoring the Republican candidate were called—and the two regular parties.

The situation became so grave that forty-six Southern white liberals felt it necessary to denounce publicly the vitriolic stirring up of friction. They urged "the leadership of the South—the pulpit, the press, the platform—and every right-thinking man and woman among us to disclaim, discourage, and discontinue such appeals to prejudice and fear." Their plea fell on deaf ears.

Ironically, the three-pronged fight between Democrats, Republicans, and Hoovercrats gave the Negro vote in the South, small at that time, status and recognition which it had not enjoyed since the days of Reconstruction, even though that recognition was surreptitious. The contest was so close that, in many areas, clandestine bids were made by Democrats, Republicans, and Hoovercrats to Negro voters because they held the balance of power.

The viciousness of the tactics used in the 1928 campaign disillusioned even the staunchest Negro Republicans and greatly accelerated the Negro's determination to say to Republicans and Democrats alike, "A plague on both your houses." This reluctance to be identified with either party had been germinating quietly but rapidly throughout the administrations of Republican presidents Calvin Coolidge and Warren G. Harding. As far back as its inception in 1909 the NAACP had urged Negroes to vote for men and measures, and not on the basis of empty party labels. But as long as the Democratic party was dominated by anti-Negro Southerners it had little attraction for Negroes. The result was the creation of a gentlemen's agreement, as James Weldon Johnson and others pointed out, between the two parties, in accordance with which the Democrats said to the Negro, "We neither need nor want you," and the Republicans treated him with no greater respect, knowing that he had no place else to go and must be content with whatever crumbs of attention the GOP deigned to throw him. The 1928 campaign, through raising such callousness to heights that had not been surpassed even in the days immediately following the Civil War, caused even such rock-ribbed Republicans as the late Dr. Robert Russa Moton of Tuskegee and C. C. Spaulding of the North Carolina Life Insurance Company to join in an "Appeal to America" against the manner in which anti-Negro prejudice had been used to sow hatred and discord. The appeal had little discernible impact on white America, but considerable on Negroes.

That effect mounted with the entrance of Mr. Hoover into the White House. His studied indifference toward the needs and wishes of Negroes was climaxed when, in an obvious effort to placate Southerners for ignoring their demand for several cabinet posts in repayment of the support they had given him in the election, he nominated to the United States Supreme Court John J. Parker, a

North Carolinian who had openly and vigorously advocated disfranchisement of Negroes.

Mr. Hoover's stand permitted no other course for Negro voters, whose influence in certain pivotal states the President had underestimated, but to fight confirmation with all the resources at their command. Admittedly, these were quite meager. But a whirlwind campaign of six weeks, aided by organized labor's opposition to Judge Parker because of decisions he had rendered in labor cases, resulted in a 41-to-39 rejection of the nomination on May 7, 1930. And in elections that year in California, Kansas, Missouri, Indiana, Ohio, Pennsylvania, West Virginia, New Jersey, Connecticut, and Rhode Island, Republican senators who had voted against the pleas of their Negro constituents were defeated.

There were two results of the successful campaign. Even the most intransigent Southern newspapers conceded that the Senate rejection of Judge Parker and the retirement from the Senate of a number of the senators who had obeyed Mr. Hoover's command marked at least the beginning of the Negro's political coming of age. And the Negro himself recognized his political power. Ever since the first slave was landed on the shores of Virginia early in the seventeenth century, the Negro had been the cat's-paw of American politics. But now his strength had grown to an extent that made it possible for him not only to protest but also to make his protests effective. His sense of futility and impotence was miraculously and gratifyingly replaced by knowledge that when his cause was just and sufficient unity and intelligence were put into a fight for principle, he had a chance of victory.

To a greater extent than even he realized, this new confidence played a dominant role in Negro abandonment of traditional Republicanism to vote for Roosevelt, spottily in 1932, and in even larger numbers in 1936, 1940, and 1944, for Harry S. Truman in 1948 and Adlai Stevenson in 1952. Confidence gained in the Parker case, and refutation of the dire prophecies of disaster to Mr. Truman for his championship of civil rights, were reinforced by the Negro vote in Ohio, Illinois, and California in 1948, which gave

Mr. Truman the margin of electoral votes necessary for his phenomenal victory over Governor Thomas E. Dewey of New York. Little recognized publicly but highly significant is the impetus that the Negro's political activity has given to greater political independence of the white voter. For years a minority of thoughtful white Southerners have advocated that the South abandon its one-party politics. These practical idealists have pointed out that the system deprives the people of any choice whatever between candidates or policies and vests control in the hands of political bosses who are more concerned with restriction of public participation in politics than with its expansion. The result inevitably, with few exceptions, had been selection of the least admirable and most unashamedly bigoted Southerners for public office. But as long as the Republican party rendered even diminishing lip service to the principle of equal justice for the Negro, the bulk of white Southerners would not listen to suggestions that they consider voting for any ticket except that of the Democratic party.

Even the gains made by the Negro through the severance of his traditional ties to the Republican party made no impression until quite recent years. There were outcries of protest when the Negro became steadily more important in the Democratic party during the Roosevelt and Truman administrations. But the defection of Southerners from Democratic orthodoxy has been almost wholly of those who wanted more power for themselves rather than for Southerners generally. Hidden alliances with Republicans came into existence wholly on the basis of extreme conservatism, not for the purpose of achieving more democracy for all citizens. Since the middle thirties, for example, a coalition between Southern Democrats and conservative Northern Republican senators has dominated the United States Senate. In exchange for Republican votes against civil rights, or the arranged absence of a sufficient number of Republican senators during votes on limitation of interminable debate on such measures, the Southerners have supported measures favored by reactionary Republicans.

Formalization of such alliances began early in the Roosevelt ad-

ministration. In 1936 a group of wealthy Southerners participated in a Detroit conference with anti-Roosevelt Northerners
opposed to the economic policies that had saved capitalism. As a
result such organizations as the Constitutional Democrats of Texas
materialized at the time of the presidential election of 1936. In
1940 and 1944 other revolts against Roosevelt on the third-term
and fourth-term issues developed in South Carolina, Mississippi,
Texas, and other states. All of them were engineered by well-
to-do conservatives and disgruntled officeholders or former officeholders who hated the New Deal.

But these measures were not popular with farmers, workers, and
other beneficiaries of the economic recovery of the South. Unable
to rally anti-Roosevelt sentiment through attacks on a program that
meant more jobs, more food, and more security after the frighten-
ing days of the depression, and a program of successful prosecution
of the war, the politicians and businessmen behind the rebellion
against the liberalization of the Democratic party were forced to
find another rallying point.

They concluded that, "to win the most votes," as Alexander
Heard wrote in his brilliant *A Two-Party South?* "they would
have to play on the race issue, and so they did. . . . Quite clearly,
appeals to white concerns over the Negro told most effectively and
accounted for the great bulk of Dixiecratic votes. . . . They saw
readily that their greatest chance for a sure, if limited, popular
appeal lay in the South's ancient fears of race. They translated their
whole opposition to the Democratic party's economic and social
programs into warnings against civil violence and enforced social
intermingling between the races. They brutally agitated racial
prejudices, a disservice to the country hard to equal. Some did it
blindly in their zeal. Others, the abler and more experienced, did it
deliberately, with full awareness of the humbug they purveyed."

This calculated use of race was the chief instrument of the forces
in the presidential election of 1952 that were determined to turn
over tidelands oil and other natural resources to the states and
thereby to private interests. Untold sums of money were ex-

pended in Texas, for example, in support of General Eisenhower, who as a great war hero born in Texas was palatable even to those who hated the Republican party. The Republican candidate made frequent trips to the South and was photographed with Governors Byrnes of South Carolina and Shivers of Texas—leaders of the white supremacists and foes of the national Democratic party. The desire for a change and the concentration on the issues of alleged communism and corruption in the Truman administration unquestionably affected some voters in the South, as they did those in other parts of the nation, and were effective in bringing about an Eisenhower landslide. But the three issues—race, tidelands oil, and opposition to the liberal social and economic policies of the national Democratic party—played the decisive role in the Republican capture of four Southern states.

Winning these states did not yet mean that a two-party South had come into being. The revolt was a grass-roots one only to the extent that the vast personal popularity of a candidate like Eisenhower could be translated into votes along with capitalization on ancient fears and prejudices based on race.

The schisms that developed in the Southern political camps materially enhanced the future power, both active and passive, of the Negro voter. It was the Negro vote in the 1952 landslide that kept Arkansas, Kentucky, Louisiana, North Carolina, South Carolina, and West Virginia in the Democratic column. More than ninety per cent of the Negroes in these and other states, both South and North, voted for Adlai Stevenson and against the Republican-Dixiecrat alliance. The Southern Negro registered vote jumped from 750,000 in 1948 to 1,300,000 in 1952, and in 1955 was growing at a rate that indicated that it would number 3,000,000 by 1956.

That vote, along with the steadily growing liberal white vote, resulting from industrialization and education, will determine the future course of politics in the South to a far greater extent than will the 1952 alliance. The new type of voter has already begun to retire the more blatant demagogues such as Rankin, whose sole stock in political trade has been race-baiting of the Negro. Others will soon pass from power through defeat or advanced age or death. The South, delighted with the new prosperity it has gained from diversification of agriculture and industrialization, is beginning to learn that it can no longer afford spokesmen who make of it a laughing stock or a symbol of bigotry.

This does not at all mean that the millennium is at hand or that powerful and greedy financial interests will not continue to use the race issue or any other which will be of advantage to them. But even they will learn that a phony two-party system will not benefit them. Here again the Negro is teaching the South a political lesson and helping it to emancipate itself from the bonds of one-party rule. Influential Southern newspapers such as the Montgomery, Alabama, *Advertiser* are sharply reminding the South that the Negro voters have demonstrated measurably greater wisdom and flexibility in politics than have Southern white voters.

"The Republican party was 'the party of his [the Negro's] fathers,' " the *Advertiser* wrote recently. "For it was the GOP that freed him from slavery. If an element ever owed eternal gratitude to the Republican party, it was the Negro. In time, the colored man decided he had fully paid the GOP for freeing him from slavery. In 1932, and particularly in 1936, the Negro forsook the 'party of his fathers' and went over to the Democrats. He did so because the Democrats offered him more of what he wanted. No blind party label held the Negro in chains. And the Negro, being an independent who might switch back to cold-eyed choosing between the two parties, is pampered by the Democrats."

The new sense of progress and power that the long court battles and the tenacious campaigns in Congress and state legislatures against disfranchisement and toward political independence and political education has given the Negro is being translated into concrete gains. In New York City in 1953 all three major parties —Republican, Democratic, and Liberal—nominated capable Negroes for the position of Borough President of Manhattan. Mention has already been made of the election of Dr. Rufus E. Clement

to the Atlanta Board of Education in a city-wide election in 1953.
In the previous ten years colored candidates won election to school
boards in Augusta, Georgia, Knoxville, Tennessee, and San Antonio, Texas, in the South, and in several Northern cities. In the
same election that placed the Atlanta educator in office two other
Negroes—one of them leader of Negro Democrats in Georgia,
attorney Austin T. Walden—were elected to the sixteen-man City
Executive Committee. By 1955 Negroes were serving on the city-
planning and governing bodies of Greensboro, Winston-Salem,
Durham, Fayetteville, Gastonia, and Chapel Hill, North Carolina;
Nashville, Tennessee; and Richmond, Virginia. All were elected by
the ballots of white and Negro voters.

These are admittedly minor successes. But, along with the presence in the House of Representatives of Negro congressmen from
New York, Illinois, and Michigan, they are important primarily
as a forecast of things to come. Certain alterations of concepts previously held are already visible. One of the old fallacies is that
Negroes can be elected only from political districts inhabited predominantly by Negroes—that is to say, ghettos created by racial
segregation. This has already been disproved in city-wide elections
in both the North and the South, where Negro candidates have
won victories that would not have been possible without the support of white as well as Negro voters.

A second misconception which is being dispelled is that Negroes
will support any Negro for office, whatever his character or ability.
Yet Negroes have not only refused to vote for candidates they
believed to be unqualified or otherwise unworthy of support, but
they have ridiculed these candidates. This has been especially
noticeable when the Communists have nominated Negroes for
public office. The sole exception to this rule of repudiation of Com-
munist-backed nominees was that of Benjamin J. Davis, supported
by Negroes in his campaign for election as City Councilman in
New York. An affable, energetic man, he was backed even by some
conservative Negro Republicans, not because of his admitted Com-

munist affiliations, but solely on the basis of his excellent qualifications and his accomplishments in the council.

A third fallacy which is being exploded is that the Negro is in mid-twentieth century as inextricably fixed in the Democratic party as he was in the Republican ranks from the Civil War to the end of the Hoover administration. Above all else the Negro voter has been taught by hard experience to be a realist. Sooner than most he saw the narrow difference between the philosophies and objectives of the two major political parties in the United States. He recognized early that reactionaries of the Republican party from the North and of the Democratic party from the South were united not only against the Negro but against labor unions, social security, housing, minimum-wage laws, prevention of exploitation of woman and child labor, and every other measure to expand the benefits of democracy. Because necessity taught him these lessons, the Negro voter is certain to remain an independent.

Finally, the Negro is a bloc voter only when outside pressures force him to be. He has no choice when, for example, a candidate who has proved himself an enemy of all Negroes offers himself for election, or when one, whatever his race, who has a good record on such basic issues as civil rights, stands for office. When disabilities and restrictions based on race are relaxed and eventually abandoned Negro voters will divide along economic or political lines precisely as do other voters. However, often—especially in the South—the Negro is forced to choose between two evils. In this case he generally votes against the incumbent, with the idea of negating the candidate's seniority rights and important committee appointments.

All these considerations entered into the Negro's thinking when, after the United States Supreme Court outlawed the "white, Democratic primary," Alabama, through such devices as the Boswell Amendment, and South Carolina, through repeal of its state laws dealing with primary elections, sought to circumvent the high court's ruling. Having worked so long to overcome previous attempts at disfranchisement, the victims were in no mood to accept these new attempts to perpetuate the injustice without a fight.

After the Boswell Amendment was declared unconstitutional by a federal court in 1949, and the United States Supreme Court upheld the lower court, a new amendment to provide more limited powers to registrars was voted in a state-wide election by the narrow margin of 369. Also, certain candidates who believed that they might get Negro votes quietly influenced registrars in the cities and larger towns to enroll qualified Negroes with a minimum of trouble or objection.

In South Carolina a turning point came when two cases were brought and won in a federal district court before the courageous jurist J. Waties Waring. The first Waring decision outlawed a color bar in suffrage; the second rendered ineffective a rule designed to discourage Negroes from voting by making them take a loyalty oath, which they could not accept. Judge Waring tartly and firmly admonished South Carolina to "rejoin the union" and threatened contempt proceedings and jail sentences if further evasions were attempted. That ended the efforts to bar Negroes from the polls.

This, then, is the story, greatly abbreviated, of the long and expensive struggle that the Negro, aided by many white Americans, has made to achieve the right to vote. Even though full franchise has not yet been achieved, the position of the Negro voter in 1955, in comparison with what it had been even fifteen years before, demonstrates a progress that has been phenomenal. Consider the accumulated barriers the Negro has had to overcome. He has gained strength through having won the rights he has achieved instead of having them given to him. Through his victory he has strengthened not only his own position but also that of democracy everywhere.

III. The Fight for the Right to Fight

One of the toughest struggles the Negro has been forced to make —and the one in which most progress has been made in the shortest span of time—has been, ironically, the fight for the right to fight for democracy.

On January 5, 1943, William H. Hastie created a modest sensation by resigning as Civilian Aide to the Secretary of War. No Negro ever held a higher post in the military structure of the United States government. The nation was engaged in the greatest war of its existence, to preserve human freedom against the threat of destruction by Nazi Germany, Fascist Italy, and militaristic Japan. Mr. Hastie's resignation, followed by publication of a series of four articles under the title, "On Clipped Wings," exposed one of the greatest obstacles to complete victory over the evil we were fighting—the continuation of racial segregation in the armed services of the United States.

On behalf of democracy, let it be said that had a member of an oppressed minority in Germany resigned such a post (granting the impossible—that a Jew had been appointed to a comparable position by Adolf Hitler), and so vigorously publicized his reasons, it is almost certain that he would have landed either in a prison cell or in front of a firing squad. It takes little imagination to decide what would happen in the Soviet Union were a subordinate to challenge and criticize his government in like manner. But Mr. Hastie returned to the deanship of the school of law at Howard University. Later he was appointed first Negro governor of the Virgin Islands, and was afterward elevated to the bench of the Federal Circuit Court of Appeals, the court second only to the Supreme Court of the United States. These facts are in themselves evidence of the progress that the American Negro has made during the last generation.

William Hastie had already made a notable record scholastically and in educational and governmental fields, having crowded much able and unselfish service into a short career. Phi Beta Kappa at Amherst College, he was graduated from Harvard University Law School with high honors. He became assistant solicitor of the Department of the Interior and was an active member of the legal committee of the NAACP. Despite their contact with him, which should have caused them to know better, the men who decided policy for our armed forces could not conceive that a Negro would voluntarily give up, as a matter of principle, a position that conferred on him such prestige. The Secretary of War, the late Robert P. Patterson, also a civilian and a man of principle, understood and admired the motivation of Mr. Hastie's act, however.

Recognizing the growing importance of the Air Force, even in 1943, before nuclear weapons had given air superiority the essential place that it has today, Mr. Hastie wrote: "Racial practices of the Air Force are of critical importance both because the air arm already constitutes almost one-third of the Army, and because it will become increasingly important and independent in this war and in the postwar period. Faith in our way of life must be based on two premises. We must believe, first, that our government is so organized as to be responsive to public opinion and, second, that the public, if properly informed, will exert pressure in the direction of complete equality for all men and full opportunity for each individual to achieve and to serve according to his own capabilities."

Thus his resignation focused attention on a weakness in our defense at a time when our need for strength was greater than ever before in the history of the nation.

There were many in 1943 who applauded Mr. Hastie's honesty and courage but believed his act to be one of hopeless idealism. Ominous stories of bitter and sometimes fatal clashes between white and Negro American soldiers were coming with alarming frequency from the European Theater of Operations. A few of the reports were so grave that even military censorship was unable to suppress knowledge of them at home. Both at home and overseas a rigid pattern of segregation was maintained, assigning Negroes without regard to intelligence, education, training, or choice to menial service units, such as construction (engineering), ship-unloading, sanitation (janitorial), and truck-driving crews. White combat soldiers believed in an extraordinary number of instances that Negroes asked for such noncombatant service because of cowardice. Negroes, on the other hand, bitterly resented not only the implied deprecation of their valor and patriotism, but also the humiliation of being set aside as presumably inferior human beings.

Here are a few of the startling facts Mr. Hastie related with characteristic careful documentation. Immediately preceding the presidential election of 1940, and following a series of disastrously inept acts and statements by a Southern-born White House press-relations secretary and others in high official position, a long-postponed promotion to the rank of brigadier general was given for the first time to a Negro; Mr. Hastie was named Civilian Aide; and an order was announced by the White House that, "Negro organizations will be established in each major branch of the service."

This was the first breach of the wall of racial segregation, which had been inaugurated as a fixed policy of the United States armed services during the Civil War. In the Navy, since World War I, Negroes had been assigned to menial service as messmen. They had been barred altogether from the Marine Corps. In the Army they were restricted to two cavalry and two infantry regiments that had won fame with Teddy Roosevelt in the Battle of San Juan Hill during the Spanish-American War and with General John J. Pershing on the border of Mexico. But now they were used chiefly as grooms and flunkies to serve white officers and even enlisted men.

During World War I New York's famous all-Negro 369th Regiment was sent to France, but the United States Army refused to use it. The regiment had to be attached to the French forces, where it so covered itself with glory that the entire regiment was decorated with the Croix de Guerre for gallantry in action. After returning to the United States the troops received a tumultuous ovation when they marched down New York's Fifth Avenue in a memorable parade. But their deeds had had no impact on Army policy, and there was even some resentment among the top brass— much of it Southern-born—against the Negro soldiers who had disproved the contention that Negroes were too emotional or too cowardly to make good combat soldiers.

The quite modest advance toward greater utilization of Negro man power which the 1940 order to establish Negro organizations in each major branch of the armed services represented was regarded by Mr. Hastie and other Negroes merely as an instrument to open a little wider the door of opportunity. The newly established Air Force had refused to enlist Negroes at all; now it only grudgingly bowed to the new order. Under compulsion, the Air Command enlisted twenty-five hundred Negroes and put them into ten "Aviation Squadrons (Separate)," issued no guiding statements for their use, as was invariably done with other units, and contented itself with assignment of the two-hundred-fifty-man units to air fields for whatever use the commanding officer chose to make of them. The result in most cases was delegation to menial chores or —even more wasteful and humiliating—complete idleness.

It was even later that the Air Corps under public and White House pressure accepted applications from Negroes for aviation-cadet training. To train them as pursuit pilots the Army spent millions of dollars to establish a segregated Army air base at Tuskegee Institute for the primary training of Negroes. Caught unprepared by the outbreak of war in Europe, and lulled by isolationists into the dangerous belief that the United States would not have to fight actively to stop Hitler, Hirohito, and Mussolini, the Army found itself in desperate need of specialists such as pilots with training in civilian aviation, meteorologists, mathematicians, and other technical experts. Even then, Negroes with such skills and experience as fitted them to fill these needs were bluntly turned down.

Negro and interracial organizations brought every possible argument and pressure to bear on the Army, Navy, Marine Corps, and White House to abandon the wasteful and harmful practice of segregation, with little discernible effect. At a White House conference in 1941 some of us urged as a beginning the formation of a volunteer non-segregated Army division, which would be assigned to maximum perilous duties, to find out whether integration would eliminate friction, inefficiencies, and waste caused by segregation.

We were told that the Army would not initiate such a move but that it would consider the creation of such a division if sufficient public support for it was made evident. Robert P. Patterson, at that time Acting Secretary of War, heartily favored such an experiment, but told me shortly afterward that even he was unable to overcome the adamant opposition of the regular Army top brass in the Pentagon.

But the public reaction to the proposed new division was phenomenal. I remember well reporting the proposal a few days after the White House meeting to a large convocation audience at the University of California in Berkeley. No sooner had the meeting ended than a handsome white giant with a heavy Southern accent rushed to the platform to say, "I want to be the first man, as a Georgia 'cracker,' to volunteer!" But the Army, when given evidence that more than enough qualified men were willing to serve in a non-segregated division, dropped the idea on the ground that "A time of war is not suited to social experimentation."

At another White House meeting President Roosevelt suggested to Secretary of the Navy Frank Knox that a beginning be made to familiarize white personnel aboard ship with the presence of Negroes by assignment of Negro bands to ships. Mr. Knox promised to look into such a possibility but admitted a year later, when asked by the President how the experiment had worked out, that he had done nothing to implement the suggestion. Even the heroic act of Dorie Miller, a Negro Navy messman who helped remove his dying captain from the bridge of their bombed and burning ship at Pearl Harbor on December 7, 1941, and then manned a machine gun against Japanese planes—for which he later received posthumously the Congressional Medal of Honor—did not alter Navy policy on limitation of opportunity to Negroes.

Having labored indefatigably from October 27, 1940, to January 5, 1943, to effect at least a willingness to consider changes of policies that had clearly manifested since the Civil War that they were breeders of conflict, waste, humiliation, and lowered effectiveness, and having found that little could be done by remaining inside the military apparatus, Mr. Hastie submitted his resignation.

"Prejudice is based on ignorance," he stated bluntly. "Let men get acquainted with each other in training and there is no great problem of their harmony later on." Commenting on a memorandum concerning the needlessness and expense of segregated training that he had submitted in December, 1940, and which had been read and ignored, Mr. Hastie wrote caustically: "There are none so blind as those who do not want to see. And the Air Command just does not want to see the advantages of training white and colored flyers together. I believe this blindness will continue until public criticism and condemnation of the segregated training policy becomes so strong that it can no longer be ignored."

The uncompromising and unanswerable documentation of the facts was widely read and caused more critical discussion of the policies of the armed services than any statement made up to that time. Public awareness of the situation slowly developed, particularly as the costs of new weapons and other instruments of global warfare rose to astronomical heights. Impetus was added to the pressure for change as more and more Americans flinched when barbed criticism was made by foreigners of the arrant contradiction of two American armies, one white and the other Negro, fighting presumably against the racial doctrines of Nazism.

The grave crisis of the Battle of the Bulge in December 1944 forced action. So close did General Von Rundstedt come to overwhelming the Allied forces in his breakthrough that every man capable of handling a weapon was desperately needed until reinforcements could be flown across the Atlantic to stop the onrushing Germans. General Eisenhower, at the urging of Lieutenant General John C. H. Lee, Commander of the Service of Supply troops, which was composed chiefly of Negroes, issued a call for volunteers. The response was so overwhelming that the call had to be rescinded not long after it was issued. Soldiers, both colored and white, who had handled bulldozers and trucks instead of combat weapons since their basic training, took hasty refresher training, moved into the front lines, and aided notably in stopping Von Rundstedt's drive.

It had been Generals Eisenhower's and Lee's plan to use the volunteers on a completely integrated basis. But orders came from the Pentagon to permit integration only down to the platoon level. Both apprehensive and interested in how integration would work, the Army sent psychological observer teams to study and report on the reactions of white and Negro officers and soldiers to one another under the pressures of battle. Their findings disclosed that the overwhelming majority of each race emerged from the battle with measurably altered opinions of the other, best expressed nine years later by a Southern white infantryman in Korea who declared, "If a man can fire a rifle and knows his job, he's my buddy. I don't give a damn what color his skin happens to be."

But when the Battle of the Bulge was over and the danger past, the Negro volunteers, some of whom had given up ratings as corporals and sergeants, and some commissions, in order to fight as combat soldiers, were returned to duty in segregated non-combat units.

Three years later the President's Committee on Civil Rights was able to report only moderate progress. "Within the services," it said, "studies made within the last year disclosed that actual experience has been out of keeping with the declarations of policy on discrimination."

In the Army, less than one Negro in seventy held a commission, while there was one white officer for approximately every seven white enlisted men.

"Similarly, in the enlisted grades," the report stated, "there is an exceedingly high concentration of Negroes in the lowest ratings, particularly in the Navy, Marine Corps, and Coast Guard. Almost 80 per cent of the Negro sailors are serving as cooks, stewards, and steward's mates; less than 2 per cent of the whites are assigned to duty in the same capacity. Almost 50 per cent of all white enlisted Marines are in the three highest grades; less than 2½ per cent of the Negro Marines fall in the same category. The disparities in the Coast Guard are similarly great.

"Many factors other than discrimination contribute to this result. However, it is clear that discrimination is one of the major elements which keeps the services from attaining the objectives which they have set for themselves."

The late James Forrestal, as Secretary of the Navy, and W. Stuart Symington, first Secretary of the Air Force and later United States Senator from Missouri, initiated action during the latter part of World War II to abolish segregation in their branches of the service. Forrestal ordered that racial barriers, which Texas-born Admiral Chester Nimitz as Chief of Operations in the Pacific had done much to lower, be done away with swiftly and immediately. He dispatched his fellow alumnus of Dartmouth College, Lester B. Granger of the National Urban League, on a tour of inspection of naval installations to report back on what specifically needed to be done.

At the request of President Truman, I talked with Mr. Forrestal and other heads of the military services prior to a trip to Europe in 1948. I found him quietly determined to achieve full integration while he was Secretary of the Navy. Stuart Symington was equally firm and sincere. A serious imbalance of trained personnel had developed after the war. Because of re-enlistments, new enlistments, and the choice given to draftees to select the branch of the service in which they wished to serve, Negro air units were overstaffed with pilots, navigators, and other personnel. On the other hand, white air units, because there were so many more of them, were woefully undermanned. Symington ordered the all-Negro air wing at Lockbourne Field in Ohio disbanded and its personnel distributed wherever they were needed anywhere in the world. Colonel Benjamin O. Davis, Jr., who commanded the Lockbourne base, was assigned to the Pentagon to direct fighter-plane tactics for the entire Air Force. The vast majority of those under his command were white.

The Marine Corps began to abandon the all-white policy to which it had adhered from its inception. There is now complete integration even at Southern bases such as Camp Le Jeune in North Carolina and Camp Quantico in Virginia. Because of its former policy of exclusion, as noted by the President's Committee on Civil Rights, there is still a great disparity between the number of white and Negro officers in this branch of the Service. But barriers to commissions for Negroes have been dropped, and, barring any setback, that disparity will be gradually eliminated.

Impetus to speed up integration in all the services came primarily from the White House. President Truman issued an executive order on July 26, 1948, calling for "equality of treatment and opportunity for all persons in the armed services without regard to race, color, religion, or national origin." To implement and to chart the course for that order he appointed a civilian committee, with Judge Charles Fahy as chairman, which was named the President's Committee on Equality of Treatment and Opportunity in the Armed Forces.

As the armed services moved toward a non-segregated pattern, and public opinion became steadily more insistent that reforms be instituted, one branch of government steadfastly refused to act. Not only did the Congress refuse again and again to enact legislation against segregation, but, in at least one instance, it even attempted to re-establish the old pattern. On one occasion in 1951 it was necessary to bring to Washington at considerable expense delegations from key states to oppose an amendment to the Universal Military Training bill introduced by William A. Winstead, a Democratic congressman from Mississippi. This bill would have permitted continuation of segregation in the Army and re-introduction of it into the Navy and Air Force. Fortunately the amendment was defeated.

It remained for the outbreak of war in Korea to accelerate the movement for a more truly democratic Army. Once again, as has been true throughout American history, armed conflict and national danger brought the Negro advancement toward his goal of full citizenship. The Fahy Committee had reported that, because segregated Negro units could utilize only a limited number of specialists, Negroes were being refused permission to attend specialist training schools and courses, which inevitably circumscribed their opportunities for advancement. Six months before the Korean war erupted, Secretary of the Army Gordon Gray ordered that Negroes be admitted to all specialist schools. When the North Korean forces crossed the Thirty-eighth Parallel to launch a bloody and costly conflict, the United Nations, and in particular the United States, was called upon to rush to the combat area ground, air, and naval forces, along with vast quantities of ammunition and supplies. There was neither time nor money to set up separate training camps and units.

Deaths and casualties mounted during the first two years of the fighting as the United Nations forces were driven almost into the sea at Pusan. But for some inexplicable reason General MacArthur refused to use to their fullest capacity the American Negro troops that were available, or to integrate them. Very bad morale resulted. White troops—exhausted, injured, humiliated by repeated defeats,

saddened and angered at seeing their comrades killed in action—
naturally resented seeing Negro soldiers in rear areas, where the
fighting was less dangerous and constant; the Negro troops were
bitter at the impugning of their ability to fight and the slurs they
encountered whenever they came into contact with white soldiers.
A rash of courts-martial of Negro soldiers broke out, frequently
for offenses that would not have caused even the arrest of white
soldiers, and many incredibly harsh sentences were inflicted.

The situation reached such critical proportions that it was deemed
necessary by the NAACP to send its Special Counsel, Thurgood
Marshall, to the Far East Command to check the facts and to take
whatever legal steps were possible to correct the conditions of
friction that were adding greatly to the already grave danger of
defeat for the United Nations forces. Marshall was at first refused
permission to enter the war zone. Fortunately the acquaintance I
had formed with General MacArthur in the Pacific during World
War II, and later in Japan, enabled me to persuade him to reverse
his order and permit Marshall to visit the Far East Command to
interview the accused and convicted men, their officers and associates, and to inspect officials records of courts-martial and other
pertinent proceedings.

Marshall's findings were astounding. After eliminating all cases
in which the accused was clearly guilty and his punishment not
unduly excessive, a distressing number of cases were uncovered in
which innocent Negroes had been summarily convicted by drum-
head courts-martial or given sentences entirely out of proportion to
the charges that had been made against them. One of them was
the sentence to death of a Negro lieutenant who had refused to
obey an order to go back up a hill where he and his men had been
under round-the-clock fire for twenty days, during which period
all but 80 of the original group of 189 had been killed or wounded.
Suffering from exhaustion, hunger, and dysentery, the officer admitted he had lost his judgment and temper when a superior officer
fresh on the scene ordered him to return to what he believed would
be certain death. On appeal by the NAACP and by lawyers re-

tained by his wife, his sentence was reduced to twenty years by President Truman. He has since been released and reunited with his family.

Ten life-imprisonment sentences were reduced on appeal to ten years each, one life sentence to fifteen years and another to ten, another to five years, and other shorter sentences to brief terms or dismissal of the charges and sentences. Equally important was the diminution of use of court-martial machinery to pillory and intimidate Negro soldiers.

It cost five thousand dollars to send Marshall to Korea and Japan and in excess of ten thousand dollars more for the legal and other appeals of unjust court-martial convictions. So stirred were Americans, particularly Negroes, that they again contributed generously to the NAACP request for funds for the investigation and for appeals through the Army boards and courts. The citizens of the Bay area in California, under the vigorous leadership of Franklin Williams, West Coast Regional Secretary of the NAACP, for example, contributed the total cost of Marshall's trip, raising $6100. Thus another item was added to the price of freedom that Negroes have been forced to pay.

But all such efforts were merely ameliorative as long as segregation continued, which was the case until General MacArthur was replaced by General Matthew Ridgway. As soon as Ridgway assumed command he requested and received permission to integrate all American troops under his command. He did so not only as a matter of principle but also because as an efficient administrator he objected strenuously to the waste of man power of competent, over-strength fighting units behind the lines because of idiotic race prejudice, while other units were being wiped out because their white skins ordained them to fight in advance posts.

The effect of integration on combat effectiveness and morale was as instantaneous and spectacular as Roman candles on the Fourth of July. With none of the anticipated friction during the period of adjustment, white and Negro soldiers and officers were eating, sleeping, fighting, and dying side by side. White officers and enlisted men from the Deep South who had never known any relationship with Negroes except that of patronage or hostility accepted the command of Negro superior officers. Lee Nichols of the United Press quotes a Maryland-born division officer who was assigned to a battalion commanded by a Negro colonel. "I am from Baltimore and have been filled with all kinds of race prejudice from the time I was old enough to listen. Imagine how I felt. But the colonel turned out to be one of the finest gentlemen I have ever known. I would serve under him any time. Because of him and other colored officers, I have changed my feelings about colored troops."

The effect upon Negro soldiers was no less spectacular. The story of Sergeant Cornelius Charlton is more typical than is generally supposed, because only a few of the many cases of heroism in war, whether displayed by white men or Negroes, become known unless there happens to be an alert officer or war correspondent on the scene to report what happened.

Sergeant Charlton was the son of a Negro coalminer in West Virginia who moved to New York in the hope that there he would find more remunerative employment—which he didn't—and better educational and other advantages for his children—which he did. When the commissioned officers died or were wounded in an attack on Hill 543 in Korea, Sergeant Charlton assumed command, helped tend and evacuate the wounded, and then led the charge by the twelve unwounded men left on the third platoon to take the hill against murderous machine-gun fire.

Eleven men were killed, leaving Charlton alone to charge the last impediment. He charged, throwing his last grenade and firing his last clip of ammunition as he fell with a gaping chest wound. It would be dramatic to say that Charlton's singlehanded act of courage routed thousands of the enemy. Unfortunately, that sort of thing usually happens only in fiction concocted by writers many miles away from military action. But the next day reinforcements of the 35th Infantry Regiment took Hill 543 and counted five hundred thirty-five Chinese Communists dead on the slopes where Charlton and his comrades had made their gallant stand.

The case of Sergeant Charlton can be overplayed and overemphasized as proof that the issue of race in America's armed services has been wholly and satisfactorily settled for all time. Such a hasty conclusion would be exceedingly dangerous and premature. Judge Hastie's warning of 1943 on the perils of separating human beings solely on the basis of race in a democracy still has a valid application to civilian life. Even as the Cornelius Charltons were fighting and dying in Korea with their fellow Americans, Chinese Communists were using with sadistic cruelty the stories that the United States was supplying almost daily—stories of mobs rioting in Chicago and Cleveland and Miami to keep the families of men like Sergeant Charlton from living in decent homes outside the ghetto. I have mentioned that Negro prisoners of war in Communist camps were regaled with the undeniable story of the bomb slaying of the Moores, who had, among other similar things, urged a new trial of another Negro, believed by many to have been unjustly convicted of a crime. A few Negroes succumbed in despair to indoctrination, and abandoned, possibly forever, return to their homeland. Most, however, clung stubbornly to their faith in the free way of life that is called democracy.

That may have been true because innumerable men and women with the faith and courage of William Hastie, having experienced in the anti-Negro South the racism that is typical of totalitarianism, want no part of any regime in which one man or a small group of men hold power over all other men. That an iniquitous system like racial segregation in as regimented and formidable a system as the armed services of the United States could be almost totally abolished gives them the courage to continue to believe in democracy. For nowhere has the fallacy of incompatability between Negroes and whites been more decisively and rapidly proved than in the armed services, where integration is working.

Leo Bogart, in an article in *The Reporter* of December 30, 1954, told how it has worked. He cited all the classic objections that had delayed integration for so many years: it would result in violence between white and colored soldiers; it would lower military standards; it would be impossible to get white enlisted men to take orders from Negro officers; it would create social problems; Negroes prefer not to mix with whites.

He then proceeded to show how, one by one, the arguments have been demolished by the acquaintanceship and mutual understanding that integration has brought about. One officer is quoted as reporting that it took about two hours after Negro soldiers had moved into his company before the members of the two races were treating one another exactly as they would treat anyone else.

As to morale, officers in Korea after integration reported three to one that mixing Negroes with white soldiers had no effect, or actually a favorable effect, on performance.

In the matter of how a white soldier would react to orders from a Negro officer it was found that, as always in the Army, the enlisted man accepted the authority conferred by a commission, an impersonal thing that was a recognized part of Army life. It was not, in effect, a Negro or a white man, a good guy or a stinker, who gave the order. It was a lieutenant, a captain, a major, voicing authority that was the backbone of the Army system, running from the Commander-in-Chief down through the ranks and grades, from the lowliest corporal to the enlisted man—who might, if he chose to try, work his own way up the ladder. "I figured," one white sergeant said, speaking of his Negro lieutenant, "if he gave me an order I would just have to do the job because I know it would come down from higher headquarters. I knew there would be someone over him all the time."

It is amusing to note in the Army's study of the effects of integration the frequent recurrence of one of the oldest clichés—that while Negroes as a group are inferior, this or that Negro is "different." One white GI in Korea said, "The type they mix with us are something different. I bet the Army picks very carefully the guys they put with whites. They're the cream of the crop."

One of the most significant and heartening facts which came out of the survey during the transitional period of integration was that men in mixed units, whether from the North or the South, were

consistently more favorable to integration than were those in units
in which the pattern of separation continued. "Hell," one white
GI said, "the first night they were drinking out of the same can-
teen cups! We treated them like another guy." Here, as elsewhere,
acquaintance with reality has dispelled fantasy and created understanding and appreciation.

Today all the armed forces of the United States of America demonstrate to the world that the direction of democracy's movement
is forward. Here Negro and white citizens work together, play
together, eat together, share living quarters, and die side by side
fighting for the same values. Integration, so long fought for and so
long denied, is now an accomplished fact.

If integration has not worked with absolute smoothness in every
detail, what in the Army—or for that matter in any aspect of human
life—has? The Negro soldier is undoubtedly at times still the victim
of injustice. So is the white soldier. Probably the Negro gets more
than his share of this too-plentiful commodity in an imperfect organization set up in an imperfect world. But today he can gripe
about it to his white as well as to his Negro buddies, have a sym-
pathetic audience, and hear plenty of comparable gripes that prove
that he has not been singled out for frustration and disillusionment.

All movements, whether backward or forward, are like snow-
balls. The significance of desegregation in military units extends
far beyond the boundaries of life within the armed forces. The
typical American lad is a civilian at heart, a soldier only of necessity, by nature honest and loyal in his friendships, and ready to
admit a mistake when he discovers that he has made one. The white
youth who has shared a barracks, a tent, or a foxhole with a Negro
youth, the fellow whose affection and admiration has gone out
spontaneously to a buddy whose skin happens to be pigmented
differently from his own, will find nothing surprising or disheartening in the fact that such a person has moved into the house next
door to his own, or that his children are going to school with children of a different skin color. Nor will the children.

The white GI who has taken orders from an able and respected

Negro officer will not, on his return to civilian life, say, "The Negro is all right as long as he keeps his place," but will meet Negro civilians in responsible positions with the same attitude of respect that he would feel for a white man in the same place.

Similarly, and of no less importance, Negro GIs who have almost inevitably come, during their own experiences in life and through knowledge of the history of their race, to distrust white people *en masse*, will have learned before they return to civilian life that in true brotherhood race and skin color have no pertinence.

One by one the long-assaulted barriers crumble, and the light that shines above the Promised Land comes more brightly into view for the hosts—both Negro and white—who march toward it.

IV. Work to Do

It would seem a simple thing to expect that everyone should have the opportunity to work at the kind of job for which, by temperament and talent, he is best fitted, and that such opportunity should be his regardless of race or color, church affiliation or lack of it, place of origin, or nationality.

Some years ago my wife said something of the sort to nine-year-old Claudia, trying to explain to her the reason for my all-too-frequent trips to Washington, the filibusters in Congress, the FEPC, and so forth.

"But, Mother, I thought that was what America is about," said Claudia.

We agreed with her. It is puzzling that the right to the right job should have become one of the most controversial subjects of our generation.

Yet significant gains have been made since 1940 in the campaign to establish equality in the work status of Americans. Through increasingly unified efforts of disadvantaged minorities—Negroes, Jews, Catholics, the foreign-born, and women—more employment has been opened up than ever before. A period of high employment since the beginning of World War II, during which more than sixty-three million Americans have had jobs, is one factor of measurable importance. The urgent demand of industry for workers to make the products needed by consumers and the armed services has caused employers to use many workers previously denied employment because of factors that had no bearing on their fitness as workers.

This is not to say that all employers had to be persuaded or forced by necessity, governmental action, or pressure of public opinion to hire workers on the basis of skills alone. Corporations such as the International Harvester Corporation, the General Cable Corporation, the Western Electric Company, the Ford Motor Company, and a few others have long operated on the principle that a man's ability to do the job required, and not his race or creed, is the determining factor in his desirability. The final report of the wartime Fair Employment Practices Committee made the surprising statement: "When challenged, private industry eliminated discrimination much more readily than did unions."

Much progress, however, toward breaking down barriers to employment is due to labor's active opposition to discrimination, chiefly at the national level. Since its formation in 1935 the Congress of Industrial Organizations has been consistent in continuing the open-door policies of the mass-industry unions of which it was formed. The late Philip Murray of the CIO and William Green of the AFL were both vocal and active against discrimination during the 1940–1953 period. Walter Reuther and George Meany, their successors, are continuing that campaign. At mid-century a radical change had occurred in the attitude of labor leaders and unions, except in the railway brotherhoods and a few AFL unions which have stubbornly refused to alter constitutional or ritualistic provisions barring Negroes from membership.

Some unions, however, have created special departments to work on eradication of racial and religious prejudice both within unions and in the national economy. Although the demonstrable results of their efforts vary widely, their existence has shown the determination of unions to clean up their own practices. Whereas many trade unions by one method or another actively practiced discrimination in the thirties, in the fifties they at least were on record as favoring equality of job opportunity. That fact is one of the basic reasons why more and better jobs have been opened to those previously shut out of all but unskilled and poorly paid employment.

At the center of this struggle since 1925 has been scholarly A. Philip Randolph, who looks and speaks far more like a college professor or a minister than a labor leader. Randolph organized the Brotherhood of Sleeping Car Porters and Maids in 1925 and has been its guiding spirit ever since. As a chartered unit of the AFL, the brotherhood has spearheaded the battle within the trade-union movement against any and all restriction of membership, responsibility, or benefits because of race, color, or religion. As its spokesman, Randolph has more often than not stood alone. In the face of efforts to persuade, discourage, or intimidate him, or to force disaffiliation of the brotherhood from the trade-union movement, Randolph has been adamant. His has been always an eloquent and unanswerable demand that labor live up to the democratic principles on which its own case was founded.

His battle for many years was two-pronged. Outraged by any union, and particularly a predominantly Negro union—all Pullman porters and maids except a few Filipinos were Negroes—the wealthy and politically potent Pullman Company exerted every possible pressure to cajole or intimidate Randolph into abandonment of his efforts to organize Pullman employees. (At that time the railroads did not have to meet the competition of airlines, buses, and automobiles, whose challenge as public carriers later reduced materially the profits and monopoly the railroads enjoyed.) These efforts included hiring venal Negro politicians to attack Randolph's integrity and socialist views and placing costly advertising in the Negro press in an effort to influence its news coverage and editorial treatment of the new union.

But Randolph's influence on the Negro's economic status has extended far beyond that which he wielded as the head of one small union. His impassioned pleas year after year at AFL conventions slowly won some converts, shamed other opponents into silence, and made others more subtle in their discriminatory practices. His example influenced many young, trained Negroes to enter the trade-union movement instead of turning to the professions. An indefatigable lecturer and writer, Randolph spoke not only to his own union and the labor movement, but also to churches, colleges, trade associations, and professional groups of both whites and Negroes whenever he could manage to be invited to their meetings.

Dramatic impetus to liberalization of the trade-union movement on the issue of race was given by organization of the CIO in 1935. Sixteen years previously a great steel strike had been broken when the industry hired Negroes, who up to that time had been shut out of the labor movement almost totally, to replace white strikers. CIO leaders such as Philip Murray remembered that setback to labor organization. The United Mine Workers, the Amalgamated Clothing Workers, the International Ladies' Garment Workers, and some of the other unions that formed the CIO had always welcomed Negroes into their ranks, in sharp contrast to some of the craft unions. The CIO from its inception aimed at organizing workers in the mass-production industries such as steel, iron, automobiles, and rubber, as well as mining, longshoring, shipping, and the garment industries. They therefore purposely set out to enroll workers without distinction of race, creed, color, craft, or nationality, since all these were included in the ranks of the unorganized they hoped to organize.

Another circumstance had increased Negro labor's importance, which in turn added to Randolph's power as its most effective spokesman. One of the greatest internal migrations in history resulted in the movement of nearly two million Southern Negroes to the North during and following World War I. Many of these people might have been forced to return to the South when war plants shut down had not the great tide of European immigrants, which had averaged around a million and a half since the beginning of the twentieth century, been reduced by drastic new immigration laws to a fraction of what it had been. Both employers and trade-union leaders were thereby faced with the certainty—although many of both groups closed their minds to it—that the Negro in industry had gained a toehold which he was never to relinquish. Even the most conservative of AFL unions began to awaken to the new situation.

But the onset of World War II found the Negro worker still low man on the totem pole. Despite gains won through his own efforts, and his greater integration in the labor movement, Negroes were either excluded altogether from most of the government-patronized plants filling contracts for munitions and other supplies of war for Great Britain and other friendly powers fighting Germany, or limited to a few menial jobs such as those of laborers, janitors, truck-drivers, and cafeteria workers. Despite continuing efforts by such agencies as the NAACP and the National Urban League, and repeated appeals to Washington, this practice continued.

As allocations of defense contracts were announced, for example, the NAACP rushed copies of them to each of its twelve hundred branches, with instructions to pass on the information to qualified workers so that they could make application for the many jobs the contracts opened. Branches were asked to report the details of all refusals to qualified Negroes. These soon began to pour in as the defense program rapidly expanded. They were placed before Washington officials, some of whom, such as Secretary of the Interior Harold L. Ickes, did what was possible under the existing law. But the pattern continued.

I wrote an article for *The Saturday Evening Post* titled, "It's Our Country Too," about the gross discrimination in the national-defense program, with particular emphasis on employment. It opened the eyes of readers to a gratifying degree, but again official Washington procrastinated even as an alarming shortage of skilled and semi-skilled workers grew, to the endangerment of the defense program.

Eventually the crisis reached the stage at which four influential senators, two of each party, introduced a resolution to create a Senate investigating committee to get the facts and to recommend remedial procedures to end discrimination. But foes of the program blocked it.

It became clear that forceful action was necessary to effect any change in the situation. Philip Randolph proposed a march on Washington, which instantaneously captured the imagination of Negroes and many whites—with the exception of the Communists, who, characteristically, were using every possible means to turn the deplorable condition to their own political advantage. Because I have told the story in *A Man Called White* (New York: The Viking Press, 1948) I shall not repeat the details here. It is sufficient to record that President Roosevelt, to avert the march, issued on June 25, 1941, his famous Executive Order 8802, creating the first Fair Employment Practices Committee. Although severely limited both in authority and operational funds, the FEPC materially changed the pattern of employment of minorities during its five years of life, until enemies of the agency in the United States Senate succeeded on February 8, 1946, in cutting off the appropriation for its work.

The FEPC helped to establish ineradicably certain important facts during its short and turbulent career. Numerous industrial plants, such as the Sperry Gyroscope Company, which had not employed Negroes and some other minorities previously, found that they were capable of as skilled performance as any other group. Another fact which the FEPC program brought to light was that not all white, native-born Americans object to working with other Americans of different color. And, third, it helped to speed the eventual victory in global war by reducing friction, producing more materials, and turning them out at lower cost per unit. There is little doubt that had not there been such a government agency as the FEPC, more—perhaps many more—disastrous riots like the one in Detroit in 1943 might have occurred.

The FEPC did not, of course, open every available job to every qualified American. A continuous and expensive campaign had to be continued in Congress to re-establish some form of official body to insure compliance with the clauses forbidding racial or religious bias in employment that Congress ordered put into all government contracts and sub-contracts. (Creation of these clauses was one tangential beneficial result of the long fight for equality.) The campaign for such laws was not, however, futile, even though the FEPC was discontinued. Public support for the fight had so grown over the years that fifty-three national organizations joined together at the invitation of the NAACP for a civil-rights mobilization in 1949. Representing powerful church, labor, fraternal, and minority organizations, the group voiced the practically unanimous endorsement of corrective legislation and action of approximately eighteen million Americans. This did not mean, of course, that every member of every participating organization endorsed each item of the program on which the mobilization leaders were agreed.

But four thousand delegates assembled in Washington in February, 1950, to press for congressional action. The nationwide press and radio coverage of the mass mobilization, under the leadership of Roy Wilkins, Acting Secretary of the NAACP, added its quota to the education of America on civil rights. Another conference in 1951, this one restricted with difficulty because so many interested persons wished to attend, continued the crusade. Continuous emphasis in the journals and other publications of the participating organizations, appearances before committees of the Senate and the House of Representatives, literature, radio and television programs, and vigorous united demands on civil rights before the platform committees of the Democratic and Republican parties in 1948 and 1952 were some of the methods of educating and persuading the American public to make good the guarantees of equality and freedom to which they were dedicated.

This mounting public opposition created sufficient political pressure to bring about enactment of laws and ordinances establishing state and municipal agencies, modeled on the federal FEPC, to expose and end employment discrimination. The states of New York, Connecticut, Massachusetts, New Jersey, Washington, Oregon, New Mexico, Rhode Island, and Colorado, as well as the Territory of Alaska, adopted FEPC laws with enforcement powers.

Several states such as Wisconsin, Kansas, and Indiana established agencies without such powers, relying instead on persuasion and compromise.

Numerous cities passed ordinances barring discrimination in either public or private employment or both. Among these were Cleveland, Akron, Campbell, Girard, Hubbard, Lorain, Lowellville, Niles, Steubenville, Struthers, Warren, and Youngstown, Ohio; Gary and East Chicago, Indiana; Minneapolis, Minnesota; Pontiac and River Rouge, Michigan; Richmond, California; Phoenix, Arizona; Sioux City, Iowa; and Philadelphia, Sharon, and Monessen, Pennsylvania. Some sixty million Americans now live in cities and states with some form of FEPC legislation. But meanwhile the legislatures of a number of the larger industrial states such as Pennsylvania, Illinois, Ohio, Michigan, and California defeated FEPC bills again and again, despite the fact that both political parties were pledged through their platforms to enact such legislation.[1]

The courts, and in particular federal courts, were meanwhile appealed to as an instrument of social progress with success. In 1944 the United States Supreme Court in two cases (*Tunstall* vs. *Brotherhood of Locomotive Firemen, et al*, and *Steele* vs. *Louisville and Nashville R.R., et al*) declared invalid the practice of railroad brotherhoods pretending and claiming to represent all employees of a particular class while excluding Negroes of that class from membership in the union. These cases were brilliantly argued by the late Charles H. Houston, Chairman of the National Legal Committee of the NAACP. The twin victories also produced court rulings declaring an agreement discriminating against Negroes, which the brotherhoods and railroads had entered into, unconstitutional and invalid.

In 1949 the Supreme Court upheld an injunction against the Brotherhood of Locomotive Firemen and Engineers to restrain it from discriminating against Negroes.

In 1950 a federal district court in Alabama found the Gulf, Mo-

[1] Since this was written, Minnesota and Michigan have adopted effective FEPC legislation. (Editor's note.)

bile & Ohio RR and the Brotherhood of Locomotive Firemen and Engineers guilty of discrimination and awarded damages to the Negro plaintiffs for the total wages they would have earned if the jobs had not been denied them because of race.

In North Carolina in 1951 the United States Court of Appeals reversed a lower court decision that allowed railroads to deny or restrict jobs as firemen to Negroes.

In 1952 the Supreme Court ruled that Negro railway porters doing the work of brakemen must receive the title of brakemen, must receive the same pay as white men doing the same job, and must be represented in collective bargaining by the Brotherhood of Railway Trainmen.

In a few state courts bias by employers or unions was outlawed —as in California, where the Machinists Union was denied the right to bargain collectively for Negroes who had been forced to join a separate all-Negro local, where they paid dues but had no voice in the affairs of the union.

The combined effect of all these forces was increasingly reflected in news and editorial coverage in the daily press, in magazine articles and books, in sermons, in radio and television discussions and debates, in study groups of churches, in labor unions, colleges, high schools and grammar schools, and in debate on the floors of Congress and state legislatures. Although it had been bitterly assailed by certain Southern members of Congress, by spokesmen for conservative business associations, and by one or two choleric columnists, "To Secure These Rights," the report of the President's Committee on Civil Rights, acted as a valuable textbook on the facts and on remedial action that needed to be taken.

The constant insistence on action by the executive branch of government in the face of consistent refusal by the legislative branch to do anything about the problem is exemplified by President Truman's Executive Order 10308 of December 3, 1951, creating the Committee on Government Contract Compliance. The committee consisted of five representatives of official government agencies—the Department of Defense and the Department of

Labor, the Atomic Energy Commission, the General Services Administration, and the Defense Materials Procurement Agency—and six members representing the public. The committee was charged with the responsibility of investigating compliance (or non-compliance) with anti-discrimination clauses in government contracts, and was instructed to "confer and advise" with any contracting agencies to effect compliance.

When deemed necessary, the committee was allowed to submit recommendations for correction of conditions to the Director of Defense Mobilization, who, "when he deems it appropriate," could pass on the information with a statement of his views to the President. President Truman had wanted some procedure and machinery much less impotent than this. But he dared not go further. The coalition in Congress of Southern Democrats violently opposed to any action of any nature whatsoever on civil rights and of Republicans already anticipating election of Robert A. Taft, or someone similarly conservative, as president in 1952, forced President Truman to the realization that it might not be prudent to give the new committee greater power.

The committee under the chairmanship of a distinguished industrialist, Dwight R. G. Palmer, whose own corporation, the General Cable Company, had established an admirable record against discrimination in its plants, conducted several hearings and many conferences with government agencies and those who held contracts with the federal government. Hamstrung by its limited power and staff, it could do little more. However, its final report made a number of excellent proposals.

These included recommendations that a permanent agency be created to receive and investigate complaints of violation of the non-discrimination clauses; that monetary penalties and, if necessary, cancellation of contracts be imposed for violations; that existing legislation be amended to include safeguards against use of federal funds where there is discrimination; that state employment services financed by the federal government be required to administer their facilities without discrimination; and that a continuing educational program against bias be conducted. The committee's most forceful statement condemned segregation based on race, religion, color, national origin, or ancestry and recommended that "industry, labor unions, and the public cooperate in combating all forms of segregation in employment."

But this detailed, thoughtful, and basic report was lost sight of in the welter and heat of the presidential campaign of 1952. The reactionary element among those who backed General Dwight D. Eisenhower took lightly the Republican candidate's declarations that he would use his utmost power, if elected, to rid the United States of every vestige of racial segregation, discrimination, and second-class citizenship. They believed that such statements were merely the usual campaign oratory, which is forgotten even before the last ballot is dropped into the box. Their confidence was deepened by General Eisenhower's fraternization with such anti-civil-rights figures as ex-Senator, ex-Secretary of State, ex-United States Supreme Court Associate Justice, ex-Director of War Mobilization, Governor James F. Byrnes of South Carolina. Assurance was bolstered by President Eisenhower's nomination of Governor Byrnes as a member of the United States delegation to the Eighth Assembly of the United Nations.

Cold water was dashed on such hopes by the President, however, when he issued an executive order establishing a new contract-compliance committee, headed by Vice-President Richard Nixon, with powers more sweeping than those given in 1951 by President Truman. Mr. Nixon, on being sworn in as chairman, announced that the federal government in disbursing forty billion dollars a year was responsible for one-fourth of the nation's total expenditure for production and that his committee intended to be one of action and not one of hazy promises. As this is written the results remain to be measured. But formation of the committee, the caliber of its membership, and its political potentialities mark a new peak in recognition of the importance of the fight that men like Philip Randolph and a host of other Americans have waged to achieve industrial democracy and equality of employment opportunity.

Perhaps nowhere is there a better example of how much has been won, and how much still remains to be done, than Detroit, formerly a powder keg in employment race relations.

The pattern here is widely varied, but with some bright spots. These oases of enlightened employment policies are due to the aggressive non-discrimination policy of the UAW-CIO from its beginning, which is militantly pushed by Walter Reuther and employers who have taken the lead on fair-employment policy, such as Ford; the Detroit Telephone Company; Sam's, Incorporated, Detroit's second-largest department store in terms of volume of trade; and a few others. The Kaiser-Frazer Company and the Great Lakes Steel Corporation have better-than-average policies. The Detroit Edison Company employs Negroes in its commercial outlets, placing them on the basis of ability in any store without regard to the population of the district. The National Bank of Detroit in recent years has employed a number of Negroes in various classifications, including tellers. The pattern, however, varies from these instances to those of some other large firms that have the reputation of hiring Negroes only when the bottom of the barrel of white employables has been scraped.

Efforts to persuade employers, either collectively or individually, to examine and alter their employment practices too often have met with little success. Most of them became conscious of the problem only when a fair-employment-practices bill was introduced in the Michigan legislature. The reaction of some of the employers was anger and opposition sufficient to defeat the bill. But organized and united church, labor, and minority groups continue the battle and it is quite probable that the legislature will enact a law within the near future which will accelerate the process of racial integration in Detroit's industry.

It has been fascinating to note the interrelationship of integration in employment with the other community problems of Detroit. During the bloody race riots of 1943, the only places in Detroit where there was neither friction nor fighting were the plants in which management and the UAW-CIO had achieved some degree of integration. During the past decade white workers, even many of those who come from the Deep South, have learned to accept Negroes as co-workers in the plants and as co-members of the unions. Some support fair-employment-practice legislation and regulations. Many are less willing to accept Negroes as neighbors, and some are vigorously opposed to doing so. But the materially increased earning and spending power of Negroes, which is quite literally enabling them to buy their way out of the ghetto, has created a situation where whites can neither resist nor afford to run away.

Malcolm Bingay, dean of Detroit's newspapermen and editorial director of the *Detroit Free Press*, attributes his city's growing maturity on race to a factor that may shock the intelligentsia. He believes that Joe Louis has done more to teach mutual respect between human beings than all the social scientists put together. "The people who go to the Detroit Arena Friday nights," Bingay believes, "go there without thought of social and economic problems" —which seems reportorially accurate. "There's never been the faintest hint of anything crooked in any of Joe's fights, which is markedly different from almost every other fighter. He has never struck a foul blow, although many have been thrown at him. No other fighter has ever been as decent and sportsman-like as Joe. The lesson hasn't failed to be learned by the kind of fellows who never before have known a Negro except to hate him."

Another city worth looking at in appraising the advances made by the American Negro in employment is Washington, D.C., "Capital of Democracy," and until recently one of the most shameful showcases of racism.

Here, as in Detroit, the Negro's job status has vastly improved during the past two decades. For many years Washington was one of the few places where educated Negroes could obtain some white-collar jobs, although many college and university graduates served as messengers or clerks to other Americans of less intelligence and with less scholastic training. Negroes were forced to accept these positions because their color barred them from other employment.

Beginning with the Roosevelt administration the number of Negroes in government employment expanded greatly, and the trend has continued. In the decade from 1940 to 1950 colored stenographers and typists increased from 1 per cent of the total to more than ten times that ratio. Printing craftsmen almost quadrupled, from 3.4 to 12.3 per cent. Librarians more than doubled, from 3.1 to 7.4 per cent. Telephone linemen employed by the government also doubled, from 1.7 to 3 per cent. A number of large private employers still refuse to hire qualified Negro men and women even as they comb the nation for competent men and women craftsmen.

What does all this add up to? What is revealed by totting up gains won against bigotry and comparing them with the job that remains to be done? Is there a sound and reasonable basis for hope that the American Negro—and other colored peoples all over the world—can put their trust in an imperfect democracy against the glittering promises of communism or some other form of monolithic totalitarianism?

I do not presume to answer such questions except for myself, as a solitary individual who has been privileged to devote most of his adult life to the hope that in some fashion or other we can build a lasting society in which no man is oppressed because of the color of his skin or the place of his birth or the way in which he worships—or does not worship—his concept of a divine being.

Here is a trial balance sheet of the Negro's employment status in American democracy, circa 1954, as I see it. The credit items outnumber and outweigh the debit ones; but the sum total of progress is not sufficient to permit relaxation of efforts to further it.

These are the steps forward since 1940:

1. The average annual income of Negroes has trebled, while that of white Americans rose 158 per cent. But a word of caution —the average yearly income of Negro Americans in 1940 was so much lower than that of whites that percentagewise gains are not as significant as the actual dollar increase of income.

2. In 1939 only 0.1 per cent of the 13,500,000 Negroes in the

United States earned $5000 a year or more. In 1950, 5.4 per cent of 15,500,000 Negroes had attained the $5000-or-higher income bracket.

3. In 1950 there were three times as many clerical workers and twice as many salesmen and craftsmen among Negroes as there were in 1940, reflecting both the rise in the number of educated Negroes and the results of the constant struggle to open new avenues of employment.

4. In 1940, 66 per cent of Negro workers were classified as unskilled; in 1950 the percentage had dropped eleven points to 55 per cent. This does not mean that all those in the two-thirds bracket of the unskilled in 1940 were unskilled; many possessed skills which for reasons of color they were not allowed to use. That situation was somewhat less true in 1950, partly because the changing climate of public opinion and the expanding need of industry for skilled workers permitted Negroes to use skills that had before then been wasted.

5. In 1953 there were 2,400,000 Negroes in American trade unions as compared with 1,500,000 in 1949 and 750,000 in 1938. The number who rose to positions of leadership at the national level, especially in the CIO, and on the local level as shop stewards, officers of local unions, and representatives of their unions around the bargaining table, steadily grew. Negroes in picket lines with white fellow workers became an increasingly common sight, even in the South. As union members Negro workers benefited from collective bargaining, equal pay for equal work, upgrading under seniority rules, and in the opening up of jobs hitherto closed to them.

6. In 1940 approximately 80 per cent of Negro males were listed in the nation's working population; in 1950 the percentage had dropped to 74 per cent. Two of the chief reasons for that decline were: (a) the improved economic status of Negro families allowed more Negro boys and young men to attend school instead of being forced to leave school to go to work, so that in 1950 60 per cent of Negro males between the ages of five and

twenty-four were in school; (b) higher income, pensions and retirement plans, old-age insurance, and social security permitted some to retire at an earlier age.

7. Beginning with President Roosevelt's executive order of 1941 and continuing through those of President Truman in 1951 and President Eisenhower in 1953, official policy of the executive branch of government and that of the judicial arm as reflected in court decisions has been affirmatively for economic equality irrespective of race, color, religion, or place of birth. Despite opposition of Congress and some employers and labor unions, executive and judicial action has undergirded the American tradition of equality, in sharp contrast with the writing of inequality into the laws of the Union of South Africa under Prime Minister Daniel Malan and into those of Nazi Germany under Adolf Hitler.

8. The differential in 1940 between the salaries paid Negro and white teachers with comparable education and experience and performing equal tasks was reduced through court action and education of public opinion by approximately four million dollars by means of equalization. Increased pay enabled Negro teachers to live less insecure lives, to obtain advanced training by attendance at summer sessions of teacher-training schools, and to subscribe to educational journals and other publications. A somewhat higher type of teacher who is slowly improving the instruction of Negro youth has been attracted to the profession.

This is manifestly an admirable and heartening record, which demonstrates once more the power of the democratic process to win a victory over the foes of democracy. But even here, when gains are definite and demonstrable, the victory is not clear-cut, and it is far from total.

1. The average annual income of the American Negro, though it has improved, is still, as this is being written, only about half that of the average annual income of American white workers.

2. In 1950 Negroes constituted 11 per cent of the industrial workers of the United States. This means that there were twice as many Negroes in industry as there were in 1940, partly because of the acceleration of immigration from farms to cities during that period. But in spite of these gains, a large majority of Negroes were engaged in unskilled or semi-skilled work. Even in such heavy industries as steel, automobiles, and rubber, most Negro workers were in the foundries rather than in the more highly skilled and better-paid jobs on assembly lines.

3. Even in industries filling contracts (amounting to over forty-one billion dollars in 1952) for the government of the United States —the spokesman for and guardian of democracy—the great majority of Negroes were in such job classifications as janitor, porter, truck-driver, and so forth.

4. In order to supplement family incomes more Negro women (44 per cent more in urban cities) were forced to work outside their homes than were whites, leaving them less time to take care of their homes and families—a major factor in juvenile delinquency.

Fortunately for all workers, the United States has since 1940 been consistently in a period of high employment, which has of itself had a noticeable effect in improving the Negro's work status. But no one—and especially no Negro—who was past the years of early childhood in 1929 has forgotten what a real depression is like. And the Negro worker knows today that, despite the gains he has made in the last fifteen years, in another depression he would stand a very good chance, in many places, of being the first to suffer from unemployment, regardless of seniority or skill.

Yet although these negative factors are all too apparent to make placid acceptance of the contemporary status, or cessation of effort to better it, possible, the prospect for the American Negro worker is today more hopeful than it has been at any time in his history.

All things work together. As no man is an island, neither is any factor in the life of an individual or a race an isolated factor. Any movement, whether it is forward or backward, is powered partly by an innate force and is capable of acceleration—if it is pushed a bit. Many factors contribute to a prospect of increasing betterment for Negroes in employment. Among these are: desegregation in the public schools, which will more and more intimately associate white and Negro children during their formative years; integration in the armed forces, which will automatically develop increased understanding and deep and lasting interracial friendships between Negro and white young men; growing proof that the skills of the Negro are needed in industry, business, and the professions.

In a society which is less than ideal for all men, one learns, not to be content, but to be unsurprised if a cherished goal is not reached quickly. In Negro employment the goal is still ahead of us—as it is also for white workers. But though we have still farther to go in order to reach it, we see now that the direction of movement is toward democratic equality.

That is what matters most.

V. A Home of His Own

What sort of houses could a Negro American own or rent as he began the second half of the twentieth century? Many were shacks as primitive as the slave cabins his ancestors had occupied, or fetid slum apartments in segregated districts in such cities as Washington, Chicago, and Atlanta; a few were comparable, both in the character of the dwelling and in the neighborhoods in which they were located, with similar houses or apartments inhabited by white persons on the same economic level; some were luxurious air-conditioned houses of the most modern design or opulent country estates with swimming pools and riding stables. The number of the latter was greater than is known even by most Negroes themselves.

Since 1940 an extraordinary number of homes have been constructed or purchased by Negroes in cities and suburban areas both North and South. Frequently the acquisition and occupancy of such homes has been won only at the cost of braving the active opposition or the passive unwelcome of neighbors. Yet in fairness it must be said that in many quarters the opposition has been less than it would have been fifteen years ago, in some it has not existed at all, and in some where it has existed at the outset it has changed in time to neighborliness.

But the acquisition of such homes has been possible for only a very small minority. The overwhelming majority of dwellings that Negroes have acquired since 1940 have been situated either in Negro districts or in transitional areas where whites were moving out to new developments—the majority of which have been constructed with federal or state financial aid—in suburbs of American cities. In 1954 there was hardly any large American city which was not ringed about with such developments, from most of which Negroes and other minority groups were excluded.

It is not by the exceptional instances of wealthy Negroes who have been able to buy and live in magnificent, well-equipped houses that the housing situation must be judged, but by the conditions under which the overwhelming majority of Negro Americans must live. And in regard to these one must say sadly that, whereas there are undeniable advances in some areas, the old pattern of segregated ghettos, sub-standard housing, and opposition—sometimes violent —to the spread of Negro housing outside of restricted areas is still widespread, in spite of the markedly better position the Negro now holds in reference to employment, education, political power, and integration in the armed forces.

Because the story of the struggle of the Negro to find homes is too lengthy to tell in detail, this account will be restricted to a brief résumé of the pre-1940 fight to escape the ghetto and, against that background, a description of the victories and defeats since the inauguration of public aid to housing that began under Franklin Roosevelt.

From the Civil War to the second decade of the twentieth century, housing of Negro and white Americans followed no perceptible pattern. The Negro with few exceptions emerged from the Civil War as a freedman with nothing but his physical strength, no longer possessed of even the food and shelter he had received from his owner, who naturally was interested in keeping his property —slaves, mules, cattle, poultry, and farms—in good condition, so that none of their productivity or sales value would be lost. Except in rare instances he had little education, because the slave owners had mortally feared the power that ability to read and write would give their chattels. He had no money to buy a home, and the illusory promise of "forty acres and a mule" that the Freedmen's Bureau made never materialized.

Thus it took several decades, during part of which the Ku Klux Klan dominated the rural South, before schools established by Northern philanthropists helped give the Negro the education that enabled him to begin to climb out of the seemingly bottomless pit in which he found himself on the signing of the Emancipation Proclamation. There were some well-to-do Negro land owners, especially in New Orleans and Philadelphia, but on the whole the race was without property.

During the latter part of the nineteenth century and the first decade of the twentieth, those Negroes who could amass enough capital to buy or build homes met with only a minimum of segregation. This was due in part to the fact that not many Negroes emerged from the morass of poverty to own homes. The white South had not yet learned to fear the Negro as an economic competitor for jobs. Whites and Negroes lived next to one another all over the South and thought nothing of it until the new generation of Negroes—the sons and daughters of slaves but not slaves themselves—arose, a challenge to white supremacy!

It was after Reconstruction that all-white Southern legislatures hurriedly enacted for the first time laws requiring segregated travel on railroads and streetcars. These laws followed the "Black Codes," which imposed severe penalties on Negroes who left jobs owing money to their white employers, and prohibited Negroes from living in white districts and whites from living in Negro districts. Such laws were quickly amended, however, to permit Negro servants to live in servants' quarters. For the comfortable life must go on comfortably.

The first legal challenge to residential-segregation laws occurred in Louisville, Kentucky. A white man by the name of Buchanan brought an action to compel a Negro editor, William Warley, to fulfill an agreement to buy certain real estate owned by Buchanan. Warley answered that because he was a Negro the Louisville segregation ordinance forbade him because of race to use or occupy the property, which was located in a "white" block. Buchanan retorted that any such legislation violated the Fourteenth Amendment to the federal Constitution and should be set aside. But the Kentucky Court of Appeals ruled against him, declaring the ordinance valid.

The NAACP, at the joint request of Messrs. Buchanan and Warley, appealed the decision to the United States Supreme Court, where it was argued superbly by Moorfield Storey of Boston, then President of the NAACP. Justice William Rufus Day, in reversing the Kentucky Court of Appeals in 1917, declared unequivocally on behalf of the court: "We think this attempt to prevent the alienation of the property in question to a person of color was not a legitimate exercise of the police power of the state, and is in direct violation of the fundamental law enacted in the Fourteenth Amendment of the Constitution preventing state interference with property rights except by due process of law. That being the case the ordinance cannot stand."

This edict would appear to be clear enough to end the matter right there, but it did not do so. Two other cities—New Orleans, Louisiana, and Richmond, Virginia—sought to enforce ordinances that had the same objective but were worded slightly differently. It was necessary at considerable expense to take to the Supreme Court cases from each of these cities. Both were won by the opponents of such ordinances on the basis of the Louisville case. As late as the 1950s Birmingham, Alabama, enacted a similar ordinance, which was quietly voided by a lower court.

Three decisive defeats convinced proponents of segregation that the answer to their wishes—if there was a legal one—did not lie in legislative action by states or municipalities. They then adopted the West Coast tactic of covenants among private-property holders to forbid ownership or occupancy by any persons not of the white race on pain of heavy penalties. Whereas, on the West Coast, covenants were originated to bar Orientals, in other parts of the country their original target was the Negro. But they were soon extended against Jews, Orientals, and others, and became more dangerous than city ordinances or state laws. The political strength

of groups singled out for attack was such in the North that no
Northern city or state would have dared pass discriminatory laws
on the Southern pattern, whereas Southern legislative bodies could
enact them without fear of reprisal at the polls because of the disfranchisement of Negroes at that time and the small number of
voters of other minorities. But covenants became fashionable all
over the country.

During World War I and the twenties, when Negroes were
flocking from the South to the North (Chicago alone received
forty-three thousand of them between 1920 and 1930), interracial-
housing violence was a commonplace. Here is a partial calendar.

1918. East St. Louis, Illinois. Riot. Forty Negroes killed; innumerable stabbings and clubbings. A two-year-old child shot and
thrown into the doorway of a burning building.

1919. Various locations. Twenty-six riots, the most notorious of
which, in Chicago, sparked by a white property-owners' organization, killed twenty-three Negroes and fifteen whites and
injured more than five hundred persons.

1924. Garfield Heights, Ohio. Negroes forced out of the homes
they had bought.

1926. Denver, Colorado. A Negro's house torn down in protest
against his occupancy of it.

Meanwhile the continuous growth of cities, and the continuing
influx of Negroes into them, had given rise to a practice that had
long been used in Europe to segregate Jews in ghettos. Numerous
devices masquerading as zoning regulations were used to prevent
Negroes from moving into white areas.

Racial provisions in zoning laws were declared unconstitutional
by the Supreme Court in 1917, but, by subtle evasions, which are
discussed later in this chapter, zoning ordinances, spreading like a
rash throughout the United States, are used to keep Negroes from
adequate housing in the neighborhood of their choice. It required
twenty-two years, seven cases carried to the United States Supreme

Court, and many thousands of dollars eventually to win victory over covenants. The victory over the subtle power of racial zoning has yet to be won.

A covenant in the District of Columbia was, in effect, approved by the Supreme Court as recently as 1926 when it dismissed, "for want of jurisdiction," an appeal from a decision of a lower court forbidding a white woman to sell her home to the wife of a well-known Negro surgeon in Washington.

Fourteen years later, in 1940, the Supreme Court reversed a decision by the Illinois Supreme Court holding that a Negro real-estate operator in Chicago was bound by a previous decision upholding a restrictive covenant against the occupancy of property in that city. The court conspicuously failed to rule on the validity of covenants.

Eight years later the Supreme Court moved forward to rule in a 6-to-0 decision in five cases coming to the court from Michigan, Missouri, and the District of Columbia that covenants cannot be enforced by state courts or other agencies of governments. Three justices disqualified themselves from the cases when, to their acute embarrassment, they discovered after the cases reached the court that there were covenants in the deeds to the homes in which they lived.

But although the evil of racial segregation and exclusion in housing was being attacked here and there, the few victories for democracy were far from decisive.

It has been demonstrated over and over that two factors have played a most important part in racial prejudice in America: reasoning, often faulty, based on economic factors, and the ignorance of many who unthinkingly follow the lead established by others. In no manifestations of the ugly phenomenon have these factors been more clearly demonstrated than in those that have made it impossible for the overwhelming majority of Negro Americans to have the freedom of choice in housing which their white contemporaries enjoy. Two of the most commonplace of all clichés uttered by American white people are these: "Sure, I like so and so" (a Negro whom the speaker happens to know); "he's different from most of them," and, "Not that I have any prejudice, but I wouldn't want to have a Negro live next door to me because it would lower the value of my property." In those exceptional cases in which Negroes have moved into white neighborhoods without violent opposition, the coldness and passive hostility that have greeted them on arrival has often changed to warm friendliness and respect, once acquaintance has been established and ignorance dispelled. In such cases it is evident that the prejudice-revealing statements made by whites before any real acquaintance with Negroes are mere unthinking, parrot-like repetitions of a policy line established by leadership often unrecognized and unacknowledged by those who follow it.

The past fifteen years have seen full integration in the armed services of the United States, the Supreme Court's decision against segregation in the public schools, a vastly improved status for the Negro in employment and trade-union relations, increase in the life expectancy and general health of American Negroes—in short, remarkable progress toward full democratic equality in all fields save one, where progress has been spotty and isolated, and where the reactionary enemies of enlightenment seemingly remain firmly intrenched. This field, in which it is difficult to see much concrete evidence that any general advance has been made, is housing.

Why?

Back of the blind, unreasoning prejudices, and the oft-repeated clichés by which they are rationalized, lies a story of careful planning and propagandizing of which many Americans are unaware. Throughout the 1930s and 1940s, when enlightenment was slowly spreading and affecting public opinion to the point at which the long-overdue improvements previously mentioned could be made, in real estate, a strong reactionary force dedicated to segregation in the sacred cause of "keeping property values up," was building up its power. Before 1930 real-estate selling and management were largely unorganized affairs, in which real-estate agents and property owners operated individually or through local associations. With the formation and continuously growing strength of the National Association of Real Estate Boards (NAREB), which consisted in 1950 of eleven hundred member boards with 45,539 members paying annual dues of $420,000, the situation changed markedly.

Associated with the NAREB are such organizations as the United States Chamber of Commerce, the National Association of Home Builders, the United States Savings and Loan League, the National Association of Lumber Dealers, and others. In combination they have set up what President Truman called the most dangerous lobby in Washington.

Radio and television, the press, college textbooks on selling real estate, "city planning" and real-estate management, the real-estate lobby's incessant pressure on federal legislation—all constantly and without compromise, though often subtly, reiterate the sacred principle that members of "undesirable races" shall never be allowed to live in "good" neighborhoods inhabited, or suitable for habitation, by whites.

Such passages as this occur in texts used in training courses.

Sometimes a relatively poor location may be so improved and restricted as to greatly enhance its natural value. It is a matter of common observation that the purchase of property by certain racial types is very likely to diminish the value of other property in the section.[1]

Residential values are affected by racial and religious factors. . . . A home utility seeks location near people . . . but always near persons of the same social standing, same races . . .[2]

The prospective buyer might be a bootlegger who would cause considerable annoyance to his neighbors, a madame who had a number of call girls on her string, a gangster, who wants a screen for his activities by living in a better neighborhood, a colored man of means who was

[1] *The Principles of Real Estate Practice.* Ernest McKinley Fisher. New York: Macmillan, 1923. Quoted by Charles Abrams in *Forbidden Neighbors,* New York: Harper & Brothers, 1955. Mr. Fisher was, at the time the book was published, Assistant Executive Director of NAREB.

[2] *The Appraisal of Real Estate.* Frederick M. Babcock. New York: Macmillan, 1924. Quoted in Abrams, *op. cit.*

giving his children a college education and thought they were entitled to live among whites. . . . No matter what the motive or character of the would-be purchaser, if the deal would instigate a form of blight, then certainly the well-meaning broker must work against its consummation.[3]

In what charming company are we classed by NAREB!

A realtor should never be instrumental in introducing into a neighborhood a character of property or occupancy of any race or nationality . . . which will clearly be detrimental to property values in that neighborhood.[4]

Real-estate agents who have been adjudged to have violated this rule by selling property to members of "undesirable" races have been expelled from the Association.

This is but a mild sampling of the solemn poison that is served to students eager to earn the right to call themselves "realtors," a title that is copyrighted by NAREB and may be used only by its members. Many more examples could be cited—this, for instance:

There is a natural inclination of the colored people to live together in their own communities. . . . Property values have been sadly depreciated by having a single colored family settle down on a street occupied exclusively by white residents. . . . Segregation of the Negro population seems to be the reasonable solution. . . . Frankly, rigid segregation seems to be the only manner in which the difficulty can be successfully controlled. . . . The colored people certainly have a right to life, liberty and the pursuit of happiness, but they must recognize the economic disturbance which their presence in a white neighborhood causes, and forego their desire to split off from the established district where the rest of their race lives.[5]

---

[3] "Fundamentals of Real Estate Practice." National Association of Real Estate Boards, 1943. Quoted in *Equality of Opportunity in Housing,* New York: National Community Relations Advisory Council, 1952, and in Abrams, *op. cit.*
[4] "Code of Ethics." National Association of Real Estate Boards, 1950. Quoted in Abrams, *op. cit.*
[5] *City Growth and Values.* Stanley L. McMichael and R. F. Bingham. Cleveland: The Stanley McMichael Publishing Organization, 1923. Quoted in Abrams, *op. cit.*

And this:

> Southern cities have by hard experience evolved a method of handling the situation which may appear objectionable but which seems to be effective.[6]

One text earnestly lists what might be called "the pecking order" —that is, the degree of undesirability of national and racial groups in a white American neighborhood. In this weird classification there are ten categories, listed in a descending scale of desirability. English immigrants have the honor of being classed as the least undesirable, Mexicans are most to be avoided, and Negroes are listed next to Mexicans in undesirability.[7]

According to Herbert U. Nelson, Executive Vice-President of NAREB (as quoted by Charles Abrams in *Forbidden Neighbors*), there are now some eight hundred books on the subject. In none which Mr. Abrams examined was he able to find any deviation from NAREB's anti-Negro policy. Courses in real estate, NAREB has announced, are now given in one hundred sixty-five universities and colleges, forty of which have majors in the subject. It is from the classrooms in which these courses are taught that many of today's and tomorrow's "realtors" come, thoroughly indoctrinated with the evils of racism.

The policy of NAREB, thoroughly and constantly reiterated by the real-estate lobby, has been tragically reflected in official government policy by the Federal Housing Administration, which, ever since its formation in 1934, has openly held to a policy of segregation in housing, and has been a staunch protector of the all-white neighborhood. It has published several manuals, which echo the policies of NAREB in such passages as these:

> The Valuator should investigate areas surrounding the location to determine whether or not incompatible racial or social groups are

[6] *Real Estate Fundamentals.* Charles T. Male. New York: D. Van Nostrand, 1932. Quoted in Abrams, *op. cit.*
[7] *One Hundred Years of Land Values in Chicago.* Homer Hoyt. Chicago: The University of Chicago Press, 1933. Cited by Abrams, *op. cit.*

present. . . . A change in social or racial occupancy generally leads to instability and a reduction in values. . . . If a neighborhood is to retain stability, it is necessary that properties shall continue to be occupied by the same social and racial class.[8]

Thus, during the decade and a half in which the American Negro was, in most fields, making the most signal advances in his history, his natural desire for a decent home of his own was continuously thwarted by shortsighted economic interests, with the blessing of an agency of the federal government of the world's most powerful democracy.

A number of simple subterfuges have been found that have made it possible to use zoning laws against Negroes, in spite of the illegality of racial zoning. Zoning commissions are given a certain latitude of interpretation and the power to make exceptions. Rules that make building economically impractical, or even impossible, for all save the extremely wealthy may be inserted into the ordinances. Some of these rules may be waived when a builder for whites applies for relief from them, and strictly enforced if the building is for Negroes or members of other unwanted minority groups. Or zoning ordinances may suddenly be changed when it becomes known that "undesirables" plan to build in a neighborhood. In Miami and near Philadelphia formerly residential property was quickly rezoned for industrial use when there was intimation that it was to be used for Negro dwellings. In Birmingham, in 1949, after several Negro houses had been dynamited, a fifty-foot strip of land six blocks long, between Negro and white residences, was zoned for industrial use. In Michigan, after a group of Negroes had bought land on which to build, a suddenly passed zoning ordinance prohibited their building a house on less than a twenty-acre parcel of land!

It may seem out of place, in a book which has been written in order to record the advances made by Negro Americans during

---

[8] *Underwriting Manual.* Washington: Federal Housing Administration, 1938. Quoted in Abrams, *op. cit.*

the last fifteen years, to record in such detail and so positively the sordid story of reactionary attitudes and their baleful influence on Negro housing.

Two considerations impel me to do so. One is that the report of most heartening advances toward true emancipation for the American Negro would be unconvincing and distorted unless it included this unhappy story of one of the most important fields of Negro life, in which the slow rate of advance has not by any means kept pace with advances in other fields. The other consideration is more complicated, and perhaps more important.

In judging any movement, two often seemingly separated factors must be taken into consideration. One is the complex of physical facts. The physical facts of most Negro housing are still distressingly bad, partly, as we have seen, because of the determined and intensive efforts of a powerful minority of real-estate and associated interests. The other factor is composed of the changing attitudes of many people, who are influenced by related changes. In this aspect there is no question that the Negro's prospects of better housing have improved tremendously, along with his prospects in other fields. The outlawing of segregation in schools by the Supreme Court, the general smoothness with which integration in the armed services has worked, the steady decrease of discrimination in unions and employment, the acknowledged rise of Negro political power—all point to an inevitable eventual breaking down of housing segregation. The policy of NAREB has outlived its time, and public opinion will inevitably overcome it.

Some evidences of this may be discovered in by-products of some of the most horrible stories of violence in the housing situation that the past decade has produced.

Consider, for instance, the story of the Harvey Clarks of Cicero, Illinois. In the details of force and destructiveness, mob psychology, and support by police of lawlessness rather than decency, law, and order, it is one of the most revolting episodes in American race relations. It would be difficult for a skilled writer of creative fiction to make it seem worse than it was. Yet in the wake of the horror were evidences of the progress in enlightenment that America has made during the last fifteen years.

On July 8, 1951, Harvey Clark and his wife, pleasant and attractive, quiet and industrious, both with college degrees, attempted to move, with their young daughter, Michele, and son, Harvey Jr., into an apartment that they had rented in Cicero, a suburb near Chicago which had long boasted that it had no Negro residents. They were met by a detachment of police headed by Erwin Konovsky, Chief of Police, roughly handled, and told that no "niggers" would ever be allowed to live in Cicero.

Seeking protection from the courts, they were represented by George Leighton, a Negro, a Harvard Law School graduate, and Chairman of the Legal Committee of the Chicago branch of the NAACP. He asked for, and received, from Federal Judge John P. Barnes, an injunction ordering the Cicero police not to interfere with the Clarks' occupying their home, but on the contrary to protect the Clarks against any interference from others.

On July 12, thus "protected," as they thought, the Clarks moved in. As the news of their arrival spread, a mob estimated at from four to six thousand assembled, advanced into the twenty-apartment building, and made a shambles of it. The Clarks' furniture and other personal belongings (including Harvey Clark's honorable discharge from the Army) were thrown into the street and burned in a bonfire. A new piano, bought at considerable sacrifice for the talented young Michele, was hacked to pieces and thrown out the window to add to the flames. The Cicero police stood by, their inaction giving tacit approval to the ghastly savagery.

The physical violence was finally quelled only after Governor Adlai Stevenson rushed units of the Illinois National Guard into Cicero to take over the job the Cicero police had refused to do. A special Grand Jury was impaneled. Two months later it handed down indictments—not of the rioters or the police, but of George Leighton and others who had stood on the side of the Clarks, law, and order!

These fantastic indictments were, of course, challenged at once by the NAACP and were subsequently dismissed. The federal government then stepped into the situation, with the result that seven Cicero officials, including the president of the town council, the city attorney, the fire marshal, a police sergeant, and two policemen, were indicted. The Cook County Grand Jury also indicted Chief of Police Konovsky for misconduct in office.[9]

So much for one of the most shameful episodes in Cicero's somewhat unsavory history. That it could have happened anywhere in the world at any time is a measure of the depths of depravity and unreasoning cruelty to which *Homo sapiens*—thinking man—can sink. That it could have happened in America, the "bulwark of democracy," "the land of the free and the home of the brave," would be inconceivable to anyone who did not know the dreary history of Negro-white relationships in the United States. That it could have occurred in 1951, in a Northern state, during the fifteen years marked by the greatest progress toward full equality that the American Negro had made in his entire history, might seem, in the minds of the easily discouraged, to negate all the other advances. It might, that is, if they did not know the rest of the story.

Immediately after the event, Barry Gray, a popular and courageous New York radio commentator, invited me to tell on his program what had happened to the Clarks. While we were still on the air a woman listener telephoned to say that she was mailing a check for fifty dollars to start a fund to buy Michele a new piano. Within a few days more than a thousand dollars had been collected. Three piano-dealers offered instruments at wholesale rates. From all over the country, in indignant reaction to the story published by a weekly magazine, money was sent to enable the Clarks to buy new furniture. Norwalk, Connecticut, asked them to be guests of honor at the celebration of the three hundredth anniversary of the

---

[9] Konovsky and two others were tried and fined by a federal court, but the sentence was appealed. In 1954 the United States Court of Appeals reversed the decision, citing prejudicial error; and at the request of the Attorney General the federal court dismissed the indictments. (Editor's note.)

founding of the city. They were warmly invited to become permanent residents, and a musical scholarship was given Michele.

The Clarks, however, as a matter of principle, returned to Chicago, determined to continue their efforts until they and any other Negroes could live in Cicero in peace and safety. So universal was the nation's condemnation that Cicero authorities were reported in the press as planning to change the name of the town and employ a publicity expert to refurbish its reputation.

The Clarks have an apartment now—but in a segregated neighborhood.

Mixed with the horror and discouragement innate in the story of the Harvey Clarks and Cicero, there is an element of comfort, and a measure of the change in public attitude—in spite of the intensive and determined efforts of the NAREB and the real-estate lobby and the sporadic outbreaks of their unwitting dupes.

Fifteen years earlier there would undoubtedly have been protests and indignation against the treatment the Clarks received in Cicero. That these would have been less widespread, less voluble, and less effective, is certain. All over America today, in both North and South, non-governmental organizations and individuals are working quietly and effectively to build up public sentiment in support of the right of any American to buy and peacefully to occupy a home anywhere, without exclusion because of race, color of skin, or religion.

New York City, Detroit, Michigan, and Berkeley, California, are illustrative. In 1940 all but a very few of New York's 477,494 Negroes lived in Harlem or the Bedford-Stuyvesant area of Brooklyn. Since then many thousands of them have bought or are renting homes and apartments in various parts of Long Island, Westchester County, and the five boroughs of Greater New York. It would not be accurate to say that this dispersal of population was accomplished wholly without opposition or difficulty, or to assert that the majority of New York Negroes today live elsewhere than in the Harlem and Bedford-Stuyvesant sections. But in a remarkable majority of cases in which individual Negroes have moved into formerly all-white areas, no untoward incidents have occurred. The chief difficulty Negroes have experienced has been in obtaining mortgages and funds for construction outside the so-called Negro areas, because of the discriminatory practices of the FHA and of banks and mortgage companies influenced by the inflexible policy of the groups associated in the real-estate lobby. Several years of unceasing effort by the NAACP and others were required to have removed from the FHA operating manual the clause instructing banks to insure mortgages only in "racially homogeneous" areas.

The success of racial integration in public housing in New York is one of the reasons why its present Negro population of 775,529 is finding it easier to acquire housing in various areas of the city. That energetic champion of public housing, the late Mayor Fiorello H. LaGuardia, was equally an energetic foe of segregation. So, too, have been most of the heads of the City Housing Authority. One of the first of them, Langdon Post, was concerned when the integration program was inaugurated lest the first colored tenants admitted be met with violence or other hostility. Nevertheless, he went ahead. Today Negro and white tenants live in peace in every one of the city's housing projects.

The city's major problem rises from the acute need for housing among Negroes and Puerto Ricans. Since vacancies are allotted on the basis of need instead of race, some of the housing projects are in danger of becoming segregated simply as a result of being filled with the most needy, who are so often dark-skinned peoples.

An interesting case study of improvement, both in attitude and in the physical facts of Negro housing, is furnished by Detroit, which has variously been called "the arsenal of democracy," "the grand duchy of Ford," "the world capital of the assembly line," and many other names that it accepts proudly. But this hustling, brawling town has also been called the hotbed of race riots.

Now, however, an extraordinary change is taking place. No one would be so foolhardy as to say that other riots may not occur or to claim that the racial and religious tensions have disappeared—

tensions born of overcrowding, the vagaries of employment in a one-industry town, and the circumstance that many of its residents, both white and Negro, came from the Deep South. Yet there have been noticeable alterations in the pattern of living and of association of individuals of varied racial backgrounds that would have been impossible even five years ago.

To understand more clearly the significance of what is happening, one needs only to remember a few of the widely publicized frictions of the past quarter-century. Detroit remembers with shame the famous case of Dr. Ossian H. Sweet, whose house was attacked by a mob of five thousand persons in 1935 in a wild night of rioting. Barricaded in his home with his wife, their infant child, his brother, and several friends, Dr. Sweet was forced to defend himself. One of the rioters was killed by a bullet that fitted none of the guns in the house. Hundreds of policemen who had stood idly by sprang into action and arrested all the occupants of the house, charging Dr. Sweet and his group with murder in the first degree. Clarence Darrow defended them in two lengthy and notable trials. They were acquitted. Attacks upon the homes of Negroes lessened. They began to move out of their crowded ghetto, ironically known as Paradise Valley.

Now individual Detroiters and several agencies appear to have buckled down to the job of doing something about the eternally dangerous tensions of a manufacturing area with a polyglot population. The greatest problem faced by most Detroiters of all races is created by the still acute housing shortage. During the decade from 1940 to 1950 the population of the metropolitan area jumped 26.9 per cent, from 2,377,329 to 3,016,197. During the same period Detroit's non-white population increased 109.5 per cent, from 172,788 to 361,925. It was during this war decade of shortage of building materials that overcrowding not only in housing but in transportation, recreation and other facilities increased tensions and frayed tempers of all who lived there. Pressures were most severe on Negroes, who were denied access to old and new housing through restrictive covenants. Agreements among real-estate dealers not to show, sell, or rent to Negroes took the place of covenants, after these had been outlawed, and some mortgage companies and banks refused to lend money for building or to grant mortgages to Negroes. These forces, together with community pressures that were greatly increased by a hostile police department, combined to pen a rapidly growing Negro population in ghettos that long before had burst at their seams.

How this situation has been met in some sections of Detroit was illustrated at a meeting at the home of George Schermer, formerly the Director of the Mayor's Interracial Committee. Among those present were the Reverend H. B. Sissel, pastor of St. Andrew's Presbyterian Church, located at Twelfth and Glendale, in a neighborhood where in ten years the Negro population had increased 547.8 per cent. The white population of the census tract in which the church is located had decreased by 15,000 from 1940 to 1950, while its Negro population increased by almost 16,000.

Many of the Reverend Mr. Sissel's parishioners became panic-stricken when the first Negroes moved into the neighborhood. "I counted fifty 'For Sale' signs within three blocks of the church," Mr. Sissel told us.

At first the young pastor referred to the changing pattern only in Sunday-morning prayers, in which he sought to allay the fears of the congregation. Later he called a meeting at which he laid before the church the three things it could do: "Move out and sell the church building to 'some fringe sect' "; stay on in the area, but keep the walls up, in which case it was inevitable that the church must eventually die as the community changed; or "stay and let the church change along with the neighborhood."

He made it clear that the third alternative was "not only the Christian but the wise thing to do." He encountered the stiff resistance he had expected. Some of the church members informed him angrily that their life savings were invested in their homes, and some hinted darkly of "other means" of stopping the "invasion."

Meanwhile Mr. Sissel had made pastoral calls upon the newcomers and invited them to attend the church. At first he met only suspicion and coolness. They were not certain what kind of welcome they would receive. Later Mrs. Albert Jones, a librarian, and her husband, who was then studying for a Master's degree in social work, began to attend St. Andrew's, but with some trepidation. Not long afterward Mrs. Jones was elected president of the mothers' club of the predominantly white Longfellow School near the church. There are now five Negro families who belong to St. Andrew's. The exodus of white families from the neighborhood slowed down as colored and white neighbors began to know and like one another.

Also present at the meeting in the Schermer home was Mrs. Gustav Taube, wife of a cabinetmaker, who told earnestly of her conversion from the racial views she had brought to Detroit from the small Missouri town in which she had been born and reared. Her husband shared her aversion to Negroes. But their son brought home from school enthusiastic stories about his best friend, Gordon Willis.

"My son kept talking about Gordon all the time," Mrs. Taube said. "He thought Gordon was just about the most wonderful thing that ever happened in his life because Gordon had taught him to whistle with his fingers. One day he came into the kitchen and said that he had brought Gordon home with him. I was busy doing something or other, and I guess I just didn't look up. I said, 'That's fine.' So he and Gordon went into a room to play. After a little while I took some cookies into the room, and, I tell you, I jumped a mile when I saw that Gordon was colored. I didn't know what to think. I had never known any colored people before —well, maybe a matron in a restroom or something like that. All the Negroes in the town that I came from lived off by themselves across the railroad tracks. I had never thought of them as friends.

"Well, I didn't know what to say to Gordon or to my son. So I just walked out of the room, and then pretty soon it was time for Gordon to go home, and I walked out on the porch with him. I was afraid of what some of the people in the neighborhood would do to him, and I was worried about his getting home safely. Finally

I said to him, 'I guess you'd better not come any more when it's light.' I figured it might be safer after dark, but now I can see that was pretty silly of me."

She went on to tell how Gordon and her son got to visiting back and forth with each other, and her son insisted that Gordon join his pack of Cub Scouts. Mrs. Taube is a pack mother, and she described the three all-white dens and the two all-colored ones. It was not long before she began to use her influence to break down segregation.

"It was not all beer and skittles among the Cub Scouts," she said, "and there were several fights between the white and colored dens." She persuaded her husband to become a Cub master, and eventually he agreed that friction would be considerably less in dens made up of all the boys in the neighborhood, without separation on the basis of race or religion. Mr. and Mrs. Taube eventually won the battle not only with their own ideas of Negroes but also over the prejudices of the neighborhood.

Then there is the story of two Dorothys—one white, one colored. One is the wife of a Jewish lawyer. At the meeting she told of her horror when she learned that a Negro family had moved into the block. She called her husband at his office, and, in her own words, "wailed" about the situation. "We'll have to move out," she declared. "Where are we going to move?"

Her husband suggested, "Keep your shirt on. Take it easy. After all, I've been working with the American Jewish Congress on race relations. Let's just hold on to ourselves and see what happens."

Not long afterward a Negro family moved into the house next door. She told us how she became "sick at the stomach" in her panic. But she remembered her husband's admonition to "hold on to herself" and decided to go immediately to visit her new neighbors. She was so impressed by their dignity and appearance that she found herself saying, "You people must be awfully tired, moving and all. Won't you come in for a cup of coffee?" Today the two Dorothys are close friends and active workers on community projects.

In another section of Detroit a white family erected a fence so high they could not even see the house next door, into which Negroes had moved. In time, however, the inevitable meetings of next-door neighbors caused the white family to learn that their neighbors were among the nicest persons they had ever known. Down came the fence, and in its stead the two families built a wading pool for the use of the children of both.

It would be heartening to be able to report that friendliness and learning to live together as friends and Americans characterize all of Detroit. This is far from being true. Since World War II some 180,000 new dwellings in the Detroit area have been erected. Less than 2000, or slightly more than 1 per cent, of these have been made available to Negroes. But the housing pattern is being altered, nevertheless—at least in urban Detroit—by the combined and relentless pressures of economic changes growing out of the building of suburban developments and by the steadily increasing Negro population.

Arden Park is a case in point. Some years ago the mansion-like houses of Arden Park were occupied by affluent and socially prominent Detroiters. When newer and more modern houses were built in the suburbs, many left Arden Park and placed their former homes on the market. In numerous instances the prices were higher than white purchasers cared to or were able to pay. In 1950 some of the homes were purchased by well-to-do Negro doctors, lawyers, businessmen, and ministers.

Again there was panic among some of the white residents, which caused the unsubstantiated fear that entrance of Negroes into the neighborhood would greatly depreciate property values. Some, however, refused to be panicked. The new Negro occupants took especial pride in their new houses and lawns. In some instances they did such a good job that the neighborhood, which had begun to run down, was refurbished and became not less but more attractive. This pattern promises to continue.

In public housing the Detroit City Housing Authority maintained, until recently, a rigid policy of segregation. It required legal action by the NAACP to achieve relaxation of this policy. In one recently completed housing development Negroes were admitted on an integrated basis, although this was done with fear and trembling on the part of the housing authority. No friction accompanied the changed pattern.

Where formerly the police did nothing to protect Negro property owners who moved into new homes outside the ghetto, and in some instances even joined the mob, today wherever there is neighborhood hostility the work of the police has been excellent.

"I am ready to say any time," George Schermer stated in 1953, "that no matter what section of Detroit a Negro might move into, the police would maintain law and order. Recruiting is okay. Initial training of police is pretty good. There is a Negro teacher in the Police Academy. Police officers are now being sent for training in race relations to the University of Michigan at Ann Arbor, the University of Chicago, and Fisk University in Nashville. There are four Negro uniformed sergeants, one detective, and a hundred and one Negroes on the Detroit police force, which numbers forty-two hundred persons."

In Washington, D.C., long known as one of the worst spots in the nation in regard to Negro housing, the pattern is also slowly changing for the better, though against strong opposition. The nation's capital is the most glaring example of how the federal government has not only failed to act on this problem but has actually fostered and expanded racial segregation.

It is supremely ironical that this has been done as part of one of the most commendable governmental programs of the twentieth century—helping American citizens to build homes that they could not have obtained either through their own resources or through private industry. Washington, like many other American cities, has been encircled during recent years by new housing developments. Virtually none erected during the past twenty years came into being without some form of governmental financial assistance. But Negroes, and to some degree the members of other racial and religious minorities, have been excluded from most of these areas just outside the city, even though their taxes helped make the developments possible.

The new suburban housing for whites has, however, eased somewhat the problem Negroes face in buying better homes in metropolitan Washington. White home owners who wanted to move to the suburbs discovered that they could obtain better prices from Negro purchasers, and the Supreme Court decision against restrictive covenants freed them from agreements not to sell to colored customers.

Colonel Campbell C. Johnson told me about some of the efforts that had proved successful in cracking the iron curtain of housing encircling Negroes in Washington.

"Two important things," he said, "have happened. Exodus of white families from blocks into which Negro families have moved has been greatly decelerated. These white owners are more and more saying to real-estate agents who try to persuade them to sell, 'I am perfectly satisfied with my home and I do not care who my new neighbor is as long as he is respectable and maintains the character of the neighborhood.' Second, an increasing number of apartment buildings which were taken over with the idea that they would be converted to all-Negro use have not had the expected change in racial composition. Some white families have not desired to move, with the result that a number of excellent apartments in the better sections of the city today have mixed racial occupancy."

Colonel Johnson was named by President Truman in 1950 as the only Negro member of the National Capital Housing Authority after citizens' groups had campaigned for many years for such representation of one-third of the city's permanent population. Shortly after taking office, Colonel Johnson introduced a resolution to end segregated public housing within the city of Washington and to include all low-income people in such housing on the basis of need, without restriction as to race, religion, color, or national origin. Time and time again over a period of eighteen months his resolution was decisively defeated. It was argued that

segregation was the general pattern in Washington and that therefore school and recreational facilities would not be available to
Negroes in areas where white housing projects were located or
being erected. It was feared that Congress, holding the purse
strings, would be made even more hostile to public housing as a
whole if integration was practiced under its very nose.

Colonel Johnson, however, would not be discouraged. After a
year and a half his resolution was passed unanimously. A campaign
was undertaken to educate and prepare tenants in each project and
in the neighborhoods in which the housing projects were located.
In 1954, he reported, eighty-seven per cent of all public housing
in the District of Columbia—as distinguished from suburban housing—operated under an integrated policy, and this was expected
to apply shortly to all such projects. White families had gone into
housing formerly restricted to Negroes and Negro families into
buildings originally intended for whites—and none of the dire predictions of disorder had been fulfilled.

"Not a single racial incident has occurred as the integration program has gone forward in public housing," Colonel Johnson reported.

This is remarkable in view of the fact that Washington is more
Southern in its racial patterns than Chicago, Cleveland, Cicero,
Illinois, or Kansas City, Missouri—in all of which cities friction
occurred when Negroes moved into white neighborhoods.

The status of housing for minorities can be most effectively and
simply observed by listing the action taken in the years 1951–52.
This includes legislative, legal, and administrative action along with
the continuing changes of public attitudes, for good or ill. Such
a summary gives a sense of the continuing struggle being waged
by those in need of homes from which they have been barred because of race, religion, place of birth, and economic handicaps, but
also shows considerable justification for encouragement.

During this period a nationwide legal attack was accelerated
against government agencies that continued to exclude Negroes
and other minorities from housing projects.

In Long Branch, New Jersey, the Housing Authority agreed to a consent decree barring all distinctions based on race for admission to local projects.

In Schenectady, New York, a suit to admit Negroes to a state-aided project of public housing and to prohibit all color bars in public housing induced the Municipal Housing Authority to admit nine of the ten Negro applicants and to institute a program of integration in all other projects.

In Birmingham, Alabama, a city ordinance imposing residential segregation was voided by the federal district court on the basis of United States Supreme Court decisions. The Federal Circuit Court of Appeals and the Supreme Court upheld the district court's decision.

Legal actions against discriminatory practices by public-housing officials were initiated in St. Louis, Missouri, Hamtramck, Michigan, New Haven, Connecticut, Tampa and Miami, Florida, Sacramento and San Francisco, California, Evansville, Indiana, Savannah, Georgia, and Washington, D.C.

Efforts to outlaw segregation in housing in the state legislatures of New York, Rhode Island, Michigan, Connecticut, Wisconsin, New Jersey, Pennsylvania, and Massachusetts, and in the councils of a number of cities—Buffalo and Schenectady, New York, Newark, New Jersey, Los Angeles County and San Bernardino, California, Omaha, Nebraska, St. Paul, Minnesota, and others—have materially helped to ameliorate the evil.

In the light of the numerous and powerfully entrenched obstacles in the Negro's path to decent housing, the gains he has made are remarkable. Legislative, legal, administrative, and public-opinion campaigns have achieved these results.

Of 1138 housing projects erected or planned under the 1949 Housing Act, 305, or 26.8 per cent, were open to all citizens irrespective of race or religion.

In a number of cities, because of persistent efforts of non-governmental organizations and of state commissions against discrimination, previously segregated projects have been opened to all.

Of 205,706 dwelling units provided for by the 1949 Housing Act, 55,826, or 27.1 per cent, went to Negroes.

As the market for housing for whites approached the saturation point, contractors and developers, both white and Negro, began to wake up to the considerable potentialities of the Negro market. The phenomenal financial success of several integrated housing projects began to open the eyes of many who had not believed such investments either possible or profitable. Such authoritative national housing and builders magazines as *House + Home*, *The Appraisal Journal*, *The Review of the Society of Residential Appraisers*, and magazines of general interest such as *Time*, *Tide*, and others, increasingly called attention to both the need and the potentialities of the Negro housing market. The fact that the income of American non-whites had trebled, and the marked rise of their cultural status, which caused them to seek top-grade products, proved an increasingly attractive magnet for those with housing and goods to sell.

As of December 31, 1952, Negroes occupied 84,869, or 38 per cent, of the 222,487 permanent housing dwellings created with PHA aid, while another 50,000 dwellings then under contract were to be occupied by Negroes when completed. Through the persistent efforts of the HHFA Racial Relations Office, under the leadership of Dr. Frank Horne, Negroes had been paid $107,000,-000 in wages in building these houses. The agency's non-discrimination policy and procedures that had been inaugurated in the thirties and the later policy of the entire federal government was responsible for this.

At the end of 1952 more than 5000 Negroes were employed at all levels and types of positions in administration, management, and maintenance of public-housing programs throughout the United States.

More new housing for sale or rent to Negroes was available during the five-year period from 1948 to 1953 than during the entire generation that preceded that period.

But despite these advances, of the 9,000,000 new dwelling units that have been built by private enterprise in the United States since 1935 only 100,000, or slightly more than one per cent, have come into possession of the ten per cent of the population that is both Negro and in greatest need of housing.

The situation remains a mixed one. Although the degree of betterment achieved by the Negro in housing is less than that which he has achieved in any other field, there has been advance, and there is ample evidence that the plain common sense and decency of the American people is working to eliminate segregation and its attendant evils in housing.

VI. The Negro Seeks Health

A workman, concerned with his livelihood, will take care of his tools; a herdsman will see to the health of his animals as a matter of self-interest. For the same reasons, a canny plantation owner in the days of slavery took care of the health of his most valuable properties—his chattel slaves. They were fed, as were the livestock with which, in many ways, the slaves were classed in the minds of their owners, with a view to keeping them well and strong so that they could make the largest possible return on the investment they represented. They were denied alcohol, and often tobacco, as harmful substances were kept from horses and cows. Though their living quarters were as austere and lacking in luxury as were the stables, they were kept in a state of comparative sanitation, as the stables were and for the same reasons. As the veterinarian was called in to help a sick cow or horse, a doctor was in attendance for a sick or injured slave. The result was that, on good plantations, the health of Negroes was good, and the death rate low for the period—often lower than that of poor whites in the same region.

After Emancipation the situation changed markedly. Bad housing, malnutrition, lack of proper medical care—all the inevitable adverse elements that accompanied the confusion of economic and social adjustment against white opposition to the demands and opportunities of freedom—took their toll. The Negro's health established a new low in American culture, creating a major national problem. There have been gains since then—especially in the past two decades, which are the principal concern of this chapter—but Negro mortality is still higher than that of whites.

It is significant that the greatest hazards to health and life for the Negro have been from those diseases that inevitably accompany substandard housing, crowding, poor sanitation, low income, insufficient medical care, and (especially since the Negro's place in industry has been expanding) accidents.

A striking example of the reversal in trend after the Civil War is furnished by records of deaths from tuberculosis in South Carolina for whites and Negroes from 1848—during slavery—to 1890.

DEATHS FROM TUBERCULOSIS PER 100,000[1]

	Whites	Negroes
1848	268	266
1866	198	411
1890	355	686

[1] *The Negro in American Life.* Harry J. Walker. New York: The Oxford Book Co., 1954.

During the twentieth century the death rate for both whites and Negroes has fallen, but that of the Negro has been slower to respond to increasing knowledge of medicine, sanitation, and hygiene than has that of the white American, precisely because the Negro has been denied so many of the advantages of increasing knowledge and improved conditions. His average income is still well below that of the average white man; his housing is still vastly inferior to that of white Americans; his education (especially in medicine) is still substandard; and the vast majority of Negroes are still denied medical care and hospital facilities equal to those available to the average white American. These and other factors are all closely interrelated in their influence on human health; when any or all of them are improved, health improves. Such advances in health as the Negro has made reflect largely his improved status in the general aspects of life discussed in other chapters of this book.

Two factors responsible for the advances have been the slow but steady increase during the last three decades in medical and hospital facilities available to Negroes, and the broadening of their opportunities for medical education. Much of the credit for the progress made in these directions is due to the aggressive and intrepid leadership in the Negro medical world of the late Dr. Louis T. Wright.

Stepson of a handsome, successful physician in Georgia, Dr. Wright was graduated from Clark University in Atlanta and then from the Harvard Medical School, finishing both institutions with exceptionally high scholastic records. Despite the brilliance of his career, however, he learned at Harvard that race prejudice was omnipresent. A single blackball cast by a fellow student from Tennessee barred him from Alpha Omega Alpha, the medical honor society. The dean of one of the departments kept him from marching in the post of honor to which his marks entitled him. Only the pleas of his parents caused him to abandon his plan to absent himself from graduation in protest against the insult to his race.

As an intern at the all-Negro Freedman's Hospital in Washington, D.C., he buried himself in his work both because of love of science and in order to forget the Jim Crow practices of the city, which he detested. As an intern, he challenged the assertion of the famed Dr. Bela Schick that Negroes reacted differently from whites to the test for diphtheria because of difference of pigmentation. Using Schick's own methods and theories, Dr. Wright proved him wrong and guilty of highly unscientific bias. Later he devised a more effective type of vaccination, which became known as the Wright intradermal method. He was enabled to test this method when he became an officer of the United States Medical Corps during World War I.

After the war Dr. Wright decided to practice in New York City instead of returning to Atlanta, because his burning intensity was not for making money but for medical research. But neither he nor any other Negro doctor at that time could serve on the staff of any hospital or engage in research at any of the public or private laboratories or institutions. Harlem Hospital, located at the very center of New York's huge Negro population, had the worst reputation in the city. No colored doctor, surgeon, specialist, or nurse could enter its doors except as patients. Doctors of other races used the hospital to make experiments and to gain experience and reputations. Some were good; many treated their patients with cavalier indifference. Relatives of Negro patients expected the worst. Too often they were completely right!

Working with the NAACP, Dr. Wright helped form a committee which employed an able Columbia Law School graduate, William N. Colson, to make an investigation of hospital conditions in Harlem. The facts he uncovered were so shocking that Mayor John F. Hylan ordered open hearings by Commissioner of Accounts Hershfield. The New York *World*, a crusading newspaper, then edited by the brilliant Herbert Bayard Swope, featured the revelations in news stories and editorials. Other papers followed suit, with the result that New Yorkers demanded corrective action.

A gesture was made by the city fathers in a proposal to build a two-million-dollar modern hospital for Negroes. It was at this point that Dr. Wright came into prominence as the leader that he was. To the amazed New York City authorities, who could not understand why any Negro would not be delighted with their proposal, he said, "If you attempt to build a Jim Crow hospital in New York City we shall go to court and get an injunction to keep you from wasting the public's money."

This was in 1921, when the separate-but-equal philosophy dominated New York almost as much as it did Atlanta, Georgia. It was for this reason that rejection of a segregated hospital by the North Harlem Medical Society, which Dr. Wright had organized among doctors of similar views, and by the NAACP, jolted New York's officials and its white medical societies.

The threat succeeded, and Dr. Wright's stand became a turning point in America's attitude toward the Negro in medicine. But most of New York's Negro doctors, as well as many physicians throughout the nation, were either honestly puzzled or definitely angered by his act in rejecting a modern hospital, to have been staffed entirely by Negro doctors, nurses, and other personnel. Dr. Wright was wise enough to know that even the great advantages of a modern hospital for Negroes in New York would be more than offset in the long run by its deeper intrenchment of the evil of Jim Crow in medicine.

Almost as startling was Dr. Wright's relentless opposition to selection and appointment of Negro medical men and women to non-segregated institutions on any basis except that of ability. He was adamant in insisting that Negroes must meet the same standards of training, experience, and devotion to absolute standards of medical ethics as other doctors. Even some sincere friends of the Negro believed him to be too exacting, in view of the difficulties Negroes encountered in obtaining medical education and experience.

But Louis Wright stuck to his guns. More and more medical men and laymen came to agree that the real battle should be to abolish the barriers of segregation and discrimination in the realm of medical care, to the end that color would eventually be neither a barrier nor a reason for sentimental concessions to inferior Negroes. Hippocrates' oath, for Louis Wright, was more than a pledge to do all that he as a physician could do for his patient. He took on the added responsibility of seeing to it that no man capable of learning to be a good doctor should be barred from doing so because of race, color, or creed.

In 1933 the life expectancy of American Negro males was ten years shorter than that of white males, and that of American Negro women twelve years shorter than that of white females and a major cause, in addition to bad housing and unemployment, was the inadequacy of medical facilities for Negroes even in northern communities—in many Southern areas they were non-existent. Quota systems or outright exclusion from the leading medical schools were practices so prevalent that only about a hundred and twenty Negro doctors were graduated annually in the entire country.

Eighty per cent of that wholly inadequate number received their
education from two Negro medical schools—Howard University at
Washington, D.C., and Meharry Medical College at Nashville,
Tennessee. Both these schools, according to a survey made at the
time, required "considerable improvement in equipment and personnel to bring them up to the level of other Grade A medical
colleges of the country."

Internships for fledgling Negro doctors during that era were almost entirely restricted to segregated hospitals, only fourteen of
which were considered suitable for intern training by the Council
of Medical Education of the American Medical Association. Not
only the AMA, but also the state, county, and city medical associations of almost the entire nation, North as well as South, barred
Negro doctors from membership, which excluded them from practicing in tax-supported and private hospitals.

This situation led Dr. Wright and the NAACP to ask a distinguished committee of medical experts and laymen to study the facts
and make public their findings. Dr. Walter L. Niles of Cornell University Medical College served as chairman. Recognized authorities
in various fields of medicine from Johns Hopkins at Baltimore, the
New York University Medical School, the Columbia University
Medical College, the Harvard Medical College, the New York College of Physicians and Surgeons, the Boston College of Medicine,
and the Howard University School of Medicine served on the committee. Supplemental financial assistance for the inquiry was obtained by the NAACP from Mrs. Dwight L. Morrow and the
Carnegie Corporation. Dr. E. H. L. Corwin, Dr. Gertrude Sturges,
and technical assistants were employed to make the study, which
was published by Charles Scribner's Sons in 1936 under the title,
Opportunities for the Medical Education of Negroes.

The startling and distressing picture of denial of medical education and experience as well as the appallingly inadequate hospital
and clinical facilities for Negroes profoundly shocked both the
medical and the lay worlds. American universities were urged to

remove existing barriers to the admission of Negro medical students; hospitals, and particularly tax-supported institutions, were besought to open internships to qualified Negro medical-school graduates. The medical profession generally and especially the boards of municipal hospitals were urged to recognize how important it was that opportunities be provided for post-graduate study and service of qualified Negro physicians and surgeons on staffs of hospitals.

The report was particularly timely because it was issued at the very depth of the depression that followed the stock-market crash of 1929. The Negro's already disadvantaged health status was being worsened by malnutrition caused by unemployment. The eminence of the personnel of the committee that conducted the study caused the findings to be at least seriously studied by medical authorities all over the nation, although specific action was slow in materializing, except in Harlem Hospital in New York. Although the previous interracial character of that institution was preserved, more qualified Negroes were added to its staff not on the basis of their race but on that of ability.

Under Dr. Wright's direction and encouragement rigidly scientific studies were instituted and substantial contributions made to the leading medical journals of the United States and other nations on pneumonia, brain injuries and skull fractures, cancer and venereal diseases. Dr. Wright himself published during his lifetime an astounding total of ninety-six articles dealing with a wide variety of subjects in recognized medical and scientific magazines. Twenty-six of them dealt with the uses of aureomycin, the antibiotic with which Dr. Wright treated and cured for the first time in history certain internal viruses in human beings. He wrote what is now accepted throughout the world as the standard treatise on the treatment of skull fractures.

He did not, however, operate as a lone wolf in the field of science. He collaborated both in research and writing with many of his colleagues, including his two daughters, Dr. Jane and Dr.

Barbara Wright. Both by the example he set, and by his stimula-
tion of investigative and scientific effort, he helped to lift both
Negro and white doctors out of racial ruts to serve mankind. Before
he died of a heart attack and pulmonary ailments caused by having
been gassed in France during World War I, Louis Wright saw
measurable results of his thirty-one-year battle against Jim Crow
medicine.

He and his associates were also adamant in the rejection of segregated medical schools and segregated facilities offered by private
philanthropy and the federal government. When the Julius Rosen-
wald Fund, despairing of hope that private medical schools would
alter their practices of exclusion or limitation of Negro students,
proposed to build one for Negroes in Pennsylvania, Dr. Wright led
a vigorous, widely publicized, and successful fight against it, remi-
niscent of his fight in 1921 against a segregated hospital in New
York. His carefully documented pamphlet, showing how the harm
of perpetuating segregation far outweighs the immediate benefits, is
today an historic milestone in the campaign for unrestricted medical
education of all Americans regardless of race. So, too, is another
pamphlet against discrimination by the federal government in its
hospitals and other medical facilities for Negro veterans.

Eleven years after the publication of *Opportunities for the Medical Education of Negroes*, the NAACP published "Medical Care
and the Plight of the Negro" and, in 1948, "Progress and Portents
for the Negro in Medicine." Both of these pamphlets were written
by Dr. W. Montague Cobb of the Howard University Medical
School. As editor of the *Journal of the National Medical Association*, and Chairman of the National Health Committee of the
NAACP, Dr. Cobb had devoted years of study and of close association with Dr. Wright to the question of breaking down the barriers.
The two pamphlets presented a comprehensive, meticulously documented picture of the health problems of minorities, particularly
the Negro, and presented irrefutable facts to demonstrate that they
could not be solved within the pattern of segregation. Both pam-

phlets were widely distributed and read. Many of their facts and arguments in opposition to Jim Crow medicine soon found their way into the thinking and actions of both medical authorities and laymen. The walls of prejudice did not, like those of Jericho, "come tumbling down," and, for that matter, some remain standing as this is written. But the demolition of many old barriers has taken place during the past five years.

In 1949 the American Medical Association named a Negro, Dr. Peter Marshall, to its national policy-making body—the first Negro to be so honored in one hundred and three years. In that same year the medical profession in the border state of Missouri voted overwhelmingly to banish its color bar, and two Negro doctors were promptly given membership in the St. Louis Medical Association, despite a 35-to-25 vote of the St. Louis County Medical Society to retain its constitutional clause admitting only whites to membership. In December, 1949, the Arkansas State Nurses' Association voted unanimously to admit Negroes to full membership, leaving only the nurses' associations of Georgia, Louisiana, Texas, Virginia, South Carolina, and Washington, D.C., in the unenviable class of those which limited membership to white nurses.

This development in the professional nursing field led to a unique event a few months later, when the forty-two-year-old National Association of Colored Graduate Nurses decided in 1950 to disband voluntarily because there was no further need for a segregated organization. Whereas during World War II colored women could attend only twenty-eight nursing schools out of more than a thousand, in 1950 they were welcome in three hundred and thirty and since 1950 many more schools have opened their doors. Mabel Keaton Staupers, who had served as President of the National Association of Colored Graduate Nurses and who spearheaded the drive against exclusion and segregation, announced at a dinner celebrating dissolution of the NACGN that thereafter the American Nurses Association and the Nursing League of America would receive into their membership all qualified nurses irrespective of race or color.

In 1951 the St. Louis Dental Society and the North Carolina Academy of Science dropped their color bars, and vigorous action toward the same goal was instituted in the medical associations in Virginia and Tennessee. The following year the medical associations in Texas, Georgia, and Virginia extended "scientific membership" to Negroes, which admitted them to scientific meetings and courses but excluded them from social activities. In some Southern communities such as Bibb County, Georgia, and Charleston, South Carolina, full membership for Negro doctors was voted.

This process moved so swiftly that, whereas Negroes were excluded from all state and county medical societies in Southern and border states in 1947, by 1953 they were admitted and welcomed in twenty-seven of those states—including Arkansas, Florida, Georgia, Missouri, Oklahoma, Delaware—and the District of Columbia. The extent of the basic change in attitude of white Southern medical men was indicated by a poll taken in 1953 by the Southern Conference Educational Fund. Five thousand seven hundred and fifty representative doctors were chosen to be queried out of the total membership of 42,500. Their attitudes were revealed by the following: 71 per cent favored admission of Negroes to medical societies; 24 per cent opposed it, and 3 per cent gave qualified approval. Sixty-three per cent approved admission of Negro doctors to hospital staffs, 14 per cent gave qualified approval, and 23 per cent opposed it. It is interesting that opposition or limited approval was found chiefly among older doctors, while approval of abolition of restrictions based on race was highest among men who had studied at non-segregated schools either in the South or the North, and those who had served in the armed services after segregation had been attacked and eventually abolished.

The results of the long struggle were summarized by Dr. Cobb in October, 1953, in an article in the NAIRO *Reporter*, official organ of the National Association of Intergroup Relations Officials. The opportunities for medical education and internships in 1953, in contrast with those of a short seven years before, were presented by Dr. Cobb as follows:

The number of Negro medical students in the United States has increased from 350 in 1938–39 to 697 in 1951–52. The table shows that increased enrollment at Howard and Meharry represents a substantial part of the total increase, but the numerical total of Negro students at other schools has nearly quadrupled since 1939.

Sixty-five of the nation's eighty medical schools, including six of the seven schools which give only the first two years of basic science, will accept Negro medical students, but in 1951–52, the last year of record, only forty-eight of these schools had such students enrolled.

Beginning with the medical school of the University of Arkansas in 1948, 11 schools which had hitherto barred Negros have admitted at least one Negro student, namely the University of St. Louis, Washington University (at St. Louis), University of Texas, Medical College of Virginia, University of Louisville, University of North Carolina, University of Maryland, University of Oklahoma, University of Missouri, and University of Virginia. Of the fifteen medical schools which still have never admitted a Negro, eight are tax-supported and seven are privately endowed.

In 1947 there were only 158 approved internships available to Negro physicians. These were in eighteen hospitals of which ten were strictly Negro institutions and two were classed as unsegregated but had a predominately Negro patient load. These twelve institutions represented about 150 of the 158 internships. In 1952 the 134 Howard and Meharry graduates of that year served their internships at forty-six different hospitals, a number of which had never had a Negro intern before. This represents an all-time high in the number of hospitals affording internships to the graduates of these schools. This total would be slightly increased by internships of graduates of schools other than Howard and Meharry on whom data are not available. Of the fifty-eight members of the Howard graduating class of 1953 who have been placed for internships, only sixteen, or 27.6 per cent, will serve in Negro hospitals.

The contrast between conditions of about twenty-five years ago, when there were not enough internships to go around among the Negro medical graduates, and those of today, when nearly every such intern receives from two to eight acceptances, is striking. The increased availability of internships must be ascribed in part to the fact that now there are something over four thousand more internships offered than there are medical graduates annually.

As for the important matter of obtaining residencies for further specialized training, Dr. Cobb reported: "It is perhaps safe to say that it is now possible for a qualified Negro physician to obtain somewhere an approved residency in almost every field."

However, it would be distinctly dangerous to assume that the problem is near complete solution or that ancient mores have been wholly abolished. On the question of admission of patients to hospitals without segregation, the Southern Conference poll of white Southern doctors showed that only 17 per cent voted in favor of non-segregation; 64 per cent favored admittance of Negro patients to the same hospitals but only on a segregated basis; 11 per cent of the doctors advocated completely separate hospitals for the two races; while 6 per cent proposed a variety of other alternatives. Twenty-two per cent of Georgia's white doctors voted for total segregation, and only 2 per cent of the medical profession in Mississippi and South Carolina voted for complete integration.

Meanwhile the Congress of the United States has refused to enact any safeguards against racial discrimination and segregation in its grants to states for hospitals and other health services. Although President Eisenhower repeatedly asserted that he would never interfere with the spending of its own money by any state, he stated that he would resolutely oppose expenditure of any federal monies for segregated facilities. The Eighty-fourth Congress ignored both the President and widespread public opinion by refusing to include a provision against segregation in the Medical Facilities Survey and Construction Act of 1954.

If one takes the short view, represented by the Congress and the white doctors of Georgia, South Carolina, and Mississippi, the future for Negro patients and for men of science is dark. But in the longer view, based on the considerable changes over even so brief a span as the eight years since 1947, the color line in medicine is beginning to give way.

What have been the effects on Negro health and mortality of these and other related factors? It is too early properly to appraise the outcome of improvements of the past fifteen years for benefits from the gains made by one generation in matters that influence health are, alas, often not apparent until their effects are demonstrated in the next generation. Available statistics, however, show that, while the American Negro's opportunities for a healthy and long life are still inferior to those of the white American, they have improved markedly and demonstrably.

The situation is excellently summarized by Harry J. Walker, Associate Professor of Sociology at Harvard University, in the pamphlet already quoted, "The Negro in American Life."

Since the beginning of the twentieth century the death rate for both whites and Negroes has decreased, but the Negro rate is still the higher. In 1951 (according to the National Office of Vital Statistics) 1090 of every 100,000 Negroes died, whereas only 950 of every 100,000 whites did.

Deaths per 100,000 of population due to three of the most serious communicable diseases were more startlingly disproportionate:

	Negroes	Whites
Tuberculosis	51.5	15.3
Influenza and pneumonia	62.2	27.9
Syphilis	12.2	3.7

Again, it is important to note that these are diseases in the prevention and cure of which such factors as housing, crowding, sanitation, education, and early medical care are of the greatest importance.

On the other hand, in respect to two major killers, the Negro in the same year fared better than did the white American:

DEATHS PER 100,000 OF POPULATION

	Negroes	Whites
Cancer	105.2	147.5
Heart disease	486.0	515.4

The ratio of accidental deaths (other than in automobile accidents) in 1951—48.3 per 100,000 Negroes as compared with 37.5 per 100,000 for whites—is interesting as an example of how closely social factors are related to life expectancy. For while this figure undoubtedly is due partly to the fact that better hospital and surgical facilities are available to whites than to Negroes—in itself a social factor—it is even more largely a reflection that more Negroes are assigned to hazardous jobs than are whites.

The average life expectancy of both white and Negro Americans has increased markedly between 1919 and 1949. The rate of increase for the Negro has been considerably higher than the corresponding increase for the white, but, as I have said, his life expectancy is still less than that of the white American. Better employment conditions, higher economic status, better education—in general as well as in medical fields—already brought about or on the horizon; and the better housing for which the Negro must still hope, but with increasing justification—all should result in lessening the disparity in another generation.

AVERAGE LIFE EXPECTANCY OF AMERICANS, 1919–1949

	Men		Women	
	Negroes	Whites	Negroes	Whites
1919–21	47.1	56.3	46.9	58.5
1949	58.6	65.9	62.9	71.5
Per cent increase	24.4	17.0	34.1	24.1

It is obvious from the table that the Negro American's opportunity to enjoy health and to live out his allotted span is steadily improving. Here, as elsewhere, the goal of complete equality is still ahead, but thoughtful Americans, both colored and white, are more justified today than they have ever been before in looking forward with confidence to its eventual attainment.

VII. Jim Crow on the Run

It would be difficult to find in American history any greater proof that "the evil that men do lives after them; the good is oft interred with their bones" than that furnished by the effect of the United States Supreme Court's separate-but-equal doctrine. Nor has this evil ever been more visible and humiliating than in circumstances which have affected the Negro traveler.

That enforced segregation on trains and other public carriers has worked grievous hardships on Negroes is generally known. What is not usually recognized is the ironic fact that railroads and other public carriers, all controlled by white people, have themselves suffered greatly from this evil practice, through the economic loss it entails for them. Because of the Jim Crow ruling they have been forced to spend many millions of dollars since 1896 for separate cars, waiting rooms, ticket windows, restrooms and special police officers to enforce segregation—all of which, realistically speaking, has been money thrown down the drain. Had any of the so-called separate-but-equal facilities been actually equal, the cost would have been many times greater. A not inconsiderable item has been made up of the heavy costs public-carrier companies have been forced to pay in defending court actions for damages brought on by brutal or overzealous employees in the enforcement of segregation. With the growing number of automobiles and good roads, and the competition of airplane and bus travel, the railroads have lost many additional millions of revenue, to say nothing of the good will of Negro passengers. They and their stockholders have been penalized. Vast sums have been lost. All this has played a part in the fact that railroad stocks and bonds no longer occupy the preferred position they held when *Plessy* vs. *Ferguson* affirmed the right of the several states to force railroads to provide separate accommodations for white and colored passengers.

Yet there has been change. Excerpts from two publications by Negroes on Jim Crow in travel published twenty-three years apart give a most interesting and valuable picture of the progress that has been made. The first (1929) is the book *What the Negro Thinks* by the late Dr. Robert Russa Moton, who succeeded Booker T. Washington as Principal of Tuskegee Institute in Alabama. The second (1952) is "Segregation in Inter-state Railway Coach Travel," a ninety-one page mimeographed report by Professor Herman H. Long of Fisk University of a 1952 study of railway segregation by four field investigators, two white and two Negro. The purpose of the study was to provide documentation on existing practices, to consider the effects of segregation upon the public and the railroads, and to supply a basis of facts for further action by government, public carriers, legislative bodies, and the public to abolish segregation.

To buttress his assertion that segregation not only retards progress but "touches all Negroes, irrespective of their means, education, character, or position, and in actual practice subjects them all to embarrassment, humiliation, and injustice," Dr. Moton cites the following facts as of 1929:

In actual practice . . . the principle of segregation seems to apply only to colored passengers. There are trains upon which Negroes are confined strictly to the Negro coach; they cannot leave that compartment to go into any other part of the train whatever. They cannot so much as board the train by way of the coach for whites. On the other hand, white passengers as well as the train crew have free access to

all parts of the train. White men have been known to come into the
Negro coach to smoke and drink liquor without protest or interference
from the train conductor or any of the train crew. . . . It is practically
impossible for the average Negro to . . . secure Pullman accommodations of any sort.

On a few trains in 1929, Dr. Moton wrote, Negroes could enter
the dining car to purchase food, but only after all white passengers
had been served; on most trains they could eat not at all. Negro
travelers were forced to ride in a car or a half-car—the other half
usually a baggage car or smoking room for whites—next to the
engine, where it was not only dirtier but most perilous, since the
Negro coach at that time was usually an antiquated wooden one,
while the rest of the cars were steel. When the Negro passenger
arrived ahead of white passengers to buy his ticket before the rush,
he would be told he was too early. When the train was called,
according to Dr. Moton, "he takes his stand at the window for
Negroes, and there waits and waits and waits until every passenger
is sold a ticket and is then impatiently asked, 'Where are you going?' with barely time enough to get his luggage and board the
train. Sometimes there is not time enough left to purchase the
ticket, and the hapless passenger is rebuked by the gate man for not
having a ticket; the porter at the train growls his reproaches and
the conductor voices his contempt for the stupidity of anyone who
boards a train without a ticket."

Subsequent to 1929, however, the campaign against both gross
inequality and segregation on all public carriers was stepped up
steadily by legal actions, legislation, complaints from stockholders
of money wasted in enforcement of segregation, the bringing of
carefully documented and authenticated cases before administrative
agencies such as the Interstate Commerce Commission and the
Securities and Exchange Commission, and a relentless campaign of
publicity.

Professor Long does not report the problem solved in 1952. Far
from it. But he and the Annual Reports of the NAACP, as well as

the yearly *Balance Sheet of Civil Rights*, published by the American Jewish Congress and the NAACP, could list the following changes:

Negroes in 1953 could purchase and occupy Pullman accommodations anywhere in the South as well as in other parts of the United States.

They could eat in diners, unhumiliated by having to wait until white passengers had been served and without being required to eat behind a drawn curtain or at segregated tables.

In interstate travel they could ride in unsegregated coaches on some railroads in the South; and the continuing pressure of court decisions, administrative rulings, adverse publicity, and economic loss by railroads was making it certain that the end of Jim Crow travel was in sight.

Led by the Pennsylvania Railroad, considerable progress had been made in the abandonment of restriction of Negro passengers to a specified car or cars on reserved-seat trains originating in Northern cities and bound for Southern cities. Reservation clerks and ticket-sellers had created costly resentment among both colored and white passengers by their questions, which attempted to pierce the veil of anonymity on race, when reservations were made by telephone. Adamant refusal of Negroes to move to Jim Crow coaches had resulted in numerous legal suits for damages, some of which were won, when railroad employees or police officers arrested or man-handled colored passengers. In many cases, such as some of those involving Professor Long's investigators, Negroes who refused to move were permitted to remain in non-segregated coaches.

Here is a brief summary of the persistent struggle that brought about these changes. During the campaign several Negroes were killed, others beaten, still others arrested and convicted for refusal to submit to racial segregation. Professor Long reports a number of tragic cases.

In the spring of 1947 Fletcher Melvin, a twenty-four-year-old orderly at Provident Hospital in Baltimore, was asleep when the train conductor ordered all colored passengers at Enfield, North

Carolina, to move to the segregated coach. On being awakened Melvin refused to move and was shot and killed instantly by the Atlantic Coast Line Railroad conductor. The conductor claimed self-defense and was freed.

George Serrell, also twenty-four and a veteran of World War II, accompanied by his wife, refused in 1947 to move to a segregated coach at Charleston, West Virginia. He was arrested by a railroad detective and killed en route to prison for "resisting arrest."

A venerated clergyman, Reverend William H. Jernagin, Ralph Mathews, a Negro newspaperman of the Afro-American chain, and another Negro were arrested and removed from a Southern Railway train at Lynchburg, Virginia, for refusing to leave seats reserved at Philadelphia. They promptly filed suit for forty-five thousand dollars in damages.

A Morehouse College professor of English, Hugh Gloster, riding from his Atlanta, Georgia, home through Mississippi during the Second World War, asked the train conductor if some of the Negro passengers who were standing in the overcrowded Jim Crow section could sit down in the half-empty white car. At Tupelo, Mississippi, police summoned by the train conductor beat Professor Gloster and locked him up, and he was forced to sign a statement absolving the railroad from responsibility.

Possibly the most ironic episode was this. Nazi prisoners of war being transported to a prison camp were ushered into a railroad-station restaurant where a stop was made by the train for food. Wounded American Negro veterans just back from the European front en route to a veterans' hospital were told they could obtain food only if they went to the rear, to be handed sandwiches and coffee out of the kitchen door.

On the weekend of the Thanksgiving Day holiday of 1951 a tragic head-on collision between two crack trains of the Southern Railway—the Crescent Limited and the Southerner—occurred at Woodstock, Alabama. Seventeen passengers were killed. Fifteen of them were Negroes, who were herded into a half-baggage, half-coach car located next to the engine. The twenty-two-seat Negro half-car was crushed like an accordion, such was the terrific impact from the head-on crash of the speeding trains.

Despite these and other instances of brutality and intransigent insistence on complete segregation, two major developments took place during the 1940s. The most basic of these was the realization by Americans, and particularly by Negroes themselves, that segregation in travel could no longer be tolerated. Where colored passengers had silently endured being forced to pay first-class fares for third-class or worse accommodations, with all the hazards and embarrassments attendant on such travel, more of them began to fight back. Negroes were fighting and dying for freedom on battlefronts all over the world. Franklin Roosevelt and Winston Churchill were exhorting the free peoples of the world to make whatever sacrifice was needed to save the world from nazism. American Negroes identified themselves totally with the war objectives, but had one additional aim—they were determined to share the freedom for which the world was fighting.

Up to this time they had bitterly resented travel segregation, but had been content, in the main, to obtain equal accommodations. Resignation was replaced by a new resolution to utilize every legitimate means to end the abuses from which Negroes had suffered at the hands of the public carriers, the law, and the white public. To this end two developments came into being: first, to submit no longer in silence; and, second, to fight segregation itself and no longer be content with allegedly equal facilities. "There is separation but it is seldom, if ever, complete," Charles S. Johnson wrote in 1943 in his able *Patterns of Negro Segregation*, "and accommodations are seldom equal or similar." A firm resolve came unnoticed into the pattern of Negro thinking and action to end both separation and inequality.

The first widely publicized blow was the suit for damages brought in 1937 by Arthur W. Mitchell, Negro congressman from Illinois, when he was ejected from a Pullman car in Arkansas. A measure of the considerable improvement was the fact that Mr. Mitchell, even though a member of the House of Representatives, was able to purchase Pullman accommodations at all in 1937. Even in 1943, Dr. Johnson reported: "Only in exceptional cases are Negroes sold accommodations in Pullman cars; they are ordinarily obtained through some irregular procedure, such as having a white person purchase the reservation, or approaching a friendly railroad official who will sell the reservations without regard for the prohibition features of the laws. . . . The Negroes who occasionally procure Pullman accommodations on trains . . . are given 'Lower 13,' the drawing room; and this is interpreted as providing segregated quarters."

Besides enabling him to travel more comfortably, the "Lower-13" device bestowed one additional benefit on the Negro who occupied such a drawing room—he was usually charged only the price of a lower berth. The irony of such subterfuges was illustrated by the bewilderment of a Southern Railway conductor in a situation in which I was involved. In 1931 I went to Atlanta, accompanied by my four-year-old son, to speak at a meeting celebrating the signing of the Emancipation Proclamation. In discussing the problem of travel, my sister, who was registrar of the Atlanta School of Social Work, told me how she was accustomed to obtaining "Lower-13" accommodations northward out of Atlanta for such Negroes as Dr. Moton of Tuskegee and Dr. John Hope, President of Atlanta University, by telephoning a friendly official of the Southern Railway.

The conversation invariably was almost a ritual. My sister would say, "I would like a lower berth to New York for next Thursday [or whatever day passage was desired] on the Crescent Limited."

The reply would come, "I have reserved a *lower*. When do you wish to pick it up?"

My sister, being indistinguishable from a white person, would go to the office to *pay* for a lower berth but *receive* a ticket for a drawing room.

She suggested that on my return trip to New York I might as well be the beneficiary of the Southern obsession with its own racial superiority. I was delighted to do so, and was pleased to find that the Pullman porter was an old friend with whom I had gone to grammar school in Atlanta. He was most gracious in making my son and me comfortable, and we had a good time talking over old times—that is, until the conductor and his assistant arrived to take our tickets. They could not understand why passengers who were apparently white should occupy choice space costing two and a half times that of a berth.

The porter and I, being opposed also to discrimination against white Americans, did nothing to ease their embarrassment as they sought to find the answer without risking trouble through asking questions that might give offense. Thoroughly baffled, they eventually abandoned their quest and went about their business of taking tickets from the other passengers. They thought they had found revenge when they returned that evening as my son and I were preparing to go to bed. The porter had made up both lower berths. In triumphant anger the conductor told me I would have to pay for an additional full-fare railroad ticket and lower berth if we used more than one berth. When I informed him we would use only one berth he ordered the porter to unmake one berth. The man complied by folding back the mattress.

As soon as the conductors left, the porter restored the berth and told me to lock the door and use both berths. We were scheduled to arrive in Washington at four a.m., at which point the Southern Railway conductor would end his run. By the time we awakened we had left Washington and were on our way to New York, and there was, of course, no difficulty with the Pennsylvania Railroad conductor who was then in charge of the train. For a long time afterward the Southern conductor sought to worm out of my porter friend the reason for my occupying "Lower 13," but his failure was as complete as his bewilderment.

Congressman Mitchell's suit for damages sought to wipe out the practice of denying Pullman accommodations to Negroes. After three years of litigation in lower courts his case was considered by the United States Supreme Court and decided by it in 1940. The court ruled that whether the demand by Negroes for Pullman accommodations be great or small, failure of the railroads to supply equal-though-separate accommodations violated the equal protection guaranteed by the federal Constitution. The court further made it clear that that protection was an individual instead of a group right, which answered the defense contention that the cost of dual service would be prohibitive, since not enough Negroes bought Pullman space to warrant providing an extra Pullman and an extra dining car for each train having such accommodations for whites.

Dr. Johnson described the device used to comply with the court's order this way: "A curtain was hung in the dining car, and it was exposed only enough to indicate the intent to segregate."

But the war played its part in making even this subterfuge difficult to operate. For reasons of climate, many military installations had been located in the Southern states, and more were being erected. These included non-segregated officers' training camps in places such as Fort Benning, Georgia; Fort Sill, Oklahoma; and Fort Hood in Texas. Vouchers for Pullman berths and meals on dining cars were supplied by the War Department in many, if not most, instances to white and colored officers alike and to many enlisted men of both races, especially returning wounded veterans. The number of such military personnel, added to the number of Negro civilians able to travel in Pullmans because of increased employment and wages due to the war, so increased travel that the cost of separating curtains for diners became a sizable item of expense in itself.

There were other problems for the railroads, though unfortunately these were not as frequently encountered as would have been desirable to speed the abolition of silly devices and stratagems.

One of the greatest heroes of the war was a gallant young white Mississippi airman who received nationwide acclaim when he returned, gravely wounded, to the United States to receive from President Roosevelt at the White House the Congressional Medal of Honor. The members of Congress from Mississippi arranged a press conference for the young hero when he reached Washington, at which he related with modest reluctance the experiences that had brought him fame.

The late Senator Theodore Bilbo sought, as was his wont, to bring the race question into the discussion. "Captain, I suppose you had the usual trouble with the niggers overseas, didn't you?" he queried. To Bilbo's dismay, the veteran replied, "No, Senator, I didn't. On the contrary, I learned something—that Negroes can fight just as well and die as bravely as white Americans. And I've been shocked on getting home to Mississippi to see something I've looked at all my life but never really *saw* before—those signs, 'White' and 'Colored.' "

Bilbo tried to shut off the confession of the earnest young man, which was bringing delighted smiles from the newspapermen. But the veteran was not to be interrupted until he could cleanse his conscience.

"What's more, Senator," he went on, "I'm worried about this whole business of segregation. On the train coming up here I asked to be seated in the diner with a Negro Captain of Infantry. He was one of the most intelligent men I've ever talked with. We've got to do something about this race question, because what we've been doing isn't right."

Unable to take any more, Bilbo hastily terminated the conference.

There are many incidents revealing the broadening of attitude of some white Americans because of having fought on foreign soil with Negro Americans in defense of freedom.

The colored members of a Merchant Marine crew were ordered by the train conductor, on reaching the Mason-Dixon line en route to New Orleans, to leave their white companions and move forward to the Jim Crow coach. The white crew members objected so vehemently that the conductor speedily retreated from the car, in fear of bodily violence from the men who told him, "We've faced death together fighting for so-and-so's like you, and we're not separating now."

Not all Americans came out of the war for democracy imbued with such determination to practice it at home. But enough did do so to make an impact on the pattern of segregation.

There were other factors at work. A federal agency that should have been concerned with the problem of inequities caused by the practice of segregation is the Interstate Commerce Commission. Judge Margold had observed in 1930 of the ICC that it had rendered two liberal decisions on the issue "not very long after the Civil War. In 1909, however, the commission rendered a decision which was based on the rule that colored passengers have no right to complain of accommodations actually inferior to those furnished white passengers on the same train, so long as these accommodations are not worse than the worst accommodations furnished to whites on *any* train operated by the carriers. Since then, the commission has consistently failed to find sufficient proof of real discrimination in every case that has come before it."

Despite its abysmally poor record, however, a succession of carefully authenticated cases was presented to the ICC. It is the specific duty of that agency to correct gross abuses. The commission continued to evade the issue and to avoid action, but it became less arrogant in its rulings as a result of public pressures and court decisions. If the ICC did little to correct injustice, it did not do as much as formerly to protect and bolster it. One cause of its change in attitude may have been the growing public opinion that more liberal members, including a Negro, should be named to the commission to replace those who were so manifestly biased in behalf of segregation and the public carriers.

More court actions for damages resulted in awards to Negro plaintiffs. In 1943 the Reverend J. C. Jackson of Hartford, Connecticut, prominent and beloved Baptist leader, received a settlement of $3750 from the Southern Railway for indignities inflicted upon him en route to a church convention in Memphis, Tennessee. A suit was filed by Mrs. Berta Mae Watkins, who was ejected from a train for refusing to move to the Jim Crow coach. Similar actions challenging segregated travel were brought in numerous other cases all over the South. Some were won or settled out of court by the defending railroads. Some were lost, but the railroads were put to increasing expense to defend these actions, even as they saw their revenues from passenger travel diminishing as patrons turned to other modes of travel.

The second notable case involving segregation in transportation to be decided by the United States Supreme Court was that of Mrs. Irene Morgan. Decision was handed down on June 3, 1946. While traveling on October 18, 1944, from Virginia to Baltimore, Maryland, Mrs. Morgan had refused to move to the rear seat of a Greyhound bus, on order of the driver. She was arrested and charged and convicted of violation of Virginia's segregation laws and of "resisting arrest." Her case was carried by the Virginia State Conference of the NAACP through the Virginia courts and up to the Supreme Court of the United States, which ruled that state segregation statutes place an "undue burden" on the carriers, and therefore do not apply to interstate passengers on interstate motor vehicles. The decision materially broadened the principle laid down in the Mitchell case, which applied primarily to Pullman cars and diners, but not to travel in buses. It affected many more Negroes—those who could not afford to ride in Pullman cars or eat in diners. The Morgan case and the court's ruling on it directly affected all modes of travel, including railroad coaches and airplanes as well as buses.

A further attack on segregation was made by the Supreme Court in the case of Elmer Henderson, where there was direct challenge of the validity of the separate-but-equal accommodation in interstate travel, which the Supreme Court had inferentially approved in Congressman Mitchell's case. Following the Irene Morgan decision, railroads and bus companies had concocted their own rules and regulations to continue segregation wherever possible, thereby bypassing the courts with the implicit blessing of the ICC.

Henderson had refused service at a segregated table on a Southern Railway train. The ICC held that such restriction of Negroes to designated tables was not discriminatory, and its ruling was upheld by a federal appellate court. Both the federal Department of Justice and the NAACP filed friend-of-the-court briefs in the case, which was financed and handled by the Alpha Phi Alpha fraternity, of which Henderson was a member. Justice Tom Clark of Texas abstained from participation in the decision because as Attorney General of the United States he had filed a brief in the court urging abandonment of segregation. The other eight justices avoided ruling on the valid claim that both the Fifth and the Fourteenth Amendments were involved, but ruled instead that the segregated tables violated the Interstate Commerce Act.

But the decision did bring about considerable relaxation of the practice of segregation, and abandonment of the objectionable curtains. The Southern Railway sought to evade strict compliance with the spirit if not the letter of the decision by adopting a rule that young people be seated with young people, whites with whites, Negroes with Negroes, but that no person should be denied a vacant seat. Running true to form and tradition, the ICC voted that this rule was not discriminatory.

But while the ICC stood still, and lawyers in the employ of the railroad companies collected fat fees for efforts to devise means of circumventing the courts, the nation's Supreme Court continued to hack away at segregation, on cases which Negroes continued to bring before the court.

William C. Chance, a Negro high-school principal in Virginia, was forcibly removed on June 25, 1948, from an Atlantic Coast Line train—which took over temporarily from the Southern Railway the dubious distinction of leading the fight to maintain and perpetuate segregation. Chance was convicted of "disorderly conduct" for refusing to obey an order to move to a segregated coach. In this case a new note was registered when the Circuit Court of Appeals reversed the district court instead of leaving that chore to the Supreme Court.

Another new element in this case was withdrawal by the railroad of its charges, but Professor Chance took the initiative and sued the railroad for breach of contract, unlawful arrest, and unlawful incarceration. His action and the affirmation by the United States Supreme Court of the Circuit Court of Appeals' decision constituted an important step forward in establishment of the principle that an

injured and aggrieved Negro passenger can successfully sue for
redress when penalized for refusal to obey segregation rules and
regulations. Chance's victory in winning a judgment for damages
and two refusals by the Supreme Court to reverse that judgment
were considered as effectively outlawing the application of rules
and regulations by interstate public carriers to segregate passengers.

Air travel has, from the start, been less segregated than the older
forms of transportation, but even the airlines are not without traces
of the evil. Toilet facilities are still separate in most of the cities of
the South. Negro passengers are not served in many airport dining
rooms, though the Knoxville City Council voted in 1953 to accord
equal courtesies to all. In Houston and Memphis limousine service
to and from airports is not available to Negroes.

Negroes today press forward toward total abolition of segregation
in travel. On the basis of gains won in this field, it is not unlikely
that all separation based on race will be eliminated on public carriers
within a few years.

Closely related to segregation on public conveyances has been
the exclusion of Negroes from "white" hotels, restaurants, moving-
picture houses, theaters, dance halls, and so forth. Here too the situation, while still highly conditioned by prejudice in many places, and
far from ideal in others, has improved noticeably during the past
fifteen years.

It is not within the purpose of this book to attempt a country-
wide survey, but a few facts about one Northern city and one
border city are revealing.

New York City has for many years been one of the most enlightened cities in America in regard to the acceptance of Negroes in
public places. Yet in 1940 a Negro who needed a hotel room in New
York would in many places have been told that there was no va-
cancy. Even if he had wired ahead for a reservation, and it had been
confirmed, he would often be told when he arrived that there had
been a mistake and no room was available. Today there are very
few hotels in New York in which he is subjected to this humiliation.

Most New York restaurants have for many years served Negroes along with white people, though many of them have found ways to lead their Negro customers to inconspicuous tables, to delay serving them, and otherwise to embarrass them. This too is changing.

In 1949 a small group of people living in the eastern part of mid-Manhattan, in an area that was about to house the United Nations offices, formed The Committee on Civil Rights in East Manhattan and made a careful survey of every eating place between Thirty-fourth and Fifty-ninth streets and between Fifth Avenue and the East River. Sixty-two representative restaurants chosen from two hundred and forty-eight medium-priced eating places in the area were then checked by having both white and Negro members of the committee eat in them. A Negro team entered each restaurant first, and a white team followed a few minutes later.

In 42 per cent, or 26 of the 62 places tested, the Negro pair met obviously inferior treatment in various ways. They were led past empty tables to be seated next to a kitchen or a lavatory or in a place where they would be less visible to other diners; or they were treated rudely, made to wait out of turn for a table; or service was delayed; or they were hurried through their meal and made aware that their quick departure would be welcomed.

After the survey the committee instituted efforts to improve the situation. Conferences were held with restaurant associations and individual restaurant owners, and many of them gave pledges to discontinue discriminatory practices.

In 1952 a check was made on the same restaurants. Whereas in 1949 42 per cent had practiced discrimination, it was found in 1952 that in only 16 per cent of the restaurants was there any noticeable difference between the treatment given white patrons and that accorded to Negroes.

Washington, D.C., has been an especially interesting place to study changing race relationships—particularly in respect to the reception accorded dark-skinned peoples in public places. Distinguished colored foreigners, as well as American Negroes, have been embittered by the refusal of Washington's hotels, restaurants, theaters, and concert halls to admit them.

As recently as 1945, Ras Imru, Ambassador of Ethiopia, angrily departed from Constitution Hall when an usher barred him from the official box that had been assigned him for a meeting of the American Association for the Advancement of Science. Dr. Ralph J. Bunche, destined to become winner of the Nobel Peace Prize shortly afterward, declined the post of Assistant Secretary of State because he would not force his family to undergo the daily humiliation of Washington's Jim Crow customs. Even more recently, Thava Rajah, Malayan labor leader, guest of the State Department in its program of bringing visitors to America to enable them to learn at first hand what democracy means, was bluntly refused service in both a Washington drugstore and restaurant. He was told, "We don't serve black people here"! The episodes were gleefully reported by *Izvestia* and the Moscow radio.

Another view of Washington is one an American Negro Fulbright scholar obtained recently in Egypt. He was attempting to interpret American democracy to a group of Egyptian friends. One of them who had served in the diplomatic corps of his government answered the Negro's defense of America by telling him that when he had lived in Washington he had to use his passport continuously to keep from being considered and treated as an American Negro. "Isn't it ridiculous," he asked the embarrassed American, "that just because I had a passport I could be treated better than you, a citizen of the United States, even though I am brown too?"

But such incidents have lessened materially during the past few years and, if the present trend continues, are destined to become even more scarce in the years ahead. The complete abolition of racial discrimination and segregation in America has not yet been achieved, but the democratic process has manifested its ability to correct its shortcomings in a fashion that is genuinely encouraging. Washington has taken the revolutionary changes in its stride, with but little of the friction that opponents of change or the fainthearted predicted. And the perturbation of the State Department and other government agencies over what might happen to important dark-skinned visitors from other countries has materially lessened.

To understand the nation's capital, and to evaluate intelligently the true significance of such recent developments as abolition of the color bar in restaurants and movie houses, a little history is necessary.

One of the most baffling contradictions in American history is that the advent on the Washington scene of Woodrow Wilson, a man proclaimed as a great intellectual liberal, caused the most abrupt descent of the Negro's status in the District of Columbia. Up to that time Negroes had been admitted to theaters, restaurants, and hotels. It is true that, although a considerable number of Washington Negroes were college graduates, most of them were restricted, under Republican administrations, to jobs as clerks and messengers. Yet there had been little segregation based on race, according to Judge James A. Cobb, of white and colored clerks in governmental restaurants, toilets, and other facilities.

Then Woodrow Wilson, gifted exponent of a liberal philosophy, entered the White House. His first wife focused her attention on less global points of view. She visited the Government Printing Office one day shortly after her husband's inauguration, to find, to her dismay, that white and colored employees were using the same facilities. She launched an attack against "such un-American practices." Postmaster General Albert Burleson, of Texas, was assigned the task of ending these practices. He summoned to his office several prominent Negroes and announced that if they would accept segregated divisions in government, more Negro supervisors would be appointed.

The bait failed to attract. But despite the stand of Negro leaders, Negroes were barred from the restaurants of both Senate and House. Bills were introduced in Congress to establish segregation on streetcars and other public carriers. There was an increasing demand for the rejection of every concept of racial equality that had been inaugurated since the Civil War.

In 1913 the United States Supreme Court, reflecting the temper of the times, ruled that the Civil Rights Acts of 1875 did not apply to Washington. The rout was on. Negro residents of the District of Columbia and dark-skinned visitors to the nation's capital were progressively subjected to greater and greater restriction of rights until the administration of Franklin D. Roosevelt in 1933.

Two individuals who came to Washington with the new administration were shocked by what they found. One was Mrs. Eleanor Roosevelt. Through the spoken and written word and by example she advocated the integration of colored Americans in all aspects of government and in American life as a whole. In incident after incident she acted and spoke her mind in a forthright way. It took courage to make such a stand in a city that had become completely Southern in its mores and practices. Members of the Congress from Southern states and some members of the Cabinet brought all manner of pressures on the President to stop Mrs. Roosevelt's campaign against the color line. President Roosevelt, however, knew his wife too well to make such an attempt, even though he occasionally ran into political squalls because of her position on segregation.

The other newcomer who acted specifically against the Washington pattern of race discrimination was Harold L. Ickes. He was astounded to find a rigid pattern of segregation in the Department of the Interior. With characteristic impetuosity, he ignored the customary predictions of calamity and ordered immediate abolition of all segregated facilities. When an angry delegation of white employees called on him to demand restoration of segregation, Mr. Ickes ordered a secretary to take the names of the protesters and informed them that he would hold them responsible if any trouble developed. The rebellion ended there.

As Secretary of the Interior, Mr. Ickes had jurisdiction over many of the parks, picnic grounds, tennis courts, and swimming pools in the District of Columbia. After abolishing racial segregation in the Department of the Interior itself—an example which eventually was followed by other governmental departments and agencies—

Mr. Ickes and Assistant Secretary Oscar L. Chapman tackled Washington's Jim Crow recreational facilities.

Here are some of the precautions that were taken, on Chapman's instructions, when Washington's swimming pools were desegregated. Carefully selected park-service policemen and policewomen were assigned to the most pleasant job imaginable in tropical Washington—swimming in the pools controlled by the Department of the Interior. Without uniforms or badges, they could not be distinguished from other swimmers. When a white man acted obstreperously a white policeman would quietly swim alongside the troublemaker, identify himself, and suggest that he either behave or leave the pool. White policewomen did the same with white female swimmers, while Negro Park Department employees performed similar duties when Negroes of either sex acted improperly.

The extent of Washington's reformation is illustrated by a recent luncheon, attended by seven hundred Negro and white guests, held in one of the city's top hotels to celebrate the ninetieth birthday of Mrs. Mary Church Terrell, an Oberlin graduate and the widow of Washington's first Negro judge. Mrs. Terrell had played a major role in the famous Thompson restaurant case. The decision of the United States Supreme Court in that test case had opened the doors of the District of Columbia's restaurants to Negroes for the first time since the Woodrow Wilson administration.

Mrs. Terrell had, with two white friends and a distinguished Negro clergyman, been refused service in a Thompson restaurant in 1951. A suit for damages was promptly instituted under laws that had been enacted in 1873 but mysteriously "forgotten" at the turn of the century. These laws required restaurants to serve "any well-behaved and respectable person." The late Charles H. Houston had brought to light the "forgotten" laws, and legal action was commenced by the corporation counsel of the District of Columbia on behalf of Mrs. Terrell as she neared the tenth decade of her life.

A municipal judge reached the odd conclusion that the "forgotten" laws had repealed themselves through non-use. But the United

States Supreme Court handed down a unanimous decision that "well-behaved persons" could not be denied service because of race or color. An excellent friend-of-the-court brief in support of the old laws was filed by the Department of Justice as the first governmental action by the Eisenhower administration implementing President Eisenhower's campaign pledge to continue the drive against segregation in Washington.

All manner of dire predictions were voiced, even by Washingtonians who were ashamed of and opposed to denial of restaurant service to dark-skinned patrons, yet very few unpleasant episodes occurred. In one small restaurant two intoxicated white men beat a colored woman and tore her dress. In another low-priced neighborhood lunchroom the proprietor told a colored man that he had been served "only because the court says so, and we don't want your trade." There was no great or immediate rush of Negro customers into the more expensive restaurants and hotels, and when they did enter them they were served like anyone else.

The relative ease with which the restaurant ban in Washington was erased emboldened other places of public accommodation to initiate new policies. Long and continuous efforts against discrimination in theaters, swimming pools, tennis courts, government restaurants, and Constitution Hall had created a climate of opinion for compliance with the Supreme Court's decision in the Thompson restaurant case. Not long after that decision was handed down, downtown Washington moving-picture theaters abandoned their policy of refusing to admit Negroes. All but a few hotels accepted Negro guests, and there was extraordinarily little protest, even from white Southerners.

Changes in the Negro's status in sports have been less striking than have those in his reception in public places, for the Negro athlete has for years been an accepted and respected figure. Yet here too he has been hounded by the shadow of Jim Crow, and here too the shadow is noticeably fading.

As far back as 1895 the late William H. Lewis, who later served as Assistant United States Attorney General, was the outstanding player on the Harvard University football team. In the years since, great Negro players have starred on college and high-school teams of Northern and border states, a number of them being chosen as all-Americans. Among the better known are Paul Robeson of Rutgers and Fritz Pollard of Brown.

There is, similarly, a long tradition of great Negro prize fighters, from Joe Gans and Jack Johnson to Joe Louis, Henry Armstrong, and Sugar Ray Robinson. After 1909, when Jack Johnson won the World Heavyweight Championship, until the meteoric rise of Joe Louis, Negro heavyweights were denied by subterfuge the opportunity to fight for the championship. But Louis's great skill and his impeccable behavior destroyed that taboo. In a profession peopled by many unscrupulous and unsavory characters, Negro boxers are frequently exploited and cheated. But this is done in precisely the same fashion as and to no greater extent than it is to white fighters.

As in other sports, the paying public has come to accept athletes on the basis of their ability and character, except in a few Southern states such as Mississippi and South Carolina. The most striking advance of recent years has been the almost total abolition of the color bar in the highly remunerative field of professional baseball. Prior to 1947, when Jackie Robinson was brought from Montreal by Branch Rickey to play with the Brooklyn Dodgers, the only colored players in professional baseball were a few who claimed to be Indians, or who adopted Spanish names, learned to speak Spanish and passed themselves off as Cuban, or those who were light-skinned enough to pass as white.

Jackie Robinson's role as pioneer was as heroic as it was difficult. Threats to kill him if he played in certain cities were made. Players, not all of them Southern-born, called him vile names and attempted to spike him or hit him with beanballs. A majority of the players on one team said they would refuse to play if Robinson played. They changed their minds when the President of the National League told them they would be suspended and boycotted so that they could not work at the only profitable trade they knew—baseball. They played.

Robinson told me one experience of those early days. The first time he was at bat in a certain border city the opposing players loosed a big black cat to run across the field past Robinson as he stood in the batter's box. Derisive comments on his race and color by the opposing team were almost, but not quite, drowned out by the laughter of the crowd.

"I was so angry, my immediate impulse was to use my bat on the fellows who were taunting me," Robinson related. "But then I remembered my promise to Branch Rickey not to lose my head. Thinking I would be rattled, the pitcher threw me a nice fat pitch right down the middle, and I leaned into it for a home run. I felt better then, and nobody has tried the black-cat trick on me since." In 1947 Robinson was chosen in a poll of sports writers as Rookie of the Year—the first of five Negroes to be so honored in a sport from which they had been totally barred throughout the long history of America's so-called "national pastime." The following year he was selected as the Most Valuable Player of the Year in the National League.

The speed with which changes are possible in a free society is strikingly evidenced by what has happened since 1947, when Robinson became the first acknowledged Negro in major-league baseball. Within seven years, nine of the sixteen major-league clubs had Negro players, many of them among the brightest stars of the game, such as Willie Mays and Monte Irvin of the New York Giants; Robinson, Roy Campanella, Jim (Junior) Gilliam, and Don Newcombe of the Dodgers; Larry Doby of the Cleveland Indians; and many others.

Among the seven major-league teams that have not, as this is written, employed any Negroes, the policies of two are most inexplicable, inasmuch as they are located in two of the most metropolitan and liberal cities of the United States. One team is the New York Yankees, which does, at least, have Negro players on some of its farm teams;[1] the other is the Boston Red Sox—in the home of the

---

[1] Since this was written, the New York Yankees have announced the signing, on October 15, 1954, of Elston Howard, a Negro catcher and utility outfielder. (Editor's note.)

Abolitionists—which refuses to hire colored players even for its minor-league subsidiaries.

The phenomenal success of Negroes in big-league baseball is not entirely due to sentimentality or to an abstract sense of fair play. American baseball is as hardheaded a business operation as is General Motors. Owners and managers have learned to their delight that there are not only an abundant number of excellent Negro ball players but that, because of them, attendance at games, not only by Negroes but also by other Americans, is measurably increased. Thus excellent profits fortuitously combined with American precepts of fair play have created a major change of racial mores, which has percolated even down to minor leagues in the Deep South.

In 1945 any person who dared predict that colored professional baseball players would soon play on Southern teams would have been thought insane. By 1954 Negroes were playing professional ball on local teams in Florida, Oklahoma, Virginia, Tennessee, Louisiana, Texas, and Georgia. However, the Attorney General of Mississippi ruled in 1953 that "it was against public policy" to permit two Negro players of the Hot Springs, Arkansas, Class C Cotton States League to play against white players in Mississippi, although there was no law against such playing. The bitter quarrel that was thereby set off brought widespread disapproval of the Mississippi official's action. George M. Trautman, President of the Minor Leagues, bluntly declared: "Any provision by any league against the employment by any club of any individual because of his race, color, or creed, cannot and will not be approved." Nevertheless, Mississippi was adamant, even when a Negro player of the Jacksonville, Florida, team was named Most Valuable Player of the Year in the Class A South Atlantic League.

Meanwhile Birmingham tried to repeal an old ordinance against interracial sports. The regulation was repealed by the council, but reinstated by a city-wide referendum, leaving Birmingham one of the few Southern cities where such sports events are forbidden.

The additional burdens and responsibilities of Negro professional baseball players, beyond those of their white teammates, are not yet over, as the Mississippi episode shows. But in 1954 there remained no doubt that the major obstacles had been overcome, as far as Negro players of talent were concerned, in the lucrative business of professional baseball.

During the same short period the American Bowling Congress voted in 1950 to eliminate its "Caucasian Rule," which, as its name implies, restricted membership to white Americans. This limitation to tourney competition had long been the object of attack by the United Automobile Workers of the CIO, the NAACP, and other organizations. The color bar in tennis began to fade, and at least one Negro professional has competed in a Professional Golf Association Tournament. Swiftly and permanently, in most sports—both amateur and professional—the color bar has been breaking down.

More rapidly than anyone would have dared to predict a decade and a half ago, in travel, in restaurants and hotels, in theaters and in sports, Jim Crow is fading to a shadow of his former baleful self.

VIII. Labor Unions and the Fight for Racial Equality

It was as logical as it is forgotten that the beginning of effective trade unionism in the United States was virtually simultaneous with the emancipation of Negro slaves. Organization of white workers was impossible as long as they had to compete with unpaid slave labor. Slavery was ended in 1865 by the Thirteenth Amendment to the Constitution; the following year the first nationwide attempt at organization of workers was made, by formation of the National Labor Union at Baltimore. The fledgling union advocated what was then the revolutionary idea of an eight-hour day. It set about organizing unskilled as well as skilled workers and foreign-born as well as native-born wage earners.

But the new movement stubbed its toe—as organized labor was destined to do for another seventy years, to its own detriment—on the Negro question. At the end of the Civil War the major part of the skilled work of the South was done by Negro artisans. This was an understandable result of the fact that the warped reasoning and unhealthy social customs which accompanied slavery held that physical labor was demeaning to white men of "culture." "Poor whites" lived largely on land which had been exhausted by the wasteful system of slavery, finding this eking out of a miserable existence more in keeping with "white dignity" than learning and practicing a manual skill. Under such conditions, wresting a bare subsistence from the soil was a perpetually difficult task. Meanwhile Negro slaves were the carpenters, brick masons, blacksmiths, and workers in iron—the most notable of their work in that metal being the exquisite, lacelike ironwork of New Orleans, Louisiana, and Charleston, South Carolina.

But when slaves were transformed into freedmen, employers refused to hire them except for menial jobs or, when they were employed at their skills, paid them lower wages than those of white workers. Fear of Negro competition and consequent hostility among white workers was everywhere. Thus the National Labor Union—except for a few of its leaders such as William Sylvis, who argued against the color bar because it is "a sheer impossibility to degrade one class of laborers without degrading all"—was as hostile to black labor as were employers.

Meantime the world-wide search for raw materials needed by the industrial revolution was having its impact on the attitude of the organized European labor movement toward colored workers in the colonies. This new colonialism on a gigantic world scale, particularly after the partitioning of Africa among European nations following the Franco-Prussian War, led to fear among the white workers of Europe and America that their own standards of wages would be jeopardized through competition with miserably paid workers in Asia, Africa, and the West Indies. Thus an alliance of interests came into being between employers and employed against "colonial" workers. This is illustrated by England's refusal to permit the manufacture of cloth from native cotton in places like India, since this would have lessened employment of mill workers in England. The world trend of union organization of workers in their own interests was thus influenced by the economic philosophy of employers who used the color line to frighten and weaken white labor and to keep black, brown, and yellow labor at the bottom of the ladder.

Exclusion from the National Labor Union moved Negroes to

form in 1869 the National Colored Union, which in some respects anticipated by forty years formation of the NAACP. The new organization did not concentrate on the problems of Negro workers alone, nor did it confine itself solely to trade-union issues. Unlike its white counterpart, it opened its doors to all workers regardless of race or religion. It advocated what had never existed in the South for either whites or Negroes—public education for all citizens regardless of color. It sought equality before the law and a homestead act to provide land for the emancipated slaves. Isaac Meyers, energetic and courageous organizer and president of the union, traveled throughout the South, often in the face of threats from the Ku Klux Klan, forming local units and opposing exclusion of white Southerners from the union as vigorously as he advocated that all workers join it. Although the National Colored Union eventually failed, as a result of pressures and fear, it set during its brief history a wiser pattern of trade-union organization than any other union of its era.

Possibly because of the program of the National Colored Union, the Knights of Labor, which was organized in Philadelphia in 1869, and soon replaced the extinct National Labor Union, adopted and pursued a markedly more liberal position toward Negroes. While it, of course, did not wipe out the color line, it did succeed through energetic idealism in organizing craftsmen and dock workers in a number of Southern cities, and it narrowed the breach between white and Negro workers in other places. But the Knights of Labor also failed to last, primarily because the craftsmen in the union eventually took control and established an "aristocracy of labor," with control and special privileges for themselves as self-appointed "aristocrats." This philosophy was destined for many decades to dominate the Knights of Labor's successor, the American Federation of Labor.

Another and equally potent cause of the collapse of the Knights of Labor was the organized opposition to it caused by its success in unionizing upwards of seven hundred thousand members, of whom some sixty thousand were Negroes. Between the depression of 1873

and the 1887 Haymarket Riot in Chicago, employers and government agencies united to destroy the Knights by labeling them
anarchists and using organized violence against the union.

Samuel Gompers, who rose from the position of penniless immi-
grant to become the most successful labor leader up to his time,
and other founders of the AFL in 1886, began that organization
with lip service to the principle of non-discrimination. But it was
not long before it launched an attack on the Knights of Labor for
organizing unskilled workers, many of whom were immigrants
or Negroes, and permitted its constituent unions to include constitutional or ritualistic provisions in their by-laws to exclude all
but the "white aristocrats" of labor.

The AFL's difficult struggles following the depression of 1907,
the violent opposition it encountered after World War I, and the
disastrous failure of the steel strike in 1919 (lost by the AFL partly
because of Negro strike-breakers who had been denied membership
by some of the unions participating in this joint effort) did not alter
the union's anti-Negro policy. Nor did the depression of 1921-22,
the widespread use of violence against trade unions—which spread
dangerously during the twenties—or even the stock-market crash
of 1929, which brought on the greatest unemployment crisis in history, cause the AFL to alter to any material degree its racial policy.

Meanwhile the workers in mass-production industries such as
steel, automobiles, aircraft, electrical appliances, fertilizers, tobacco
processing, meat-packing, garment making, and the needle trades
grew greatly in number. The great migration of Negroes from the
South and their entrance into Northern industry accentuated their
very great need for organization as an effective means of helping
them rise above the unskilled or semi-skilled ranks. They were the
worst off of all Americans during the dark days following the stock-
market crash of 1929 and the mass unemployment of the thirties.
Their voices were almost alone in the demand for civil rights and
economic opportunity for Negroes.

The first real hope came with the establishment of such agencies
as the National Industrial Recovery Act and other legislation

of the Franklin Roosevelt administration—particularly the Wagner Act—which protected the rights of workingmen to organize and collectively bargain. Close behind in importance was the formation in 1935 of the Congress of Industrial Organizations, which ended the monopoly of the AFL, after the latter had voted against organizing industrial unions to bring into the organized-labor movement vast numbers of workers hitherto excluded.

From its inception under the presidency of John L. Lewis, and throughout the expansion under Philip Murray and Walter Reuther, the CIO has consistently and aggressively campaigned for civil-rights legislation and has vigorously fought discrimination within its own ranks as well as in the nation as a whole. This has been most marked at the national level. Many local unions bow to the racial mores of their communities, but numerous crackdowns by the CIO steadily decrease the number of locals that draw the color line.

Faced with a successful rival, the AFL began to alter its policies. Legal decisions forced certain AFL and independent railway unions to modify practices of discrimination against Negroes. All but a few unions, such as the railway unions and some of the AFL building-and-construction unions, today welcome Negro members. They have done so not only as a matter of ethics but for very sound reasons of enlightened self-interest—it doesn't pay to deny membership to a tenth of the nation's citizens. The American labor movement is far from perfect as yet in its racial attitudes. But it has learned the truth of what the Knights of Labor proclaimed eighty-five years ago when, referring to the racial issue, it declared: "An injury to one is the concern of all."

Today two million Negroes belong to unions, approximately one-eighth of the total membership of the AFL and the CIO. They have become an integral part of the unions' growth, even as their own status is being steadily improved by membership. Their role in union growth was responsible for the late William Green's vigorous support of a fair-employment-practices law and the strong position on civil rights and the abolition of racial barriers by George Meany, successor to Mr. Green as President of the AFL. Negroes have played their part in the uncompromising stand for civil-rights legislation taken by CIO leaders such as Philip Murray, Walter Reuther, David McDonald, James Carey, Emil Rieve, Arthur Goldberg, Sidney Hillman, and Jacob Potofsky. Both the AFL and CIO participated in the Leadership Conference on Civil Rights, the cooperating organization of fifty-four national organizations that today campaigns for needed civil-rights legislation.

Both the CIO and the AFL have filed friend-of-the-court briefs and given financial as well as moral support to many of the court victories of the past decade against educational, residential, and other segregation. Both organizations have supported federal, state, and municipal legislation against discrimination in employment, lynching, poll taxes, and discrimination in housing. The CIO maintains an active department, which is generously financed, to combat discrimination. The Philip Murray Memorial Fund made a grant of seventy-five thousand dollars to the NAACP to aid in its implementation of the Supreme Court's decision against educational segregation. The AFL Federation of Teachers has repeatedly gone on record in unequivocal support of abolition of racial segregation, not only in schools, but in all its own local unions.

It would be foolish to maintain that every member of the CIO and the AFL is in total agreement with these actions. But it is of great significance that today the repeatedly affirmed policies of both major unions are militantly against discrimination and segregation. There is still much to be done to break down racial barriers, especially in the South. There are still too many segregated locals, and too many devices that facilitate discrimination on the basis of race, religion, or place of birth in hiring, referrals, upgrading, and assignment to jobs. But it is both safe and just to say that, in the fight for civil rights and human equality, the organized-labor movement has moved faster and farther during the past twenty years than has any other major segment of the American population. Some of the effects of this progress are reported in Chapter IV of this book, which discusses the Negro's generally bettered employment status.

It took seven decades for the labor movement to shake off its prejudices and to realize that as long as Negro labor was denied its rights white labor could never be free. But the past two decades have seen greater growth and progress by labor unions on the rights of minorities than has any earlier period in American history. What effect the merger of the CIO and the AFL may have on the issue is problematical, once the rivalry that puts moral pressure on both is ended. But the large and growing number of Negroes actually participating in the labor movement, the increasing devotion to the principle of equality, not only at the level of leadership, but also within the membership itself, and the pressures on the United States as a whole of the world-wide struggle between democracy and communism will all contribute to continuation of organized labor's fight against racial and religious bigotry.

IX. Sunday at Eleven

"Never is our city more segregated than on Sunday morning at eleven," a friend said to me in Washington recently. Unfortunately this is still true, not only in Washington, but across the nation. One might think that the Christian Church, which teaches the doctrine of the brotherhood of all men enunciated by Jesus, would lead in the march of enlightenment that is slowly raising the American Negro from the inferior status to which white Jim Crow practices have assigned him. But this is not the case. In no American institution, except in the diehard segregated schools of the most reactionary of the Southern states, has separation of Negroes and whites been more widespread than in the Church. But even here the color line is cracking.

During the era of slavery all manner of convolutions of doctrine and accommodations of principle were used to justify human bondage. To answer the arguments of troubled Christians concerning slavery, theologians argued—and succeeded in translating their justifications of slavery into law—that importation from Africa of black slaves to Christian America made it easier for slave masters to teach to African barbarians the tenets of Christianity.

When logic demanded that slaves therefore ought to be given their freedom as soon as they became Christians, defenders of the slave interests sought and secured enactment of laws which held that a slave's conversion to Christianity did not change his status, since continuation of his bondage enabled his owner to continue Christian instruction.

Such a heritage of perversion of Christian principle has haunted the Church in the United States ever since. Rigid racial segregation in churches and in church institutions such as hospitals, schools, and community houses became the rule in both white and Negro denominations. There were few exceptions to the practice.

But during the 1930s the Race Relations Committee of the Federal Council of Churches instituted an annual exchange of pulpits between white and Negro ministers. Literature on the subject of race for use in church schools, women's missionary societies, and church organizations was distributed. After World War II, as the world-wide nature of the race question became more evident to Americans, various denominations began to pass resolutions and to speak out more firmly against the anomaly and the contradiction of segregated religion.

Not until the pressures of court decisions and world pressures of opinion on the issue were exerted, however, did a discernible crack begin to appear in the wall of church segregation. After the United States Supreme Court ruled in cases against the universities of Texas and Oklahoma that prospective students could not be barred from graduate schools and professional schools of tax-supported institutions solely because of race or color, many church schools began to examine their own practices. When the Episcopal University of the South at Sewanee, Tennessee, invited the Very Reverend James Pike, Arkansas-born Dean of the Cathedral of St. John the Divine in New York City, to deliver the commencement address and receive an honorary degree in 1951, Dean Pike vigorously and publicly declined the invitation and the degree, declaring that he wanted no part of "white Christianity." The nationwide publicity given this incident resulted in admission of Negroes to the university's School of Theology shortly afterward.

In St. Louis, Archbishop Joseph E. Ritter ordered all Catholic parochial schools to be opened to Negro children in 1950. When church members threatened legal action to maintain segregation, Archbishop Ritter served notice that any person who participated in such action would be excommunicated. The rebellion collapsed. In April 1953 Bishop Vincent Waters, at Raleigh, North Carolina, ordered the merger of two Catholic churches, one white and the other Negro, located one hundred yards apart. He stood adamant against protests of white communicants and two months later issued a letter declaring that racial segregation would no longer be tolerated in the diocese and that, "All special churches for Negroes will be abolished immediately." Negro Catholics became integrated in the "white" Catholic churches without incident. In 1954, shortly before the Supreme Court handed down its sweeping anti-segregation decision, Archbishop James Lucey of San Antonio, Texas, ordered immediate integration of all Catholics—Negro, Mexican-American, and so forth—in churches, schools, and other church institutions of the diocese.

Catholic University of America and Georgetown University, in Washington, D.C., have for some years admitted students on the basis of qualification instead of race, as has Washington University in St. Louis, Missouri.

But unfortunately the record of several other Catholic prelates and laymen has not been so advanced. During the destructive rioting at Cicero, Illinois, in 1951 a majority of the rioters were Catholic men, women, and youths, some of whom wore emblems indicating their religious faith. Many of them had fled Nazi or Communist persecution in Europe to find refuge in the United States. The same situation existed in 1953 and 1954 during the rioting at Trumbull Park Homes, a housing project in Chicago constructed and owned by the federal government. Without effect were efforts to persuade Samuel Cardinal Stritch to speak out publicly, if only to remind his communicants of the Pope's encyclicals about race prejudice and the edict of the Society for the Propagation of the Faith that hate of another person because of color is a mortal sin.

Catholic priests, chiefly those of Polish extraction, were actively anti-Negro in the Sojourner Truth Housing rioting in Detroit in the early 1940s and in racial clashes in Gary, Indiana, and other Middle Western industrial communities. In these areas friction arising when Negroes moved into public and private housing transcended religious principle.

What of the fifty-six million American Protestants who belonged to churches of various denominations in 1954? Less than half of one per cent of American Negroes, the Intergroup Relations Commission reported to the World Council, customarily worshiped with white Christians in non-segregated churches. This pattern of almost total segregation was the basis—or excuse—for exclusion of Negroes from at least one Southern church school, whose president stated in 1953: "I have no personal objections to admitting students of any color or creed," and: "The administration would be in favor of admitting Negroes if the Churches of Christ accepted them into regular congregational membership."

Another Southern church college reported: "Prevailing opinion is that local supporters of the college would withdraw their support were a Negro to be admitted. The college is not sufficiently secure financially to survive without this support."

Another institution replied to a questionnaire from the National Council of Churches: "We have no definite plans for admitting Negroes. We have said that we might begin to permit Negro day students, but we would begin there and not permit Negro dormitory students until the community accepted the first idea."

Still another church-college president, somewhat more courageous, answered: "We have no regulation against the admission of Negro students. We have not had applications from Negroes. Although their admission might create some problems, we would nevertheless live up to our Christian profession and act on such an application in the same way in which we would act on the application of a white student."

One of the curious anomalies that is increasingly frequent in some of these church-supported schools is their willingness to accept Indian, Chinese, Pakistani, Burmese, and other foreign students with non-white skins, while maintaining the color bar against native-born American Negroes. This is partly due to the state laws which prohibited whites and Negroes from attending the same schools— until they were held to be unconstitutional in 1954—but which were not always interpreted as applying to dark-skinned students from outside the United States.

Neither local laws nor local prejudices could stop at least some integration, however, once court decisions and moral pressures began to take effect. By 1953, 59 church-supported white Southern colleges out of 116 which answered an inquiry by the National Council of Churches reported 311 students of racial minority groups who were permanent residents of the United States. Integration in reverse was indicated by the presence of more than 200 white students in previously all-Negro colleges. Of the 59 hitherto all-white private colleges, 58 Negroes were enrolled in 6 of them; 13 Japanese-Americans in 9 colleges; 13 Chinese-Americans in 13 colleges; 33 Indian-Americans in 17 colleges; 124 Mexican-Americans in 16 colleges; and 31 Puerto Rican students in 21 colleges. The total of all these constituted only about one-seventh of the Negro students enrolled in the state graduate schools and professional schools of the South. But the number did indicate that the gap between Christian principle and practice was beginning to close in church schools, if not in the churches themselves.

Decided impetus to the trend was given by the Supreme Court's anti-segregation decision. Nine thousand delegates to the annual convention of the Southern Baptists voted for a resolution pledging compliance with the court's decree, with less than fifty voting against it. In a movingly dramatic and spontaneous fashion, the audience rose to its feet when the vote was announced. All sang fervently the old missionary hymn, "He Leadeth Me."

Even before the Supreme Court made its momentous decision on desegregation in the schools, thirteen church-related or private educational institutions, twelve Protestant theological seminaries, and twenty-one Catholic institutions located in Southern or border states abandoned racial segregation. These changes, as reported in "The Negro and the Schools," a Ford Foundation survey directed by Harry S. Ashmore, editor of the Little Rock, Arkansas, *Gazette*, were made "even though they are presumably beyond the reach of court action. . . .

"This is, of course, only a small percentage of the total of about 700,000 students enrolled annually in Southern institutions of higher education between 1948 and 1952," the report adds. But, "Even so, the presence of this comparative handful of Negroes in these institutions represents a significant change in the long-standing educational pattern in the United States."

After the court ruled, various Southern religious denominations acted swiftly to pledge compliance with the decision, with particular emphasis on their own schools. At a meeting in Montreat, North Carolina, on May 29, 1954—twelve days after the anti-segregation decision was handed down—the Southern Presbyterian Church in a 236-to-169 vote called upon its 3776 churches to open their membership rolls to all individuals regardless of race, and voted that "all of the church's institutions of higher education be operated on a non-segregated basis."

Ten days before the court ruled, the Board of Social and Economic Relations of the Methodist Church, second numerically only to the Baptists in the South, voted: "There is no place in the Methodist Church for racial discrimination or racial segregation," and reaffirmed the 1952 General Conference recommendation: "That the institutions of the church, local churches, colleges, universities, theological schools, hospitals, and homes carefully restudy their policies and practices as they relate to race, making certain that these policies are Christian."

The National Council of Church Women, representing some ten million Protestants, the Congregational-Christian Church, and a number of regional and local divisions of various denominations went on record either before or after the court decision for calm acceptance and orderly compliance with the decree. Although, of course, many individual members of these churches do not agree with the new order ordained by the court, the pledges of compliance by the governing bodies of the churches will have great effect in staying the bigots, in maintaining order, and in opening up to Negroes both church-related and tax-supported schools.

In some individual churches the issue has been faced squarely by courageous ministers who have refused to preach Christianity and practice racial bigotry any longer. One of these is the Reverend Henry Hitt Crane, famous minister of the Central Methodist Church on Detroit's Woodward Avenue. Throughout his pastorate in Detroit, Dr. Crane has steadily and quietly worked to welcome Negroes and to overcome whatever opposition existed among white members. Negroes sing in the choir, serve on various church boards and committees, and are employed by the church.

One of the leading members of the church, with some acerbity in his voice, told Dr. Crane that he did not mind a few Negroes in the church, but that the number had grown too large, and he intended to take it up at the next meeting of the board of trustees. Dr. Crane met the issue head on.

"If you want to raise this issue with the members of the official board, I will recognize you and give you the privilege of the floor, for this church is run democratically. But I think I ought to tell you what I shall do the moment you are through speaking," he warned. "When you have concluded your remarks, before I allow anyone else to speak, I am going to ask five men to follow me in a period of prayer. The six of us will then pray for you, that the prejudice which is poisoning you may be extirpated, and that you may become an honest-to-goodness Christian. And this I will guarantee—that you are going to be prayed for as you have never been prayed for in your life before—and I think God will answer those prayers quite promptly."

Startled at the reaction his threat had produced, the objector was thoughtful for a moment, and then told Dr. Crane, "Well, if you didn't want me to bring it up, why didn't you say so? Let's drop the whole matter." And he turned and walked away.

Dr. Crane was certain that he would lose a valued member. He didn't. "He is still with us," the minister told me, "and he has radically changed his attitude. We have never heard another derogatory comment concerning our policy."

An outstanding example of frontal approach to the issue of the color line in the Church is that of the Right Reverend Richard Emrich, Bishop of the Diocese of Michigan of the Protestant Episcopal Church. In June 1952 he addressed a pastoral letter to every clergyman in the diocese which is so forthright that it merits quotation and emulation. It read:

I have been requested for the sake of complete clarity among all the people of the Diocese, to write a few words at this time on the Church's relationship to the various races of the earth.

In order that we may reason correctly, let us state first that the Church is under the authority of Christ, and is here on earth to do His will. He came to save not just a part of mankind but the world, and to restore men to fellowship in Him. His Church is, therefore, a universal Church, with its missionary work in the ends of the earth. The Church is not the Church of any one race, class, or nation. It is God's family. Every Parish and Mission is in its location the representative of the universal Church, and all peoples of every kindred, nation, and tongue, are welcome in its fold.

There is not the slightest justification in Scripture or in the Prayer Book for drawing up national, class, or racial lines. I ask all members of the Diocese to remember that we did not create the faith of our fathers, but are at the moment its trustees, and to obey in this matter the will of God and the mighty tradition of the Christian Church. All people are to be welcomed in every Parish and Mission of the Diocese of Michigan.

I ask the Clergy of the Diocese to assume this in all that they do, and to stand firm against all forces in the community which would tend to keep the Church from fulfilling its great reconciling task.

Here is Bishop Emrich's story of what has been quietly happening both before and since his pastoral letter.

"Most of our downtown Detroit churches are now at least partly bi-racial. The most outstanding example of what can be accomplished is Grace Church under the rectorship of the Reverend Elden B. Mowers. This church now has a white rector and a Negro curate. Three members of the vestry are colored, nine white. The organist and choir director are Negroes, as are two members of the choir. Although the church is seventy-five per cent white, there are eighty colored children in the Sunday school, and the church's organizations such as the Girls' Friendly Society are set up on a bi-racial pattern. Other churches, such as St. Mary's, have voted to follow the example of integration which Grace Church has established. What holds us back often is not so much prejudice as the inertia of society."

These are, to be sure, isolated cases. The Protestant Churches of America as a whole can scarcely be said to offer convincing proof that organized Christianity believes in human equality. But the number of religious leaders who believe and act as Dr. Crane and Bishop Emrich have done is increasing, and the time cannot be far off when it will be a commonplace for Negroes and whites to gather without distinction in the armies of the Prince of Peace, as they now do in those dedicated to the armed defense of America.

X. The Negro
in the Public Eye

The nature and extent of the changes that have taken place in the picture of the American Negro given the public by newspapers, magazines, cartoons, comic strips, radio, television, the theater, moving pictures, and books is best seen by contrast.

Twenty years ago most newspapers, Northern as well as Southern, consistently featured the race of any Negro accused or suspected of crime. In 1955 a majority of American newspapers were presenting news about Negroes and other racial minorities, unfavorable and favorable, without racial tags.

As recently as the early 1930s a distressingly high percentage of newspapers, especially in the rural South, defended editorially, either explicitly or implicitly, lynching and other forms of mob violence, particularly if there was a charge that a white woman had been raped by a Negro. Today no more than a very small handful of publications would justify or condone lynching or bomb slayings. More affirmatively, the American press has denounced mob violence with increasing vigor.

A major factor in this trend, particularly in states where such violence was once habitual, has been the unremitting campaign for federal anti-lynching legislation. It became safe as well as practical to write that unless the states acted to curb lynching, the federal government would inevitably do so. Another reason for change has been the consciousness of harm done to American prestige and security through use by Soviet, British, and other news agencies of reports of racial and religious bigotry in the United States. A third and possibly the most potent of all reasons is the increasing maturity of the press on certain social problems, the race question being among those on which such growth has been most marked.

During the same period two interesting developments have taken place in the Negro press. An increasing amount of space has been devoted to constructive action against racial segregation, although, as in the white press, exaggerated emphasis was given to sensational stories of crime and sex. When the Supreme Court in June 1953 ordered re-argument of the school-segregation cases, Negro newspapers united in a campaign to raise funds and gave an unprecedented amount of space in their news columns, editorials, and free advertisements to the issue.

The second significant development has been the steadily increasing attention to the struggle for freedom in the West Indies, Africa, and Asia. Kwame Nkrumah in the Gold Coast, Nnamdi Azikiwe in Nigeria, Alan Paton and Z. K. Matthews in South Africa, Jomo Kenyatta in Kenya, and other fighters for justice for Africans became almost as familiar to readers of the Negro press as those who were working against proscription in the United States. But the news coverage was not limited to black men. More and more there was understanding of the fact that, although the immediate circumstances varied, there was a degree of identity of interests between colored peoples all over the world who were struggling to throw off the yoke of white supremacy and its attendant evils.

When radio and, later, television entered the business of public information they did so unencumbered by the barnacles of racial traditions, as did commercial aviation when it began to compete with railroads. All three had to buck tremendous opposition to attract enough paying customers to survive. In commercial aviation the frequent crashes of the early days made it imperative for the airlines to fill as many seats as possible. Race, creed, or color didn't matter, as long as the passenger had the money to pay for his ticket. Since many Negroes hated and sought to avoid Jim Crow travel, from the beginning they formed an important market for the airlines, which were prudent enough to refrain from segregation even in the deepest South.

Similarly, radio and television sought to attract as many listeners and purchasers of sets as possible. As fledglings in industry, they were not saddled with ancient practices and prejudices, as were newspapers. Moreover, a very high percentage of executives, writers, broadcasters, and technicians were younger, more imaginative, and more venturesome than their opposite numbers in the newspaper business. Therefore in the handling of news the new industries tended to be more objective and more sensitive to protests against racial or religious stereotyping.

This does not mean that many and grievous mistakes were not made or are not still being made by both radio and television. Caricatures of the Negro such as "Amos 'n Andy" and the "Beulah" show continue to appear. Opportunity to perform in roles on the sole basis of ability instead of being restricted to Negro characters is still denied in large part to competent Negroes. Until recently there were practically no Negroes employed as cameramen, script writers, directors, or in other technical capacities; but within the past two years the National Broadcasting Company, the Columbia Broadcasting System, and a number of independent stations have increased the number of Negro employees holding responsible jobs, with steadily expanding opportunity ahead of them.

No disparagement is intended in pointing out that such policies were recognized as sound business when responsible trade papers and weekly magazines published facts and figures showing that the purchasing power of the American Negro had grown to fifteen billion dollars a year. One of the results: in 1954 there were more than three hundred radio stations beamed directly at the Negro market. The quality of program provided by some of them was excellent. One such station—WLIB in New York City—won the 1953 *Variety* magazine award for service to the community. Others provided mediocre fare for their listeners, while a few were guilty of poor taste in their emphasis on *double entendre* music and jokes. But the attention these stations and the networks have given to the Negro and the Negro market is beginning to provide a truer concept of America's largest and most maligned minority.

The programs of CBS's great commentators, Edward R. Murrow and Eric Sevareid, provide excellent examples of how the magical medium of television has helped to wipe out stereotypes and replace them with a more intelligent and accurate portrait of what the Negro really is. In the highly successful weekly television program, "Person to Person," on which Mr. Murrow visits two guests each Friday night, he has shown America the homes and families of famous American Negroes such as Ralph Bunche, Nobel Prize-winner and Under-Secretary of the United Nations; Roy Campanella, Brooklyn Dodgers catcher and 1953's Most Valuable Player of the National League; Joe Louis, ex-heavyweight champion of the world; and others representative of the varied strata of human life. As the Supreme Court deliberated on its decision on school segregation, Mr. Murrow devoted one of his "See It Now" programs to picturing how unequal the separate schools of a small Louisiana town actually were. Following his historic telecast on Senator Joseph McCarthy, Mr. Murrow revealed the story of Mrs. Annie Lee Moss, the Negro government worker who was accused by McCarthy of Communist party membership.

In all these programs Mr. Murrow maintained his role of the objective, bias-free reporter. At no time did he indicate any motive other than recognition of the Negro as an important, integral part of the American scene. The result set an example and a standard of reporting that has not yet been matched.

Radio and television have not, of course, been consistently courageous. Sometimes they have yielded to the pressures of bigots.

on many controversial issues. Upon occasion programs dealing with the Negro carried over Southern stations have been submitted on closed circuits and withdrawn when protests were made. But when Governor Talmadge of Georgia blasted the famous Mariners' Quartet, composed of two white singers and two Negro singers, Arthur Godfrey and CBS "told off" the Georgia governor bluntly and continued the Mariners as important stars on both the Godfrey television and radio programs. It seems that Talmadge believed— or said he believed—that the appearance of an interracial quartet, even an all male one, on the television screen constituted "social equality" and endangered Georgia's white supremacy!

There were also protests, though not many, against Negro major-league baseball players' being televised on Southern screens. Obviously, individual players could not be eliminated from the telecast; the alternative would have been no television of World Series games. The protests were ignored. It became increasingly difficult in 1955 to perpetuate theories of racial inferiority, physical or otherwise, as the new media of information improved their techniques, programs, and racial practices.

Except for a brief period between 1948 and 1951, the moving-picture industry has trailed far behind other educational and entertainment media in contributing to an America more free of racial bias. The fear that had plagued it from its inception—that Southern audiences would not accept Negroes in any roles other than as menials or comedians—was accentuated by the competition of television and the loss of some of the industry's foreign markets. During the last years of his life Wendell Willkie made several trips to Hollywood, on two of which I accompanied him, to urge the film industry to show more courage and imagination in the handling of roles of dark-skinned minorities. He pointed out the incalculable harm that continued picturization of Negroes, Asians, Africans, and Latin Americans as either savages, criminals, or mental incompetents was doing both abroad and in the United States.

There are many men and women of courage and integrity in the film industry, a number of them my close personal friends. They are highly sensitive to the damage done by racial stereotypes. Among them are writers, directors, executives, actors, actresses, technicians, and publicists. Their reaction to Mr. Willkie's plea to discard harmful conventional treatment of the Negro was immediate and favorable. The more flagrantly offensive stereotypes were almost immediately eliminated from films. Beginning in 1948, a number of pictures that were forthright and a sharp departure from previous treatment were made by major film companies such as Metro-Goldwyn-Mayer and Twentieth Century-Fox, and by independent producers. Several of these films were excellent and, contrary to Hollywood's fears, made money and were enthusiastically received in all but a few backward Southern communities. The trend continued through 1952, when shrinking markets, television, and McCarthyism (in its creation of an atmosphere where anyone who believed in equal rights for Negroes must *ipso facto* be a "Communist") caused the following verdict to be written into the annual balance sheet of group relations issued by the American Jewish Congress and the NAACP:

The movie industry, which produced several pictures dealing expressly with intergroup problems during the immediate postwar years, has failed to continue this trend. No such pictures were produced during 1953. Stereotyping of Negroes and other minority groups in the movies, radio, and television decreased, though the practice has far from ended.

Two decades ago just about the only serious treatment of the Negro in magazines was to be found in an occasional article in publications directed toward the highly literate, such as *Harper's*, the *Atlantic Monthly*, the *Nation*, the *New Republic*, the old *American Mercury*, and the learned quarterlies published by universities. Even these but rarely varied from discussion of the Negro except as one so disadvantaged as to be an object of solicitude, whose problems could be ameliorated only by the slow processes of education over an interminable number of years, decades, generations, or even centuries. Publication in *Harper's* in the late 1920s of articles by the late James Weldon Johnson about the actual as well as the potential political power of the Negro—which has been amply proved since—elicited a weird assortment of scornful, unbelieving, and even indignant comments. An article I wrote for the same magazine in 1931, "The Negro and the Communists," about the Scottsboro case, aroused almost as much incredulity in its assertion that colored people were sapient enough to see through Communist designs to use the Negro race for their own ends.

When the mass-circulation magazines of that era noticed the Negro at all it was almost invariably as a quaint, lovable, not-too-bright character in a story by Octavus Roy Cohen or Irvin Cobb. About the only variation was an article by a frenetic exponent of a pre-Nazi ideology based on the theories of Gobineau warning against inundation of the white world by hordes of barbaric black, brown, and yellow peoples.

Two decades have witnessed a remarkable, even a revolutionary, change. There are far fewer articles by apologists for the South's treatment of the Negro pleading that the "South be left alone to solve its problems of segregation in its own way." Southern writers such as Hodding Carter continue to find markets for articles claiming that the reforms of Southern attitude are due wholly to some miraculous moral reformation and not to the pressures of court decisions and public opinion. But these apologies for a passing order have become less frequent both in the magazines whose circulations run weekly or fortnightly into three or more millions and in those of more limited circulation which are read by the formulators of public opinion at a different level. *The Saturday Evening Post*, for example, published twenty-three articles in a period of slightly more than two years, between 1952 and 1954, expressing varied aspects and points of view regarding the Negro question. *Life* magazine spotlighted in text and pictures affirmative as well as negative actions on the color question in the United States, the Union of South Africa, the Caribbean, and Asia. *Time* magazine and *Newsweek* rarely appear without at least one item dealing with the issue of race, whether it be of progress or setback. *Time* devoted extensive research to the preparation of a comprehensive report, "The U.S. Negro—1953," which, barring a few errors of interpretation, was an excellent report of progress and of problems yet to be solved. *Look* magazine, *Reader's Digest, Collier's,* the *American Magazine, Redbook,* and the *Ladies' Home Journal* supplied their large readership with factual articles, fiction, and photographs which, with only a few exceptions, presented Negroes and members of other minorities fairly and objectively.

With the rise of civil rights as a political and legal issue as evidenced by the presidential campaigns of 1948 and 1952, the succession of cases argued before the Supreme Court and lower courts and the struggle for federal and state legislation, the leading law journals devoted increasing attention to the subject.

This new and increasing flood of articles based on fact instead of on outmoded concepts is making a significant contribution toward re-educating the public on the subject of race.

The same admirable trend is evident in book publication. I know of no book written by either a Negro or a white writer dealing with the race question, however frank in its condemnation of American treatment of Negroes, which was not published if it met the usual standards for publication applied by publishers to any manuscript. One reservation needs to be made: even now many of the established publishers prefer novels depicting the Negro as eternally the object of oppression, frustrated by his environment, and always ending up defeated. A novel whose leading character is a Bigger Thomas stands a better chance of becoming a best seller than one whose hero is a Ralph Bunche. This is said in full recognition of the fact that an outlaw, whatever his race or nationality, provides more dramatic material than does any character who lives within the law. But overemphasis in fiction on the seamy side of Negro life in the United States has served to perpetuate concepts that fit only a part of Negro America.

No such considerations affect factual books dealing with the Negro and his problems. During the past five years, in particular, the stream of excellent books, monographs, and pamphlets has continued to grow.

In 1949, for example, the major publishing firms published six novels and seventeen non-fiction books dealing with intergroup relations, by such authors as Lillian Smith, E. Franklin Frazier, Robert M. McIver, and Arnold Rose. In 1950 such firms published ten novels and nine non-fiction titles; in 1951 one novel and twenty-four non-fiction books; in 1952 seven novels, including Ralph Ellison's outstanding *Invisible Man*, and twenty non-fiction books, among them the excellent *South of Freedom* by Carl T. Rowan; in 1953 nine novels and twenty-three non-fiction titles.

These one hundred and twenty-six books published within five years do not include those issued by the smaller publishers, or the many studies, surveys, handbooks on civil rights, and other volumes, a number of them of book length, which were issued by government and other organizations concerned with the question. The over-all total of volumes of these books sold would run into several hundred thousand, which is a barometer of the mounting concern over the issue of human rights for minorities in the United States.

XI. Why Has the Negro Rejected Communism?

During a long-drawn-out filibuster in 1937 against a federal anti-lynching bill, in which slanderous and venomous attacks on the Negro had been made by United States senators from the South such as the late Senator Theodore G. Bilbo of Mississippi, I talked one day in the Senate wing of the Capitol with a wearied and somewhat discouraged senator from Massachusetts who was fighting for the measure. The senator was Henry Cabot Lodge, who later became spokesman for the United States on the Security Council of the United Nations.

"I sometimes wonder," Senator Lodge said, "why Negroes don't join the Communist party. If I were a Negro and had listened to the speech Bilbo just made, I am afraid I *would* become a Communist."

I reminded the troubled senator that the American Negro had learned to distrust and loathe dictatorship of all kinds. During two and a half centuries of human slavery in the United States slave owners had held dictatorial power of life and death over slaves. Since the Civil War, and particularly during the last half of the nineteenth century and the early part of the twentieth, the Negro, though technically, legally, and theoretically free, had known the grim realities of being unfree. He had been taught by cruel experience that power concentrated in the hands of an individual or a small clique almost invariably results in loss of freedom, however idealistic might be the proclaimed objectives and motives which dictators attribute to themselves.

That principle was put to a great test during the second and third decades of the twentieth century. During the 1920s the American Negro shared only to a limited extent the boom prosperity that preceded the stock-market crash of 1929. But he shared fully in the depression that followed. Last hired and first fired, the Negro suffered more than any other racial group during the worst depression the American economy has ever known. While it is true that he benefited from Roosevelt's New Deal, his share was not generally in proportion to his need.

In the South he was still largely disfranchised, and it was not until 1944, when the United States Supreme Court abolished disfranchisement by means of the so-called Democratic white primary, that he began to have a voice in either Southern or national affairs. Mob violence was rampant, ranging from lynching in the South to police brutality in Northern cities, especially in connection with eviction riots, when poverty-stricken Negroes were unable to pay rent even for slum dwellings. These riots were avidly seized upon by the Communists for propaganda purposes. Congress and the state legislatures used the technique of filibustering or of pigeonholing remedial legislation designed to relieve some of the major problems from which the Negro suffered. It was a period of despair, relieved only by the Negro's faith in the democratic process and by the few benefits from New Deal legislation that trickled down to him.

It is doubtful if in all human history more fertile soil has been provided for the propaganda of Communists or any other political philosophy promising betterment of a hard lot. Then as now the Kremlin ordered its followers to propagandize in every part of the world among the most disadvantaged group in each country. The American Communist party attempted to move in and take over the direction of justified Negro protests against legitimate grievances. Various segregated Communist subsidiary organizations were created, such as the League of Struggle for Negro Rights, the National Negro Congress, and similar groups, wherever Communist-party strategy ordered the creation of such units.

From the beginning Negroes were wary of most of these efforts to win their support for the Communist cause. Their skepticism would probably have continued in any case, but it was eventually increased by the history of the Communist party's connection with the Scottsboro case during the early 1930s, though the Communists temporarily gained a little ground as a result of that case.

Nine penniless Negro boys, ranging in age from fourteen to seventeen, were accused of rape by two white prostitutes dressed in men's clothing on a freight train in Alabama. A fight developed between the Negroes and a group of white male hoboes who also were riding the train. When some of the defeated white men appealed to the police, and the two complainants were found to be women, there was the usual demand for lynching or the swiftest sentencing of the Negroes to death.

The NAACP engaged the world-famous criminal lawyer, Clarence Darrow, of Chicago, along with Arthur Garfield Hays of New York and prominent local Southern attorneys to defend the seven Negro defendants when investigation established that they were wholly innocent of the crime.

The Communists sensed immediately that the case was ideal for propaganda *and fund-raising*. Using every tactic, scrupulous and otherwise, they initiated indefatigable efforts to capture control of the case. Relying upon the fact that all but one of the defendants and their parents or guardians were illiterate (a circumstance that is itself an indictment of the Southern segregated education system), they eventually succeeded in inducing the defendants to reject the defense provided for them by the NAACP and to turn over their cases to the International Labor Defense.

The story of the Scottsboro case is too well known to need repetition. Vast sums of money were raised for the defense all over the world, and no accounting has ever been made of the total raised or the purposes for which the money was spent.

Undoubtedly more harmful than the loose handling of funds was the effective use by Communists all over the world of the Scottsboro case to vilify American democracy and to create distrust of it, especially among the dark-skinned peoples of Asia, Africa, and Latin America. Sufficient for this account is the fact that the Communist tactics of threatening jurors and judges up to and including the justices of the United States Supreme Court, and all other methods, seemed to have been planned to ensure certain death for the defendants. They almost succeeded.

But Negroes were quick to realize that the Communists were not honestly interested in what happened to the individual and that it was a part of the Communist strategy to create "martyrs." Eventually the NAACP and other non-Communist organizations took over the almost hopeless case and ejected the Communists. There followed a long and often disheartening series of negotiations and legal actions, the former handled by Dr. Allan Knight Chalmers, at the time Pastor of the Congregationalist Broadway Tabernacle Church in New York and later Professor of Theology at Boston University. These efforts over a period of nineteen years brought about the release from prison of eight of the defendants. The ninth, who escaped and was not extradited, was in effect released also.

It was as logical as it was inevitable that some Negroes, despairing of justice under American democracy during the disheartening days of the Scottsboro case and other crises, joined the Communist party. But the number was far fewer than even Negroes themselves believed would be the case. Most of those who did join either the Communist party or one of its many front organizations soon became disillusioned when they discovered the ruthlessness of Communist practices and philosophy. These groups were more than willing to use Negroes as shock troops in their efforts to overthrow American democracy. But Negroes, by and large, were not willing to be used.

At the peak of its activity during the depth of the depression in the middle thirties, the Communist party enrolled an outside maximum of eight thousand Negroes out of the total Negro population, at that time, of fourteen million, according to Professor Wilson Record. By 1951 the number had shrunk to no more than five hundred. In 1954 less than one hundred remained as avowed party members out of a Negro population which had grown to more than fifteen million.

Their abysmal failure has baffled not only the Communists but many others who find it difficult to understand why the American Negro continues to have faith in the democratic process when that faith has so often proved unwarranted. Certainly the Communist failure cannot be ascribed to lack of effort. Not only have they raised vast and unaccounted sums from Negroes and others in behalf of various Negro issues, but large amounts of money, time, and effort have been concentrated on winning the Negro to communism in other ways. While the other American political parties have considered the problems of the Negro as being tangential or incidental at most, the Communist party since the middle twenties has made the Negro question one of its major planks.

Because other writers have written so extensively on the subject, notably Wilson Record in his brilliant *The Negro and the Communist Party* (North Carolina: University of North Carolina Press, 1951), I shall not repeat here the long succession of minor successes and major failures in the Communist campaign to woo and win the American Negro. Instead I wish to give in an approximate order of importance the major reasons why, despite the denials of democracy that he has found in the United States, the Negro has rebuffed attempts of the Communists to aid or use him in his fight for equality.

First and foremost is the fact already mentioned—that having known what "boss" rule means both during and since the era of slavery, the Negro wants no part of any system in which arbitrary power is vested in one man or a small clique of men. This revulsion against dictatorship applies to all forms of totalitarian rule, whether they be Communist, Dixiecrat, or any other.

The Negro's intense loyalty to democracy is a corollary of his dislike of over-rule. The following incident illustrates the deep devotion, born of bitter experience, that the Negro has for a free society.

One day during the famous Scopes evolution trial in Tennessee, Clarence Darrow had a conversation with a white Tennessean, who argued that the Negro had been better off and happier as a slave than he was as a free man. When Mr. Darrow voiced skepticism of the Tennessean's statement, the latter sought to prove his point by escorting Mr. Darrow over to an elderly Negro who had been a slave. Asked if he had not been better housed, fed, and cared for by his former owner, the ex-slave readily agreed that he had been. Triumphantly the Tennessean asked if he would not like to return to the security he had known in slave days.

Shaking his head in as vigorous dissent as his years and deference to the racial mores of a small Southern town permitted, the elderly Negro answered, "No, sir. There's a certain looseness about this freedom I like."

Thirty years later, the descendants of slaves have learned to regard even more highly that "certain looseness" of freedom. They want none of the regimentation of thought and action that the ruthless discipline of communism imposes.

The soundness of this distaste for dictatorship, whatever its proclaimed objectives, is demonstrated, in the Negro's reasoning, by the slow but steadily accelerated progress he has made in abolishing his status as a second-class citizen in what is at least officially a free society. Even as he realistically faces the fact that the task ahead of him is still considerable, he knows that he has come so far since the era of slavery, and particularly during the past decade, that his confidence in eventual total victory is justified.

The Negro knows that the tide of world history is flowing in his direction. Where once the white Western world looked with condescension if not disdain on so-called colored peoples of the world, today white people are beginning to realize that such a course can mean only destruction for the white as well as the colored world.

After two world wars the growing demands for freedom on the part of the peoples of Asia, Africa, and other parts of the globe can be no more denied than can those of the American Negro. Knowing this, the Negro is too wise to abandon a political system under which he has made noticeable gains for one under which the issue might be doubtful, at a time when his own demand for freedom is echoed throughout the world.

Another potent reason for the Communists' failure to enroll Negroes in their struggle to overthrow capitalism is their inexplicable program to establish the Negro in a "separate black republic" within the United States. However subservient to Moscow's directives the American Communist leaders are required to be, this major error of Communist strategy cannot wholly be blamed on Russia. Had the Communist theoreticians been less doctrinaire, they would have seen that the Negro's goal in the United States has always been integration and not separation from the main stream of American life and culture. Some of the more able and sincere Negroes who joined the Communists warned against the absurd concept of the "black-belt republic," with little effect. Periodically, when party strategy appeared to call for resurrection of the idea, it was brought forth again and again, although Negroes had laughed the whole idea into the realm of the ridiculous. It didn't fit into the plans they had made for reaching their goals.

It is possible that the basic condescension of white Americans in general toward Negroes played a part in creating the notion of a segregated area for Negroes in the "Soviet America" toward which the Communists were working, and in the stubborn adherence to the idea even against the advice of Communist Negroes. To this conception, put forth with the characteristic doctrinaire approach of zealots, was added the most annoying and at times infuriating attitude of the Communists that Negroes had never been able to do much to correct discrimination and therefore should be subserviently grateful to the Marxists for coming to their assistance. Along with many other mistakes made by the Communists, this thinly disguised condescension alienated intelligent Negroes.

Closely tied in with this was the smug conviction of many of the Communists that they had come up with something hitherto unknown—concerted and militant opposition to racial discrimination and segregation. Negroes themselves had fought these evils for generations, as far back as the slave revolts of the seventeenth, eighteenth, and nineteenth centuries. As I have already noted, the NAACP had been organized in 1909—eight years before the October Revolution in Russia—on a program of all-out opposition to every form of racial proscription, and other organizations—church, fraternal, social welfare—had been fighting over the years for the same objectives. Thus what seemed like an exciting new idea to the Communists was old stuff to Negroes. Often arrogant and presumptuous attacks on all those who did not obediently go along with the ideas of the Communists stiffened resistance and developed open hostility among those Negro organizations and individuals that the Communists were attempting to win.

Jackie Robinson, the first Negro to crack the color bar in organized baseball, voiced Negro opinion on this phase most accurately when he stated, "Negroes were stirred up long before there was a Communist party, and will stay stirred up long after the party has disappeared—unless Jim Crow has disappeared by then as well."

As I have pointed out, the peak of Negro membership in the Communist party was reached in the middle thirties, when the economic depression was at its worst. Those eight thousand members and some other Negroes who were lured into joining or contributing to innocent-appearing front organizations were then both stirred by the frenzied activities of the Communists and bitter against Americans who were putting forth all possible efforts to "keep the Negro in his place." But disillusion about the sincerity of purpose of the Communists, and growing conviction that theirs was a coldly calculated intent to use the Negro when it suited the Kremlin's needs and to drop him when it was deemed advantageous to communism, grew swiftly among Negroes.

The invasion of Ethiopia by Italy in 1935 made a deep impression on American Negroes. There was immediate and deep sympathy among them for Haile Selassie and the people of Ethiopia. This feeling rose to a crescendo when Italian aviators, including Mussolini's own son, strafed and bombed the defenseless Ethiopians. That sympathy was not merely racial. Since World War I American Negroes had been developing a profound interest in the victims of colonial exploitation wherever they lived, particularly if those victims were dark-skinned. They had followed with deep concern the struggle of the people of India against British rule; the seemingly hopeless efforts of Africans for freedom and against exploitation; and particularly the plight of West Indians, many of whom had fled from the shrinking sugar economy of the Caribbean to make their homes in the United States. (This migration, of course, antedated the McCarran immigration act, which established quotas based on national origin.)

With characteristic opportunism, the Communists plunged into efforts to organize and control American public support, with particular emphasis on the Negro. A united front was called for, to raise funds to give material aid to Ethiopia, to exert pressure by Negro, labor, and other organizations to stop shipment of oil and wheat from the United States, and to back the efforts of the USSR then being directed by Maxim Litvinov against "Italian aggression and imperialism at Geneva."

Emperor Haile Selassie's dramatic but futile appeal to the League of Nations aroused great admiration and enthusiasm, which was equaled only by the despair that followed the League of Nations' failure to stop Mussolini and thereby ended its own existence and laid the ground for World War II. Unfortunately for the American Communists, they were not informed by Moscow that simultaneously with Litvinov's denunciation of Italy, the Soviet Union was selling and shipping huge quantities of oil, wheat, coal tar, and other supplies to Italy, much of which was being delivered directly to Africa for use against the Ethiopians. Embarrassed efforts by the Communists to counteract publication of the facts in such respected newspapers as the *New York Times*, through saying that what served the interests of the USSR also contributed to the advancement of Ethiopians and of Negroes in the United States, brought ridicule, denunciation, and wholesale resignation of Negroes from Communist organizations. Negroes, like other human beings, do not relish being played for suckers.

Another event that caused defection of Negroes from the Communist cause was the abrupt reversal of party policy on the Negro when Hitler smashed the pact with Stalin made in 1939 and invaded Russia in 1941. Between 1939 and 1941 the American Communists had attacked the war against nazism as "phony" and "imperialist." In the process they had played up the Negro question to the hilt in the *Daily Worker*, innumerable pamphlets, and countless meetings.

Communist-party policy and strategy reversed themselves overnight when Hitler doublecrossed Stalin and attacked Russia. On no issue was the reversal so noticeable as the Negro question. While on the day before the attack, denial of justice and opportunity to the American Negro had been almost the number-one item on the agenda of the American Communist party, on the day after, the issue had been dropped completely, in subordination to the new party line that nothing, absolutely nothing, must be allowed to interfere with the new "holy war" against the nazis.

The tremendous growth of Negro participation in trade unions and the drastic expulsion of Communists from the trade-union movement have also contributed greatly to the Negro's rejection of communism. These two factors in American trade unionism are beyond all question two of the most important and dramatic aspects of the fight for democracy in the United States.

As Negroes came nearer and nearer to their goal of full participation in the American labor movement, the Communists were confident they could use Negro union members to carry the ball for them. A few of them did do so. The majority did not.

Communists have charged that the new concern for minority rights in the trade-union movement is due to the example they have set. In justice, there is a modicum of truth in their embittered and envious accusations. Most human beings act as human beings ought to act when there are compulsions to do so. But the fact that the

labor unions of the United States are maturing on the basic issue of
equality of human beings has taken away from the Communists one
of their major appeals.

A final factor is the disappearance from the American scene of
"nationalist" movements among Negroes such as the Marcus Garvey Universal Negro Improvement Association, which was active
during and immediately following World War I. During a brief
period Garvey's grandiose plans for a Negro repatriation empire
in Africa caught the imagination of many disadvantaged and frustrated American Negroes. Collapse of the Garvey bubble had at
least one virtue—it made it clear that this vision of escape for the
Negro from his problems in the United States was pure illusion. He
awoke to the grim fact that he was not a hyphenated American but,
more truly than most, one whose roots were inextricably planted in
American soil. Various projects for the transfer of Negroes to
Africa had been proposed for more than a century. The first of
these was the one of pre-Civil War days, when the African Coloni-
zation Society was organized to send Negroes to Liberia. This
scheme had the blessing of Abraham Lincoln, among others. Other
plans that followed were ardently racial, with elements of fanatic
"black nationalism," which, fitting somewhat loosely into the Communist concept of a separate black republic, caused the Communists
to attempt to capture control of what remained of the Garvey
movement and the proposed creation of a forty-ninth state for Negroes somewhere in the United States.

Once again the Communists failed to gauge correctly the trend
of Negro thinking. In quite remarkable fashion, the more the
American Negro learned about the struggles of oppressed peoples
all over the world, the more firmly did he become an American.
Malan's antediluvian *apartheid* campaign in South Africa to establish
total segregation of the native population created much sympathy
and support for its African victims, and simultaneously it intensified
the American Negro's determination to wipe out racial segregation
in the United States. From pulpits, in barbershops and restaurants
and living rooms, in the Negro press and in classrooms, in programs

and resolutions of Negro civil-rights organizations, church, and other groups, came ever-increasing expressions of concern with the social revolutions in Asia, Africa, and Latin America against colonial exploitation and racism. But with this growth of knowledge and widening of horizons, the American Negro thought of himself and the role he might play in a swiftly changing world as an American and not, in Communist ideology, as a member of a separate-but-equal group.

These are the major reasons why the Communists have met defeat in their attempt to take over the direction and control of the amply justified protests by America's largest and most exploited minority. The most concrete roadblock in the Party's way has been the NAACP. Its record of unremitting, uncompromising attack on every proscription based on race, for almost half a century, has earned for it the faith of both Negro and white Americans. It was to destroy that faith that the Communists in the Scottsboro and other cases unleashed their most savage and sustained efforts. Leaders of the NAACP were subject to vilification and the most fantastic campaign of lies by the Communists, but through the widespread repudiation of these blatant falsehoods, the NAACP has been strengthened and enlarged.

The association's program has not been one of passive acceptance of abuse. Its national Board of Directors and staff have been empowered and directed to revoke the charter of any of the organization's thirteen hundred branches should any such local unit come under the control or influence of the Communists. This mandate has been effected by democratic methods, through action taken by the Annual Conventions in exercising their legislative function, and without hysteria or the unfair tactics used by individuals such as Senator Joseph McCarthy. Communists can be rooted out by truly democratic methods. The NAACP has proved it.

There is no doubt that *had* the Communists captured the NAACP —the largest, most militant, and most successful of America's civil-rights organizations—the perilous quarter of a century following the stock-market crash of 1929 would have been far more strife-ridden. Democracy would be far less secure than it is. Again the mistakes of the Communists and the indestructible faith of the Negro in the democratic process are the chief causes of their failure. Not even the very considerable aid given to the Communists by enforced segregation of Negroes, continuation of discrimination, filibusters against civil-rights legislation, and mob violence by American enemies of the Negro have been able to shake that faith.

The Korean War provided as severe a test of the Negro's devotion to democracy and his total rejection of communism as could be devised. According to the Department of Defense, proportionately fewer Negro than white American prisoners of war succumbed to the Chinese Communists' propaganda or to offers of preferential treatment in the form of food, cigarettes, hospitalization, and other special favors, even though the penalty for steadfastness was often brutal treatment. This rejection of favors and stubborn refusal to yield under torture were completely inexplicable to the Communists, who were extraordinarily well informed through their own skilled propaganda techniques about the mistreatment of the Negro in the United States and incredibly ignorant of ameliorating factors and gradual improvements in the Negro's status, believing that the lot of the great majority of American Negroes was one of unrelieved discrimination and oppression. They were certain that Negro POWs would welcome escape from it by rushing into the open arms of the Soviet "classless society."

Potent ammunition was supplied the Communists by the shocking incident I have mentioned before—the bomb killing of the Harry Moores. As State Secretary of the NAACP, Mr. Moore had traveled continuously throughout Florida, urging Negroes to register and vote, working for the admission of qualified Negroes to state schools and the university, and speaking and raising funds for the legal defense of three young Negroes falsely accused of rape at Groveland. One of the accused men in the Groveland case had been shot and killed on a back road by the sheriff, and another was left for dead.

All the details of the murder of the Moores—as well as those of the bombing of a Negro housing project and of synagogues and Catholic churches in Miami—were industriously pounded into the ears of the Negro war prisoners. From grim experience back home the audience knew that the facts were in all probability correct. But still the captives remained unmoved by the barrage of propaganda, persuasion, and persecution. Of more than seven hundred Negro POWs, only three chose to remain with the Communists after as much as three years of concentrated efforts by their Chinese captors.

Typical of the rejection of communism is the case of Major John Harlan of West Virginia, who was a prisoner of war in Korea for thirty-two trying months. Major Harlan had earned a Master's degree at Cornell University and had taught modern history prior to entering the Army. Severely wounded, he was captured at Kuneri in the bitterly cold December of 1950. Unlike most of the other Negro captives, Major Harlan was imprisoned with forty-nine other officers in a non-segregated camp. The fifty men, representing seven of the countries fighting in Korea in the Army of the United Nations, were housed in a floorless, rectangular building whose windows were without glass panes.

"The thermometer dropped to thirty degrees below zero and stuck there," Major Harlan told me on his return to the United States. "When I asked the Communist officer in charge of the camp if we could have glass or boards to keep out at least some of the cold, he made me stand at attention for several hours in the snow and ice at thirty below."

Once a week a North Korean doctor visited the camp to snip off frozen toes and fingers, which he tossed to emaciated dogs, who ate them ravenously. The prisoners' only medication and treatment for their mutilated feet and hands were an evil-smelling salve and scraps of dirty newspaper, which were to be applied to their wounds.

Major Harlan and three other American Negro officers were offered the opportunity to escape such privation and torture. When they first arrived at Camp Five they were the objects of solicitude by their captors. Tempting offers of more and better food, cigarettes, and other preferential treatment were made to them. Major Harlan was the special target of such blandishments, because from the very beginning he had been unconsciously accepted by the POWs as their leader and defender. In his quiet fashion he had kept morale as high as circumstances permitted by encouraging his fellow prisoners to sing, by occupying their minds with whatever limited physical or intellectual activities were possible, and, above all, by giving them strength by his own example of fortitude. The "comrade instructors" naturally sought to win Major Harlan over to their side, and their anger when he quietly rejected their overtures was as great as their efforts to convert him had been.

Especially baffling to his captors was the fact that Major Harlan differed so totally from their concept of what an American Negro should be. Instead of being illiterate, he was manifestly better educated than his jailors, one of whom was a graduate of the University of Peiping. Instead of being craven and submissive as a result of the racial prejudice they had been told was directed at all American Negroes, he was quietly assured and self-confident. When taunted by stories such as the bomb slaying of the Moores, Major Harlan readily admitted that all was not perfect for American Negroes back home—not by a long shot—but he informed the Chinese Communists that Negroes through the democratic process were fighting and winning their battle against proscription, while the Chinese were exchanging colonial exploitation for Soviet imperialism.

I asked Major Harlan and numerous other Negro POWs when they returned to the United States how they had managed to hold on to their faith in democracy under such grueling conditions, particularly when they knew that not all the stories of mistreatment of Negroes in the United States were untrue or excessively exaggerated. Major Harlan's reply is typical.

"Because racial segregation was being wiped out in the armed services, we were Americans, fighting for America, without distinction of race, creed, or color," he answered. Thoughtfully he added,

"And because we're winning our fight here at home. It hasn't been completed yet, and we've a long way to go. But we're on our way. We don't want to shift to another kind of dictatorship just as we're getting rid of the one from which we've suffered all these generations here in America."

XII. "Aye, but It Does Move!"

Galileo, after having been forced to recant publicly his belief that the earth moved, is reported to have whispered to himself, "Aye, but it does move!"

The parallel is far from exact, yet I have often found myself thinking of his words as I have been writing this book. For during the almost thirty years in which I have devoted my life to the cause of human equality there have been many heartsick moments of discouragement, when it has seemed as though the march of progress had bogged down and the submerged world of the American Negro was static. But over and over again, with increasing emphasis and conviction during the last few years, have come evidences that prove conclusively that we do not stand still, that we must go backward or forward, and that in a very special sense, as the American Negro sees it, American democracy is going forward.

This, then, is the balance sheet on the status of the American Negro in 1955 as I see it. It is not, of course, the final account of a job that is completed. Far from it. The alterations in the pattern of thought and action by both white and Negro America, though measurable and heartening, represent in many instances outward reform and not inner conversion. There are many barriers to rapprochement between white and non-white people in the United States because of tradition and enforced segregation. Even normal friendship is frequently difficult in some parts of the country, and impossible in many parts of the South. As this is being written, twenty-nine of the forty-eight states still bar intermarriage. Far too many white Americans yet cling to exploded notions of racial superiority and inferiority, and many too many Negroes are convinced that all white people are incurably prejudiced.

But more change is taking place in human relations than even most Americans realize. Twenty years ago the presence of white dinner guests in a Negro's home or vice versa was a rarity, except in metropolitan centers such as New York. Even there, some hosts or hostesses would invite a Negro writer or actor merely as proof of their "liberalism." Today, even in many parts of the deepest South, such social relationships are taken in stride. Not long ago a famous industrialist told me at luncheon that in his youth it would never have occurred to him to invite one of his Negro schoolmates to his home; today his children include their Negro friends with complete naturalness. Just the other morning I found the little station platform near our home in Connecticut inundated with healthy, laughing children who were returning to New York after a holiday at the *New York Herald Tribune*'s Fresh Air Fund Camp at Ridgefield. The whole spectrum of human skin color was represented. I noticed a blue-eyed, honey-blond girl of fourteen or so holding in her lap a younger girl whose skin was as ebon as her friend's was fair. The two youngsters nuzzled each other, chuckling over some private joke, as oblivious to any difference of race as they were of what was happening at that moment in Kurdistan.

Perhaps one of the most valuable of all the evidences of progress can be seen in the fact that now, as I am finishing this book, something seems to have been left out. It would have been impossible a quarter of a century ago, or, for that matter, a decade ago, to write a book on the status of the American Negro without devoting at least one voluminous chapter to lynching. That such a chapter no longer needs to be included reflects the changing pattern of race relations in the United States.

This does not mean that the danger is ended or the problem

solved. Nor does it mean that a serious economic depression with vast unemployment and bitter competition for jobs could not revive a wave of violence. But this much can be safely said—lynching as it was practiced not many years ago, when hundreds and sometimes thousands of white Americans participated in torturing, hanging, or burning a Negro (and sometimes a white man or woman), is now ended. It must be said, however, that another less easily detected form of violence against Negroes, Jews, Catholics, labor-union members, and even law-enforcement officers has partially replaced lynching—the use of dynamite or nitroglycerine bombs thrown from swiftly moving automobiles. Such crimes have caused death or injury to innocent persons who have happened to be in the vicinity. But this kind of violence against minorities has been less frequent than lynchings were a few years ago, and public condemnation of such crimes has been much greater.

How have lynchings—which, as I have noted before, Communist propaganda has led some of the peoples in other parts of the world to believe occur almost daily in the United States—been wiped out? The most effective weapon against the crime has been the education of public opinion to the barbarity, the frequently obvious falsity of the excuses, such as rape, given by the lynchers, and the harm done by mob violence to orderly procedures of justice. That education has come about in the main by the persistent campaign for federal anti-lynching laws conducted by non-governmental organizations. Many investigations of lynchings and race riots, sometimes made at the risk of injury or death to the investigators, have been made. The true facts thus uncovered have been publicized by the press, over the radio, in pamphlets and meetings, and on the floor of Congress. Carefully documented studies have been made to explode the falsehood that lynching is necessary for the protection of white women in the South. Church groups, especially among women in the South, labor unions, student groups, professional groups, and all the media of public information have been enlisted in these campaigns.

Lynchers who were formerly heroes in backward Southern communities found themselves less popular, particularly among property owners, because of the threat of heavy financial penalties against counties or other governmental subdivisions that permitted lynchings to take place. Defenders of the South who had long contended that they should be left to solve the South's problems in their own way found themselves on the defensive, to such an extent that they were forced to take action lest the federal government step in. Most important of all, the moral conscience of the nation, which, though often quiescent, plays a more important role in the formation of American opinion than is realized even by Americans themselves, became sufficiently aroused and organized to force a change.

There are, unfortunately, other forms of anti-Negro violence that continue and will, unhappily, erupt again until housing segregation is entirely eliminated. Great blots on our record are the riots I have mentioned—those that have occurred during the past decade in Detroit, Cicero, Trumbull Park Homes in Chicago and Cleveland; and the bombings in Florida, Texas, Georgia, and Alabama when Negroes moved out of the ghetto into what had formerly been all-white neighborhoods.

But the old patterns of violence have been shattered. Sporadic violence has replaced the sickening succession of lynchings, riots, and organized sadism that had been the rule. The change marks a major transformation in the ancient mores.

A critic might say, in appraising the present situation, that every advance the Negro has made toward full citizenship, and the concomitant advances of the United States toward the practice of the democracy it professes, must be discounted by the phenomenon of McCarthyism, the possibility of hydrogen-bomb warfare, and the past and present economic and political mistakes and failures of American democracy. I would agree instantly and wholeheartedly that the problems of the Negro American cannot be isolated from the larger problem of implementing democracy in America and throughout the world. Yet it remains clear that against a most complex and formidable array of obstacles the American Negro has in the past fifteen years made significant advances in his long and tortuous march toward freedom, and that through these advances the cause of freedom throughout the world has been advanced.

One is cheered today by such statements as the following, from a recent article in the *Saturday Evening Post* by Sarah Patton Boyle, a Virginia housewife and the granddaughter of a Confederate soldier.

Our prejudice is based simply on our misconception that all Negroes are childlike intellectually and unacceptable socially, fifty years of segregation having prevented us from contact with those of another caliber. Each of us has known many who seemingly never lift their minds above the simple chores they live by, and most of us have known not even one whose cultural opportunities have been comparable to our own.

Isn't it understandable, then, that until something happens to shatter this misconception, despite friendly feeling, we cannot imagine equality relations with them? And isn't it inevitable that, for those of us who are normally flexible, only a few good object lessons are needed to start an inner vibration which will shortly result in such a shattering?

At the annual conference of the NAACP in St. Louis, Missouri, in 1953 Dr. Channing H. Tobias, Chairman of the Board, distinguished churchman and educator, proposed a ten-year campaign to complete the job of elimination of racial bigotry in the United States by January 1, 1963, the centennial of the signing of the Emancipation Proclamation by Abraham Lincoln. The proposal immediately caught the imagination of both Negro and white Americans. Not only the NAACP but many other agencies devoting all or part of their energies to the solution of this age-old problem stepped up their efforts to complete the job. New energy and new direction were given to the campaign, and there is both hope and reason to believe that the year 1963 will witness abolition of the major forms of racial prejudice.

What I have tried to do is analogous to the objective of a writer who tells the story of a long struggle against, say, tuberculosis or cancer. He knows full well that neither the complete cure nor the preventive has yet been discovered by scientists. So he relates the history of the disease and what has been done to date to wipe it out.

He concentrates on his chosen disease and does not attempt to write a materia medica or to tell the complete story of man's battle against a great host of other ills.

The job of curing and preventing man's mistreatment of another man because of his race or color in the United States or, for that matter, anywhere else in the world is not done. But we are on our way.

ACKNOWLEDGMENTS

Many thousands of persons in all parts of the world with whom I have been privileged to talk and work during the past thirty-six years have in one way or another contributed to the content of this book. A list of them—could I remember them all—would be as long as the book itself.

There are a few specific individuals and organizations that must be publicly thanked. The first is the National Association for the Advancement of Colored People, its Board of Directors, its staff, its membership, and its friends, whom I have been permitted to serve since 1918.

I am indebted to the Ford Foundation for research, secretarial, and travel assistance.

I wish to record appreciation to Judge William H. Hastie for reading and criticizing the chapter on the armed services, to Clarence M. Mitchell, Chester Bowles, Norman Cousins, Henry Lee Moon, Channing H. Tobias, Benjamin E. Mays, and W. Montague Cobb for most valuable criticisms of all or parts of the book.

The Saturday Evening Post has been good enough to permit me to reprint parts of the articles on Detroit, Michigan, and Washington, D. C., which I wrote for that magazine, and which are integrated with the chapters on Jim Crow, Jobs, Housing, the Church, and Communications; and the Chicago *Defender*, the story of how labor unions have played a very important role in achieving more democracy in the United States.

To Misses Mabel D. Jackson, Bobbie Branche, Julia Baxter, and Earlene Reeves I am indebted for their patience and valuable assistance in digging out and checking hundreds of facts.

Finally, I wish to thank my wife for invaluable aid and criticism, especially when I got bogged down, and for putting up with my many periods of absorption and ill temper when it seemed as if I would never be able to get the book done.

Need I repeat here the ancient cliché that I alone am responsible for whatever errors of fact, opinion, or judgment may have crept into the pages of this book?

Index

INDEX

237

Damages for enforced segregation, 163,
166, 170-71, 173-76
Darrow, Clarence, 138, 214, 217
Davis, Benjamin J., 84
Davis, Benjamin O., Jr., 95
Day, William Rufus, 125
Death rate, Negro, 149, 160
Delaware, 30, 32n., 50, 52, 56, 58, 158
Democracy, xi, 20, 100, 224; American, xi,
3, 7, 10-11, 21, 23-26, 50, 117, 132,
178, 215, 217
Democratic party, 78-80, 110; in the
South, 65-85, 113; see also New Deal;
Presidential campaigns
Denny, George, 5
Depression, of 1873, 189; of 1907, 190;
of 1921-22, 190; of the 1930s, 120, 155,
213, 215-16, 219
Desegregation, 53-60; in armed services,
171-72, 226; in education, 197-98; grad-
ual, 55, 59-60; voluntary, 60; see also
Segregation
Detroit, 81, 115-16, 200-201; housing in,
136-43; National Bank of, 115; race
riots in, 15, 109, 115, 197, 231
Detroit City Housing Authority, 142
Dictatorship, 7, 10, 212, 216-17, 227
Dining cars, segregated, 165-66, 171, 174
Diphtheria, 151
Discrimination, 6, 25; in armed services,
89-90, 94-103; in industry, 104-21; in
medical profession, 151-60; see also
Segregation
Disfranchisement, 5, 22, 35, 66-73, 126,
213; see also Negro vote
Dixiecrats, 81-82
Doctors, see Medical profession

East St. Louis, Illinois, 44, 126
Education, federal aid to, 46; health and,
150; medical, 150-51, 153; Negro, 7-8,
29, 31-53, 124, 189; public, abolishment
of, 52, 57-60; see also Colleges; Schools
Egypt, 178
Eisenhower, Dwight D., 82, 93, 114, 119,
160, 182
Eisenhower administration, 52, 182
El Paso, Texas, 67-68
Emancipation Proclamation, xi, 26, 63,
124, 149, 169, 232; second, 76
Employment, discrimination in, 12, 16,
34-35, 73, 104-21
Emrich, Right Rev. Richard, 201-202
England, 188, 220; color prejudice in, 17
Episcopal University of the South, 195

Equality, racial, 6, 13, 24-26, 104, 128;
see also Separate-but-equal theory
Equality of Opportunity in Housing, 130n.
Ethiopia, 178, 219-20
Europe, 3, 7, 196; labor movement in, 188

Fahy, Charles, 95
Fair Educational Practices Act, 44
Fair Employment Practices Committee, 5,
104-105, 109-10
Federal aid, to education, 46; to hospitals,
160; to housing, 123; to sharecroppers,
73
Federal Bureau of Investigation, 57
Federal Council of Churches, Race Rela-
tions Committee, 195
Federal Court of Appeals, 22, 48, 88, 112,
135n., 146
Federal Housing Administration, 131-32,
137
Filibusters, 5-6, 73, 104, 212
Fine, Benjamin, 45
Fisher, Ernest McKinley, 129n.
Fisk University, 8, 143, 164
Florida, 20, 32n., 41, 56, 59, 76, 158, 185,
224, 231; Negro vote in, 70; school ex-
penditures in, 34; teachers' salaries in,
42, 45
Florida States Rights, Inc., 56
Forbidden Neighbors, Abrams, 129n., 131
Ford Foundation, 20, 198
Forrestal, James, 94-95
France, 9, 67, 90
Fraternities, 9, 151, 174
"Fundamentals of Real Estate Practice,"
130n.

Gaines, Lloyd, 36-38
Garfield Heights, Ohio, 126
Garland Fund, 35
Garvey, Marcus, 222
General Cable Corporation, 105, 113
George, Walter F., 51
Georgetown University, 196
Georgia, 32n., 41, 51, 53, 56, 84, 151,
157-58, 160, 185, 207, 231; Commission
on Education, 59; Negro vote in, 70,
72, 76; school expenditures in, 34, 59;
teachers' salaries in, 45
Germany, 15, 87, 119
Ghettos, Jewish, 126; Negro, 41, 84, 100,
123, 139, 143, 231; see also Housing;
Slum apartments
Gloster, Hugh, 167
Gold Coast, 204
Golf, 186